Everything is
Everything

Everything is Everything

Everything

CLIVE MYRIE

A Memoir of Love, Hate & Hope

HODDER &
STOUGHTON

First published in Great Britain in 2023 by Hodder & Stoughton
An Hachette UK company

1

A CIP catalogue record for this title is available from the British Library

Hardback ISBN 9781399714983
Trade Paperback ISBN 9781399714990
ebook ISBN 9781399715010

Typeset in Celeste by Hewer Text UK Ltd, Edinburgh
Printed and bound in Great Britain by Clays Ltd, Elcograf S.p.A.

Hodder & Stoughton policy is to use papers that are natural, renewable and recyclable products and made from wood grown in sustainable forests. The logging and manufacturing processes are expected to conform to the environmental regulations of the country of origin.

Hodder & Stoughton Ltd
Carmelite House
50 Victoria Embankment
London EC4Y 0DZ

www.hodder.co.uk

For Peter and Aunty Maizie

Contents

Prologue

THE CHERRY BLOSSOM had flowered, then died. The shroud of pink petals that cloaks Japan for a few glorious weeks a year was turning brown that late spring in 1996, and I watched the transformation wide-eyed, having moved to the country only recently. At the same time, a story came across my desk that was powerful and I knew I must get right. As the BBC's Tokyo correspondent, I was anxious to prove myself in my first full-time foreign posting for the Corporation. I also needed to start making good on all the sacrifices my Windrush Generation parents had made in their lives, and on the promises I had made to myself.

In the early 1990s, Japan was a temple to the future, with a cutting-edge electronics industry, only rivalled and surpassed many years later by America's Silicon Valley. The Sony Walkman was king, with its cassette tape spinning silently in the pockets of millions of devotees across the globe, at a time when the iPod and 'streaming' were twinkles in Steve Jobs' eye. Japan was a beacon of modernity and Tokyo a thrusting metropolis of neon and hope, teeming with people apparently all on the same page about where they were going and how they were going to get there.

I loved it. It was a city shiny and bright and new, so distinct and different from anything I had ever known. I loved the food – the tempura and sushi and hot ramen dishes and Asahi Super Dry beer. I adored Kurosawa movies and Mishima's prose, was dazzled by the cherry blossom, and the fresh, fluffy snow of winter, a seemingly purer, whiter snow than the sleety slush of a Boltonian downpour in the north-west of England where I was born. I was a lad from Lancashire, who felt he had finally been introduced onto the world stage. It was as if I had achieved something simply by setting foot on Japanese soil, a milestone in a quest to a meaningful life.

I was the BBC's eyes and ears in East Asia, a vital and strategic part of the world. If something happened that the Corporation felt the world needed to know about, I would get the call. What is going on at the Tokyo Stock Exchange, the largest in Asia and often setting the pace for the FTSE and the Dow? China is sabre-rattling again against Taiwan, how serious could it be this time? What new Japanese tech innovations could there be that might change the lives of millions around the world? I would get the call.

The big global industrial titans were Japanese, the richest people in the world were Japanese, Japan was the centre of the Universe. All the hopes and dreams and ideas I'd had as a kid were being realised. And I was doing all this, despite being black.

The post-war hopes and dreams of Japan were being realised, too. It was a living, breathing example of a nation that had bettered itself and its people, after the harrowing experience and jingoism of the descent into militarism, which characterised the years up to 1945. The self-obsession and dizzying belief in the idea that the Japanese were God's chosen people, the elect, the Masters of the Universe while others were beneath them, had all gone. The puffed-out chests and demands for the subservience of others, the air of superiority – all that had been horribly vaporised in two mushroom clouds of nuclear dust.

It was a land that, because of its crushing defeat and devastation, could properly look itself in the mirror without pretence. It could rationally analyse its failings and deficiencies, its mistakes and shortcomings, and do better. Yet there were still ghosts from a deplorable past.

* * *

With my cameraman and producer, we set out to visit a place on the outskirts of Tokyo, a filming trip that made some of my colleagues nervous. We arrived at a compound of buildings that outsiders rarely visited, and it was truly a place of anguish. The administrator of the Tamazenseien Sanatorium met us at the main entrance, a kindly looking man who bowed to welcome us, as is customary. He was smiling and looked pleased to see us. He then led us into a large, clean and well-lit room, where several people were taking part in an exercise class. Swinging their arms up, then down, up, then down.

We were told most were in their sixties and seventies though some were older, and the effects of leprosy were evident. Many had stumps where there should have been hands, others had protruding gums and teeth exposed, because of damage to their faces. Some were in wheelchairs, others had lesions covering their skin.

The facility, like the fourteen others across Japan still housing thousands of leprosy patients, was built at the turn of the twentieth century, but it was in the years shortly before the Second World War when the real purges began. Tens of thousands of people with the disease were rounded up by the national police. Their parents had disowned them and wanted to forget them. Blighted offspring, who should never have been born, despatched to leper colonies. The disappeared.

I was introduced to Yasugi Hirosawa. Leprosy had swollen his face, his large bifocal glasses magnified lesions and lumps above his nose. His left hand was similarly swollen, while his right hand was withered, hanging limp from his wrist like the dying petals of cherry blossom I had seen a few weeks before, twisted and malformed. He was a short man, maybe 5 feet 6 inches, and he had a full head of jet-black hair, which despite everything trimmed his age of sixty-eight.

He told me he had not seen his mother and father since he contracted leprosy at the age of twelve, in 1940, the height of the leper purges. When he first entered the colony, everyone was forced to wear striped uniforms like criminals and the food was no more than a mixture of wheat and rice. Some patients, he said, had forced abortions. Others were sterilised. I could tell his words meant nothing to him now; stripped of an ability to shock, they carried no weight, no pathos, they were just words, and he wasn't looking for my pity.

Yet for me listening they hung heavy, saturated with torture. As a journalist hearing testimony like this, the pain leeches into you, or at least it does with me, and I have found this to be the case my whole working life. But journalists must never get emotional. We must never *become* the story, whatever our feelings.

Had Japan really changed, I thought? Had the country moved on from its pre-war notions surrounding the purity of Japanese blood? After all, it had continued to isolate its lepers decades after the rest of the industrialised world had freed theirs, ignoring a 1950s breakthrough medical cure, which had been accepted by all other nations.

This was Japan's shame, the bitter fruit of a sick and twisted tree. But it was clear why the administrator was happy to see us. A foreign television crew was finally going to proclaim to the world that the country was moving forward and at last was joining the league of civilised nations that had turned its back on shunning those with leprosy. The year I moved to Japan, the country's segregation law was finally going to be repealed. Japan's leper colonies would be shut down.

I realise now, almost thirty years later as I write this book, that on a much deeper level, I *needed* to tell the story of Yasugi Hirosawa and the others. I had not suffered such an appalling physical disease and I had not been locked away, but as a black man, I understood their sense of being rejected and treated as outsiders. That identification with the marginalised has become more intense as I have got older. I am acutely touched by others' misfortune. I have also developed a visceral hatred of the bully or the unforgiving, the cruel and the heartless. The more pain and suffering I see, the less desensitised I become.

All this was clearly meant to be. As a black man, my perspective on many of the stories I cover is borne out of my own life experience. 'Everything is Everything' means that all is well, or everything is going to plan, so I am content with who I am.

That is what this book is about. The intersection of the personal and the professional. The twin tracks of my life.

There Are Lions and Tigers in the House

I have no idea what happened to my twin brother or sister. He or she just disappeared. You see, the doctors were convinced my mother was having twins, and with the strain on her back and her aching feet, she was convinced she was having twins too. The doctors debated whether there should be an X-ray to make sure, but it was very late in the pregnancy, so it was a risky procedure. If my mum had been carrying twins, then preparations would have to be made for delivery at Townley's General Hospital in Bolton in Lancashire, where an experienced medical team would be on hand. If she was having only the one child, then a bed was already waiting at Haslam's Mother and Baby Home, where a single midwife could cope.

My mother was worried about the X-ray, about the radiation and the possible effects on the life or lives growing inside her. She had been in Britain for little more than eighteen months from Jamaica, and a new life lay ahead as a member of what would become known as the Windrush Generation.

The connection between foetal X-rays and childhood cancers had only been proved to general satisfaction in 1962, just two years before I was born. However, the initial findings of a causal connection actually came in 1958. Dr Alice Stewart and her team at Oxford University did the work, but sexism in medical research was the norm. Her methodology was attacked and her efforts ridiculed. The problem was that enthusiasm for all things nuclear was at a high point in the 1950s, and anyone threatening the conventional wisdom was ignored, especially if they were a woman.

The establishment view was that very small doses of radiation were safe, but Dr Stewart argued a fraction of that safe dose could still lead to birth defects. Nevertheless, my mother's doctors were willing to plough on with the X-rays, and she prayed that the little ones growing inside her would be alright. 'Everything is everything,' she reassured herself. 'All is well.' Perhaps that was the first time I heard that phrase, and I wasn't even born.

Heavily pregnant, the nurse manoeuvred my mother onto the X-ray machine to lie face up with the apparatus for emitting the radiation that would peer inside her womb looming above her belly. At the time, childhood leukaemia deaths were running at about one a week nationwide. The chance of disaster was small, but it was real. Surely they know what they're doing, my mother told herself. Everything is everything, this is the Mother Country after all.

When the results came through, there was shock. My mum's belly had been so big, there seemed little doubt she was carrying twins. But the X-ray revealed only one baby, a giant, in her womb. The doctors assumed there would be complications, my mum's pelvis would not be able to accommodate the birth, and a caesarean section would have to take place at the general hospital, rather than a more straightforward delivery at the mother and baby home. Then on

25 August 1964, the doctors were again confounded; no caesarean was necessary as my mum's pelvis shifted, opening up to allow a natural birth in what was a surprisingly quick and easy delivery. I weighed in at a colossal 9lbs and 3oz. The average baby is 6lbs. What on earth had happened to my twin?

And what kind of a world was I being born into on that August day, with the slap of a midwife's hand on my bottom as she strained to dangle this porker upside down? A black boy beginning life in Britain, a land that my parents already knew could be unwelcoming to people like us. Clive Augustus Myrie is the name that was inked on my birth certificate. 'It's a good job I wasn't born in April,' I tease my mum to this day.

At pre-school, around the age of four, I was completely mute. It is hard for me to believe this now, given what I do for a living, but by all accounts, I was extremely shy to the point where I did not speak. Not a single word left my mouth. My teachers were very worried. I simply would not communicate in class. The staff could not understand it, there must be something very wrong with him, they thought. The head-teacher called my mother in to have a word. 'He won't communicate verbally with me,' she told my mum. 'He just won't respond, and I think the best course of action might be for him to see a child psychologist.'

'What for?' replied my mum incredulously.

'Well, we have to try to get to the bottom of this,' said the teacher, getting irritated.

'Don't you dare, there is nothing wrong with my son. He's an only child living in a household where his father is out at work during the day, and by night when he returns, Clive is already in bed. So, the only person he interacts with is me, his mother. He's just shy being around strangers if I'm not there. Leave him be, he'll be fine.'

For some reason, the next week was when I decided to open my mouth in class, and what I chose to say was shocking and spectacularly bizarre. 'My mum has lions and tigers in the house!' I declared. My teacher was now even more worried than when I didn't speak at all. This boy *really* needs to see a professional, maybe there is something much more serious and deeper going on. So, my mum was called to the school again, and when she was told what I had said, she could not stop laughing. 'They're my glass ornaments on the mantelpiece,' she told the teacher, who then also burst into laughter.

Even at the age of four, I had an eye for the theatrical.

I was the first of Lynne and Norris Myrie's children to open their eyes in Britain, and I was clearly a nervous child. On my first day at primary school, I even threw up out of fear. I was five, away from home and surrounded by people I didn't know. I remember the classroom at St Michael's Church of England School, the teacher being very understanding, and the other children sitting at their desks as she addressed us all with the day's lesson. I recall feeling nauseous, with a trembling at the back of my throat as it began to wobble; then sharp intakes of breath and sweating, a sense of being disorientated, and hoping the contents of my stomach would stay at bay. Thinking, I can't hold it down.

In a split second, the bitter taste of bile began hitting the back of my throat, like a caustic acid rasping my tonsils. Then out it came, everywhere, showering my clothes and the desk in front of me. No one said a word. There was just shock and amazement from the other kids, all sitting there, motionless and open-mouthed. Stunned catatonia. Fortunately, no one laughed at me and my nauseous misfortune, and I was grateful for that. The teacher led me away to get cleaned up, but I felt acutely embarrassed. All this on my first day.

Being dumbstruck, then throwing up in class, was because I was anxious and unsure of myself. Eventually I was not an only child anymore. Over the period of a few years, our household bloomed and blossomed. My two half-brothers, Lionel and Peter, and my older sister, Judith, all joined us in Bolton from Jamaica where they were born. My mum and dad then had my younger brother Garfield, and younger sisters Sonia and Lorna. A giant family, where you really had to make your voice heard and where my confidence grew.

* * *

My mother was a primary school and kindergarten teacher in Jamaica, a profession she'd had her eye on since her late teens. She taught everything; English, maths, reading, writing. Her favourite subject was Bible studies, partly because all the kids in Jamaican households had no problem getting hold of a copy of the textbook.

She loved learning and imparting her knowledge to young minds, getting a kick out of seeing pupils develop and shine, helping budding flowers open and bloom with well-chosen words and attention. The naughty, those with attention deficits, the sporty, the overexcited, the easily bored, the rebels, the can't-keep-stills – the rich and poor and lazy and determined and gifted and bright and slow. My mum loved children and they loved her classes. She knew how to 'reach' every one of them and it was her calling.

But teaching was also a profession in Jamaica that was held in very high regard, a vital, even noble pursuit. Teachers were respected because they were offering something the British overlords had denied for hundreds of years, opportunity. Black teachers were a symbol of change. British rule since the 1830s had decreed so-called 'negro education' as 'a provision for regulating the condition of the negroes as may combine their welfare with the interests of the proprietors', whose *interest* of course was to carry on the production of sugar. In other words, black people received no real education at all, except better to work the cane fields. By 1962, the year my mother left for Britain, and the year of Jamaican independence, 67 per cent of the population could not read or write.

Mum hoped that working in a school in England would give her the status and respect she enjoyed back in Jamaica. She would not be another immigrant drifting from job to job, on the outside of society; she would be a core citizen on the inside, helping fulfil the dreams of countless parents, a fundamental cog in the wheel of the community. She had nursed her dream of teaching in England while making all her plans for the big move to Bolton, and teaching would underpin her new existence.

Unlike Hortense in Andrea Levy's novel *Small Island*, mum knew before she flew to England that her Jamaican qualifications would not be considered good enough for a teaching post in Britain, and she would have to retrain. But she told herself it would not be a problem. She would take evening classes if necessary while working during the day, perhaps as a seamstress, to bring home a little extra money. Teaching was something my mum had set her heart on, and in Bolton she would work to achieve that goal.

However, my mum did not fully appreciate how much time the retraining would take to get the right qualifications. In those first few months in Bolton, my dad was struggling to hold on to work, and mum was beginning to realise that she needed to contribute forcefully to the family income. My dad's work contracts would end not long after they began, because after a certain point, basic labouring work would finish, and more skilled contractors would be needed on a construction site. Often if there was labouring still to be done, this would be carried on by white workers at the expense of black people.

My dad had also chafed at the fact that he was not his own boss, as was the case in Jamaica, so work in the UK was a problem for him to begin with, until he got used to the way things were going to be, having to work for others. Back in Jamaica he was a cobbler and shoe repairer, an apprentice after leaving school, and he was on his way to becoming a skilled shoemaker when he made the journey to England. But he never pursued the career he had begun back in the Caribbean, and never settled on a line of work that gave him satisfaction in all his years in Britain.

A move to the Midlands around Nottingham might have furthered a career in shoe making, but he was in the north-west, where garment factories dominated industry. Labouring jobs came and went, and nothing fired his imagination. It was not long before mum understood that taking the time to retrain to become a teacher would not be possible. That career would have to wait for a while, which was fine, as she began working as a seamstress to bring in a little extra money. Then something happened that changed her life for ever and meant the teaching job in Bolton that she craved would probably never come. My mum fell pregnant with me.

My dad realised he now had to knuckle down to feed the growing family, and for the bulk of his working life in Britain, he was at a company called Lorival, with the factory so close to our home, you could hear the morning klaxon calling people to work. Six o'clock and off it would go, the signal to us kids sound asleep that we had just one more hour to luxu-riate in our dreams or recover from our nightmares, before having to rise for school. At Lorival, my dad helped assemble the car batteries that went into British Leyland vehicles.

Because he was never truly fulfilled at work, he always seemed unhappy to me. Frustrated and resentful to the point where he felt it had been a huge mistake to move to England, a view he holds even to this day, long in retire-ment. His dissatisfaction with work magnified the other things he was unhappy with here, especially the rainy Boltonian weather – the result of the town sitting beneath the western Pennine Moors, an ideal dumping ground for clouds pregnant with moisture looking for somewhere to unburden themselves.

A country boy from rural Jamaica, industrial landscapes and urban living were alien to him, the colour of life now viewed in different shades of grey, in contrast to the vibrancy of the colours of the Caribbean, with its yellows and deep greens and browns and reds and blues. He never acclimatised to the cold and the sharp cut of the wind blowing down from the Arctic in deepest winter.

All that rather sadly, I believe, made his personality a little cold too, because by all accounts in Jamaica my dad had a sunny disposition. He was good-looking, outgoing and urbane, a happy person, a man to fall in love with, as many women apparently did. But in England he was a big man brought low by his circumstances, a giant bear wandering around aimlessly in an unfamiliar forest, unable to carve a place for himself in his new world. He created a home and lived among us, but he was remote and distant to his children.

However, there was one treat we used to have as kids – if any one of us was ill with a sore throat or cold or feeling under the weather, we were allowed to climb into bed with mum and dad and sleep with them. It was a moment we all loved as children, warm and nurturing, a sign that perhaps he did love us after all.

He tells me now he did not come to Britain to have fun, it was all about work, and that attitude left him interested in experiencing very little beyond the four walls of our home in Bolton. He avidly watched and devoured television. That was his window on the world. Though my father was rather taciturn, never really engaging in conversation with his children, he did talk a lot, usually to voice some deeply held opinion on any number of subjects. He would forcefully rant, as if getting things off his chest, directing his words at no one in particular.

I recall him railing against the Conservative prime minister Edward Heath and the three-day week and blackouts in

9

the early 1970s. 'We need Harold Wilson,' he would say, 'we need to stop this foolishness.' In the summers when the West Indies cricket team would tour England, the BBC's televised coverage was always on in our house as my dad marvelled at the brilliance of Michael Holding and Viv Richards. It made him proud to see his own people doing well. He voiced his opinions on Donny Osmond and David Cassidy too – 'Why do they make so much money for producing sheer rubbish?'

Of course, he also had opinions on the anti-immigration MP Enoch Powell, and not the kindest. But there was a perversity to his view. England had accepted him as a Windrush Generation immigrant, yet he did not really want to be here. Enoch Powell did not understand why my dad was in Britain, and my dad was not sure either.

It was complicated. In Jamaica he was a skilled, small-scale artisan and there was a dignity for him in that work. In England he made car batteries on an assembly line in the British Leyland factory at the end of the street and had several mouths to feed. In a way, he resented England for facilitating the life he was leading. Perhaps curiously, if England had not been so welcoming to Commonwealth immigration, he would not be enduring this existence. In a way, he hated England for taking him in.

The joy of a new child tempered the upset that my mum felt at not being able to follow the career path she had longed for, and having always had a flair for dressmaking, she was in the right place in the north-west of England to look for more permanent work as a seamstress to help feed her growing family. There were advertisements every week in the local paper looking for workers in the numerous clothing factories of Bolton and Mum had no problem, most notably making shirts, blouses and trousers for Marks and Spencer, the rain-coats for the company that Harold Wilson used to wear, and all kinds of garments including Mary Quant's famous miniskirts.

In fact, my mum was so good and reliable after a while, she was allowed to work from home, as a so-called 'utility machin-ist', which meant she was entrusted with putting together a *complete* garment and not just a section, combining the sleeves, the lining, the shoulders and so on. Mum made our school uniforms, and they were better than anything other parents could buy in the shops. It meant she earned a relative fortune working at her own pace. She could make the waist-band, lining, darts, fly, pockets, any section of any garment, stick them all together and Bob's your uncle! She earned much more than a typical machinist working on the factory floor, and she did it from the comfort of her own home.

I have distinct memories of the van from the factory turn-ing up in the morning with the various materials and drop-ping them off, then returning early evening to pick up the finished garments. Because she could work from home, child-care issues were never a problem and so my mum worked full-time, while raising seven children.

Along with the money my dad earned working at Lorival, my parents were able to buy their own home, and later the house next door, which they rented out to students studying at the local technical college. The work and the money helped Mum and Dad achieve their dreams for their children and vindicate their passage to Britain. Mum was determined that as many of her children as possible would get the chance to go to university, because it was something she could not do. Talking to her now, is there any resentment she did not become a teacher in Bolton? 'No,' she says firmly. 'Never look back!'

Indeed, my mum has only ever looked forwards, which is why at the age of almost sixty, with her kids all grown up, in 1995 she donned a black gown and mortarboard hat to receive her Certificate of Education in a graduation ceremony at the University of Huddersfield after three years of study. She was the oldest member of her class and she was qualified to teach at last. My mum needed to prove to the world and to herself that she could do it. It was never a lack of ability that meant she could not be the person she had wanted to be.

–2–

The Windrush Generation

THE WINDRUSH GENERATION are fabled now to be sure, but it was certainly not always like that. In fact, it has only been in the last few years that the contribution of this magnificent collection of people to the very idea of what it means to be British, has truly been recognised. The Windrush Generation are named after the ship, the *Empire Windrush*, which set sail from Jamaica in 1948, with a passenger list including hundreds of Caribbean migrants. Two ships had arrived the previous year with West Indians, but *Windrush* had by far the most passengers and is the symbol of Britain's post-war shift towards multiculturalism.

When it finally docked at Tilbury in Essex, the Caribbeans aboard the *Windrush*, thankful the three-and-a-half-week voyage was over, were now on UK soil courtesy of Parliament passing the British Nationality Act in 1948. This allowed Jamaicans, Barbadians, Trinidadians and many others from the Caribbean and other Commonwealth countries full rights of entry and settlement, to work and help the British economy.

My parents, when they arrived here in the early 1960s, were now invited to live as 'citizens of the United Kingdom and Colonies'. This is an important point to make. My mum and dad were not in fact 'immigrants' under the law. They were full British citizens. Their journey to live in the UK from Jamaica was in legal terms the equivalent of someone moving from Manchester to London, or Edinburgh to Leeds.

Those early black pioneers were part of a social experiment that no other Empire had tried since the Romans. The total acceptance of all its subjects, black, white and brown, from different races and cultures and religions and heritage, with various ideas and attitudes and feelings, and neuroses and prejudices and baggage . . . the total acceptance of all these many millions of people, from across the globe, as citizens under *one* flag, that of the United Kingdom. On the surface, it was the very essence of inclusivity, though bizarrely that was not the intention.

Be under no illusions, the 1948 Act was primarily an attempt to keep Britain's colonies and independent Commonwealth states together, to fend off a complete break from colonialism. At the same time, there was a basic economic need for a programme of inward migration, because of chronic labour shortages in Britain after the war. The likes of British Rail and the newly created National Health Service were crying out for workers. In fact, one of those leading the charge for Commonwealth migration, was the Minister of Health from 1960–62, a Tory MP by the name of Enoch Powell.

My mum believed the 'mother country' might need teachers too. She had been working at a school in Jamaica, and after much thought, boarded a BA flight to come to Britain. She had saved the airfare over several months, but had been planning for years for her new life. The plane ticket cost just under a hundred pounds, a lot of money, and she felt lucky she was able to fly across the Atlantic Ocean in only six hours. But she ended up hating the journey, because she had never been on an aeroplane before, and she felt claustrophobic and trapped. She was glad to get out at the other end and has blanked all memory of the trip from her mind.

My father had arrived a year earlier in 1961 to prepare the ground. He had sailed from Jamaica's capital, Kingston, to Southampton, a journey that lasted seventeen days, much quicker than the *Empire Windrush* more than a decade earlier. My dad remembers it being a bumpy journey across rough seas. Three Jamaicans were on board from the same town, Sheffield in Westmoreland, where my father was from, so he had good company for the voyage. The bunk beds were comfortable and the food was rather good. It was the life he was about to begin in England that would prove unpalatable.

There was a degree of wishful thinking about the 1948 Nationality Act, on the part of British policy makers, that not many black and brown people would want to move to Britain to take advantage of their newly acquired citizenship status. Ministers believed it would mostly be *white* people who would make the journey to a white-dominated land, with the numbers of non-whites being manageable. By the time the *Empire Windrush* docked, they had realised their mistake too late.

A dozen Labour MPs tried to stop the ship, calling on the prime minister, Clement Attlee, to implement controls on immigration. In a letter, they said the British people 'are blest with the absence of a colour racial problem. An influx of

15

coloured people domiciled here is likely to impair the harmony, strength, and cohesion of our public and social life and to cause discord and unhappiness among all concerned.'

In the mid-1950s, a ministerial committee was set up to investigate migration from the colonies, and it suggested: 'The principle that the United Kingdom should maintain an open door for British subjects grew up tacitly, at a time when the coloured races of the Commonwealth were at a more primitive stage of development than now. There was no danger then of a coloured invasion of this country . . . In the meantime, circumstances have changed . . .' The report continues: 'We clearly cannot undertake to absorb . . . all the coloured immigrants who may wish to come here.'

The minutes of one Tory cabinet meeting in November 1955 reveal the prevailing view that 'if immigration from the colonies . . . were allowed to continue unchecked, there was a real danger that over the years there would be a significant change in the racial character of the English people.' That view, along with pressure from some white communities, explains the failure of successive Conservative and Labour governments right up until the mid-1960s to outlaw racial discrimination in employment, housing, and public places. It also ultimately explains the Windrush Scandal, which would shame Britain and ensnare my own family, more than half a century later.

The true feelings of ministers were unknown to the *Windrush* travellers, including my parents. Those who arrived in Britain in 1948 had sent back word of what life was like in the new land, and economically there was no doubt it was better than living in the Caribbean. There was employment for the industrious, though it was cold and windy to be sure, compared to sunny, balmy Jamaica. The reception in some areas was not welcoming. A black person in a white town or village was always a curiosity, an endlessly fascinating exotic creature, to be stared at and scrutinised, and this was unsettling and unexpected for many moving to the so-called motherland.

At times there would be naked hostility. But the economic imperative trumped the overt racism of colour bars and discrimination. Coming to Britain was an opportunity to earn some decent money and give your children a good education. The plan for so many of my parents' generation was always to make some cash for five or six years, then head back to the sunshine of the Caribbean. That was the plan my parents held in their hearts too, having been lured to Britain by my uncle Cecil, my dad's brother, as well as my mum's cousin Rennie, who had both served in the RAF during the war. They were the ones prodding my mum and dad with letters and telegrams, saying come to Britain and make a new life.

This should have been an exciting time for the country. These were decent people who *wanted* to make their homes here and were willing to come. At least *they* were excited about Britain's future. They brought enthusiasm with them and a work ethic, not having been ground down by years of rationing, or exhausted by war. They also brought optimism and hope, ideas and fresh thinking. They were an injection of adrenalin into the body politic of Britain. They were here to help, not hinder, and in lifting themselves up, they could lift the country up too.

Yet in October 1964, two months after I was born, there was a General Election, and the worsening mood of the nation over immigration became all too clear. It was marked by race-baiting and vitriol. My mum remembers hearing on the radio about the Conservative Party slogan in one constituency in the West Midlands: 'If you want a nigger for a neighbour, vote Labour!'

'I ignored it,' my mum says. 'I had mouths to feed, this kind of nonsense didn't affect me one way or the other. I had much more important things to worry about.' But this was the clarion call of a party that could soon be in government. It was not some obscure fringe outfit on the margins of society or political life. This was a mainstream political party. Labour was not much better. They talked about 'immigration quotas' and restricting future entry, and also denying equal rights for those immigrants who were already in Britain.

Not the rosiest of futures for yours truly, but this was how mainstream politics was being conducted in Britain at the time I was born. Tory Party leaflets proudly stated that once in office 'the Conservatives would bring up to date the Ministry of Repatriation, to speed up the return of home-going and expelled immigrants.' Words not a million miles from the 'get back on your banana boat and go home' language I endured from time to time growing up.

It seemed Britain was at war with itself over the new *Windrush* arrivals. What on earth was going on in this land that my parents had ventured to, despite it literally begging the members of its Commonwealth to come and help rebuild the country after 1945?

* * *

The former mill town of Bolton in Lancashire was largely trouble-free in the years after I was born, though racial tensions surfaced during the depressed economic climate of the 1970s. My father, now well into his nineties, and my mother now in her mid-eighties, will not relate to me stories of the racism they faced.

'Is this a bit like First World War veterans not wanting to talk about the war?' I once asked my mum. 'Not at all,' she insists. Despite Britain's colour bars, neither Mum nor Dad recall being denied housing or employment because of their skin colour, and while I am sure overall there may have been experiences or struggles that they had to endure that I might view as having been the result of animosity, hindsight is a wonderful thing. Perhaps for my parents there may not have been anything too overt, and the slings and arrows of micro-aggressions were not important enough to obsess over.

They were after all in a strange land and had mouths to feed. Comments that might roil the well-fed and watered of today, paled in significance alongside finding work or a roof over their heads for a growing family. I do recall Mum coming home angry one day from work, after someone had asked her where her tail was, because all black people are monkeys. Other relatives tell of verbal abuse while waiting at bus stops in the 1960s and off-hand comments at their places of work. My mum's sister, Aunty Chris, was a trainee NHS nurse trying to help an elderly patient one day and the woman shouted, 'Take your dirty black hands off me!'

My parents' strategy was to avoid situations where they could be abused, keeping their heads down. When I was growing up, I don't think they ever once went out for dinner or to the pub. They tried to stay out of trouble. There were visits to relatives' homes but not very often, as family tended to come to us.

Our house did not feel small even with seven kids all over the place, and compared to your average new-build nowadays, with their paper-thin walls and small sized rooms, our house was positively a mansion. Three up, three down, kitchen, garage, backyard. We were in the heart of the community, right opposite the Burnden Park Football Ground, home to Bolton Wanderers. Match days were noisy and fun, especially if Manchester City were playing, as they were my team, and travelling home after a win took a barely noticeable sixty seconds.

We had a splendid front room for entertaining, which was kept spick and span. As kids, we were not allowed to enter, it was only for adults. It was a room that these days might be described as 'maximalist,' a look that I am sure cost a fraction of what it might now, if 'curated' by a trendy young interior designer.

Every surface had something on it, a glass figurine or an ornament. There were two multicoloured large glass blowfish at either end of the fireplace, and in-between were carefully placed little china figures, or the aforementioned lions and tigers in glass. There was patterned wallpaper and a thick patterned carpet with a three-piece black, button down leather sofa and armchairs. Cream-coloured, crocheted doilies sat on the arms and on the backs. Two blue peacocks made of wire, their tailfeathers fanning out, sat above the fireplace.

In one corner of the room was a radiogram for playing records. Mum and Dad loved the old crooners, Val Doonican,

Engelbert Humperdinck, Bing Crosby, Nat King Cole and their favourite, Jim Reeves. He had a song called 'Welcome to My World,' which instantly transports me back in time to those days growing up on Manchester Road. There was a large TV set acquired on HP, with the thick sticky-outie curved screen housed in dark brown, mock mahogany wood. Family pictures were placed on top along with a giant conch shell, like the ones Ursula Andress found in the azure warm waters of the Caribbean off Negril Beach in Jamaica, in the Bond film *Dr No*.

But the prize piece of furniture in the front room was the corner bar, where the magic really happened. It was a brown, curved unit with a shelf on top and shelves on the inside. It was stocked with all manner of spirits depending on who the visitor was. My uncle Rennie loved whisky, while there were others who often craved Guinness punch. But you could never go wrong with rum. Wray & Nephew White Rum and Captain Morgan Black Rum. There was a pineapple-shaped ice cube holder, which was very cool, and coasters with pictures of Jamaica on them highlighting the main tourist spots, Ocho Rios and Montego Bay, Negril Beach, Kingston, Morant Bay and Black River.

My uncle Cecil would come round for dinner every Saturday night, seven o'clock regular as clockwork. We loved him coming over because he always brought one of those big multi-bags of crisps, sometimes Quavers, but usually ready salted, cheese and onion, or salt and vinegar. We would all sit down to eat dinner – traditional Jamaican fare, rice and peas and chicken or fish, plantain, and coleslaw. Then he and my dad would retire to the front room to drink rum and put the world to rights. We would hear laughter and Jamaican patois, for there was no need to enunciate as if among white English people.

The front room was for Jamaicans being Jamaicans, it *was* the Caribbean, allowing reflection on lives left behind. Maybe it was in the confines of those four walls that they talked about the difficulties of being black in Britain. Perhaps then, just between them, they railed against prejudice and racism. Or maybe they simply talked about cricket. Whatever happened in the front room, tended to stay in the front room. Those four walls encased memories and longing.

Our home on Manchester Road had become an oasis, and the troubles of the outside world only intruded via the nightly television news, or my father's rants about Edward Heath not doing this, or Harold Wilson not doing that. I got the impression my parents were happy with the way they approached life in Bolton, by letting the world come to them. Their temperaments seemed to suit this way of life. They were homebodies and that was okay.

My mother says her faith kept her insulated from the worst of people. A God-fearing woman, brought up in a God-fearing household in Jamaica, she has always believed in the fundamental goodness of Man. In those early days on British soil, selected passages from the Bible were a constant reminder of something she held close to her heart, that most people do not mean to do harm, and that forgiveness is a virtue. The Bible's teachings on right and wrong, on charity, love and compassion, and how helping others can bring its own rewards, were principles she hoped her children would take on board.

She also tried to seed a work ethic in every one of us. If our grades at school were below what she expected, we would get a telling off. Being a teacher herself, she instilled in us the importance of a good education; after all, this was why she left Jamaica in the first place, because she understood the worlds of possibilities that could be opened up by the classroom, what new opportunities might come our way as adults, and a British education was second to none. Her drive to get her children the best education came in part because she was denied that herself in Jamaica. She was a smart pupil with perfect 'A' grades, but sadly her parents could not afford the fees to go to university, so mum was determined that *we* would go.

I will never forget her telling us that we had to work twice as hard and be twice as good to succeed in a white-dominated world, words I took to heart. But I did not see them as a warning, a declaration that life could be cruel and unfair. I saw those words as a call to do my best whatever I decided to turn my hand to. That is all anyone can ask. If my best was twice as good as a white person, bravo. If it was not, at least I had tried my very hardest. I saw those words as designed to inspire hope that my life could be joyful and fulfilling. For me, they amounted to the battle cry of Henry V on the eve of Agincourt. And yes, we know that for many, life is a struggle because of their skin colour. For others, it is a war.

—3—

Take This Letter to the Priest

MY MOTHER, LYNNE, was baptised a Catholic, and she was brought up a Catholic. Yet I only found that out at the age of thirty-four, when I was about to be married. She had taught Bible studies at the local Catholic school in the parish of Westmoreland in Jamaica, where my family are from. After meeting my father, they both decided their future lay in Britain and her faith would be more important to her than ever in the new land. It would be something solid and stable that she understood, while all around was alien.

The cold climate, the buildings, the food, the shops, the motor cars, the factories, the noise of the city, and the white faces, scores of them, hundreds, thousands, millions. Some smiling and welcoming, some snarling, most indifferent. She figured that the church would be a rock to cling on to, as her world was transformed, far away from everything she knew. Her God would at least be by her side.

She had asked her local Catholic priest in Westmoreland, Father Pashby, for a letter of introduction to the priest leading the church closest to her new home in Bolton in Lancashire, some six thousand miles away. Father Pashby was more than happy to oblige, and he wrote out a little note, folded it up and popped it in an envelope for my mum, which she placed in her handbag. She was in her mid-twenties at the time. She never peeked at the note, and the envelope lay undisturbed during the packing of her belongings and during the flight from Jamaica to Britain, until she handed it to the priest in Bolton.

My mum wanted to give a good impression when she first met him, putting on a smart floral dress that she had brought from Jamaica. It was a warm Sunday morning in September, and she had only been in Britain for a few weeks, so was yet to experience the driving cold of a northern English winter. She arrived at the church and took up a place at the back so as not to invite too many stares, and after the service she asked to see the priest. Images filled her head of her religious future.

Back in Jamaica, Father Pashby, having welcomed her into his flock when she first joined his church, introduced her to the rest of his congregation so everyone could get to know each other, and down the years he had offered support whenever needed, taking confession, and baptising my older sister Judith as soon as she was born. That was important because she entered this world with a congenital heart defect, so she could have died before reaching the usual baptismal age of three months old without having been through the Sacrament, liberated from Original Sin, and welcomed into the community of the Church. My mum describes Father Pashby fondly, as a good man.

Mum thought the English would look after her in the same the way, and she had every right to expect this. She told me she imagined the priest in her new home would be just as welcoming as Father Pashby, introducing her to his congregation, greeting her every Sunday as one of his flock for years to come. He could even perhaps be the man christening her children, marvelling every week on the church steps after service at how tall the kids were growing, turning into 'fine young men and women'.

He would be a kindly priest, taking her confession, hearing her angst over this new life she was trying to create in this place called Bolton. Was it the right decision to leave Jamaica? How best to cope with the racism and bigotry that would surely now sometimes scar her life? Out of their deep conversations, perhaps the new priest might become a trusted friend.

After another parishioner pointed out the vestry, my mother approached and knocked on the door. She introduced herself and produced the note from her handbag. The priest opened the envelope, read what it contained, and asked my mum where she was living. She said on George Street, not far away. He then asked her what number, and she told him. He then folded up the note, popped it back in the envelope and handed it to my mum, saying he was sorry, but the address fell outside his diocese, even though it was within a five-minute walk. The nearest Catholic church in the correct diocese was several miles away.

I can guess what Father Pashby had written in the note: 'To whom it may concern, Lynne Myrie is a former teacher at the Catholic school here in Westmoreland. She is God-fearing and a true Catholic. Please welcome her into your flock.' Yet he said no. Why? Was it truly the suggestion that her home was on the wrong side of the road to his church by a few yards? Or was there something more sinister, something un-Godly, cruel and nasty, wicked and wrong? Although Father Pashby did not personally know the man in Bolton, they were both messengers of God in the same church, so he must have believed he knew the kind of man the English priest would have been.

Because of her kindly nature, my mum never doubted the priest's version of events in Bolton, that it was simply a matter of geography which determined whether she could pray in his church. She had travelled six thousand miles to worship, so perhaps an added bus journey would be no big deal, she told herself, and perhaps the priest thought the same. But it was a long way to travel, and my mum began visiting the nearest Church of England church, bringing up her children as Anglicans.

It is an underappreciated trauma that many of the Windrush Generation endured, unable to pray in surroundings where they felt welcome. One of the early Windrush pioneers was a man called Revd Dr Oliver Augustus Lyseight. He was from the neighbouring parish to my parents in Jamaica, called Hanover, just north of Westmoreland. In 1951, he made his new home in England in the West Midlands, preaching to other newly arrived Caribbean immigrants as a Pentecostal minister, and he eventually helped establish British chapters of the New Testament Church of God, to which many of the Windrush Generation flocked. One of those was my mum, who got to know a husband-and-wife team from Jamaica, Brother and Sister McFarlane, who established a Bolton branch.

At first services were held in their living room, before they were finally able to rent a hall on the outskirts of Bolton, and their parishioners were all black. My mum went to some of their services until I was born.

I relate these details to you as my mother related them to me in 1998, thirty-six years after the events took place. That was the year I married Catherine, or Mary Catherine to be precise, a Catholic. Her older sisters are Mary Bernadette, Mary Theresa and Mary Winifred, her older brother is John Joseph, and her younger sister is Mary Joanne. Convent-educated, Catherine's childhood was ruled by the church calendar – feast days, holy days, saints days, Benediction, Novenas and Rosaries (and she still enjoys a good Stations of the Cross).

For her family, our wedding had to be a proper Catholic one, and Catherine chose the beautiful early English Gothic church, Corpus Christi, in Maiden Lane in Covent Garden, not far from where she lived. It features in the film adaptation of the Graham Greene novel, *The End of the Affair.* 'I hope that's not a bad omen,' I told her. The church was the first built after Catholic Emancipation in 1829 and had a big statue of St Patrick with his foot on a snake in the entrance. There was only one catch. I had grown up in the Church of England, so I assumed I would need to convert, or at least get the permission of the local bishop to enter a so-called 'mixed marriage', if I was to exchange rings in a Catholic setting.

I told my mum the situation and she revealed something startling. That I had been baptised a Catholic because that was *her* religion, something I knew nothing about. It was then that her memories of Father Pashby and the handwritten note from Jamaica came tumbling out, a story locked away for decades. I had grown up an Anglican, because the local C of E church that was attached to my primary school was close to our home, and they welcomed us with open arms, after my mum made sure I was baptised a Catholic first. So geography had dictated my faith.

I was horrified that the priest in Bolton had turned my mum away. Was this perhaps *God* rejecting my mother? I thought of the irony of what had happened. The early part of the nineteenth century saw a programme of Catholic church building in England, catering to the needs of newly arrived Irish immigrants after Catholic Emancipation. They were places of worship and solace for Irish Catholics in a potentially hostile new world, and my Jamaican Catholic mother hoped to find solace there too. The church that had rejected my mum would have been built around this time. St Patrick with his foot on the snake was supposed to be crushing evil, not fellow Catholics.

* * *

In 2021, I was approached to make a provocative documentary for the BBC's flagship current affairs programme, *Panorama*. It was entitled 'Is the Church Racist', and while it was a look at the Church of England, my mother's experience was not far from my mind while making the film.

We spoke with Michelle Delves, a junior vicar at All Saints Church in Hartlepool. Mixed race and working class, she said she was shocked by the lack of diversity in the Church when she first joined. 'I'd never felt as black or as poor in my whole life. I felt like I'd landed on an alien planet,' she said. Michelle enrolled at Cranmer Hall in Durham in 2016. It is a Bible college that has been training students for more than a century. But only one in ten accepted for training into the Church of England are from minority backgrounds.

Michelle had grown up in Bradford in the 1980s, where racism was a fact of life. She told us that some horrible things had been said to her, but at least it was to her face and she could deal with that. What really scared her about joining the Church was the subtle, institutional racism, which she says was pernicious. During the two years of training, she grew more and more isolated. She did not feel she could dress the way she wanted, wearing ethnic wraps on her head for instance, and she toned down the colours that she wore. There was an atmosphere of gentle hostility, a covert, silent threat suggesting she did not belong.

Airing her views with senior tutors and lecturers led nowhere and so on leaving college, she took her complaint to the very top, writing to the Archbishop of Canterbury. His office replied highlighting the Church's 'anger and sorrow' on hearing of her experiences, and said that 'much more needs to be done to tackle institutional racism'.

One junior vicar told us she was racially abused in class at Bible college by a white student. When she made a complaint, she was told to turn the other cheek. She felt isolated and alone in the Church of England, just like Michelle. She feared losing her job if she was identified and so requested anonymity when speaking to us. There were other examples in our *Panorama* film of black and brown clergy scared to speak out about racism, worried they would be seen as troublemakers, frightened they would lose the opportunity to fulfil their mission in life, a career ministering in the Church.

It was a painful documentary to make, to see the Church admit a fundamental inability to fulfil Christ's teaching, that we are all made in God's image and all one Christ. That there is one body, and we are all members of the same body. The problem is that too often the Church seemed to believe only *white* people were made in God's image. It's now set up an anti-racism task force to ensure greater equality. While some in the black community are literally praying for change, others aren't holding their breath, having seen numerous high level inquiries into racism in the church over the last almost forty years, barely affect any structural transformation.

Despite her experience with the English priest, my mum still wanted me baptised a Catholic. It happened at St Gregory's Church in Farnworth in Bolton, and I was the first baby baptised there under new rules designed to modernise the church. The service was directed in English not Latin, which was a monumental step, given the primacy and power of Rome, and the role Latin had played in unifying a disparate global communion. The changes were the result of the Vatican opening its doors to the modern world, including updating the liturgy, giving a larger role to lay people, and starting a dialogue with other religions. The Church understood it had to adapt to survive, and *that* is the lesson it must take away, Catholic or Anglican, from the accusations of racism.

As the author and theologian Professor Robert Beckford told me in the *Panorama* documentary, the Church faces an existential crisis. Most people attending worship on a Sunday morning are white and elderly. Quite frankly, they will not be around in a decade or two. But it does have these large numbers of black and brown people who are eager to participate in the life of the Church, to contribute to its minis-try. Appointing black bishops would go some way to engag-ing these people and telling them that they matter.

As I write there are forty-two senior bishops in the Church of England, with only one from an ethnic minority background. Out of twenty-two Catholic bishops in England and Wales, there are none.

* * *

It was a couple of years after our Catholic church wedding in 1998 that Catherine and I moved to Johannesburg. I was appointed the BBC's acting Africa correspondent, and we spent much of the time trying to understand how white South Africans had reconciled their politics of exclusion with God. The National Party, which won elections in 1948 and ushered in the period of apartheid, was led by a former minis-ter in the Dutch Reformed Church, to which most whites belonged. As the prime minister, Dr D.F. Malan legalised and enforced the apartheid laws, in part justified by the belief that God was a Great Separator.

The Afrikaner poet, Totius, was responsible for much of the translation of the Bible into Afrikaans, and in the 1940s he argued that the scriptures saw God separate light from darkness, the dry land from the seas, and so on. He used the same rationale for people, arguing black and white should not be put together. Totius also believed that whenever the word 'unity' crops up in the Bible, it is in the context of a spir-itual unity, not the literal unity of human beings.

How very different all this is to the Methodism of Nelson

Mandela or the Anglicanism of Desmond Tutu. Their God's idea of unity makes sense to me, that we are all made in His image, regardless of colour. I first came across Mandela at the press conference he gave on his visit to London after being released from prison in 1990. He held the room of jaded journalists from all over the world in the palm of his hand. It was his moral clarity that was unsurpassed, and his powers of forgiveness, even of the white authorities who had locked him away for a large part of his life.

Almost a quarter of a century later, I was despatched to South Africa to report on his funeral in 2013. His body lay in state at the Union Buildings in Pretoria, the seat of South African power and where he was sworn in as president in 1994. His open casket was at the centre of a temporary structure erected under a white canopy, with giant bouquets of lilies everywhere and chandeliers dangling from above. Around two thousand people an hour filed past to pay their respects, and I was one of those who gazed upon his stilled face beneath a sheet of glass, his hair white, his shirt trademark loud. Others made the sign of the cross as they walked by, some gently wept.

I felt a profound sadness that a good man was no more, but hoped his story of courage and sacrifice would somehow live on in this new South Africa, along with his insistence on forgiveness, borne out of his faith, and the teachings of the Methodist church.

His willingness not to seek reprisals on whites, but to have them talk about the sins of apartheid, underpins his creation of the Truth and Reconciliation Commission, chaired by Desmond Tutu in 1996. It allowed victims of gross human rights violations to give statements about their experiences, some at public hearings, and the perpetrators of violence to give their testimony and request amnesty from civil and criminal prosecution. It was an attempt at restorative justice, rather than the retributive justice of say, the Nuremburg Trials.

I thought it was a brave, inspired and difficult thing to do, genuinely to try applying the teachings of the Church in such a context to bring communities together, to prevent them being driven apart. Mandela's God is the one my mum would recognise.

Do I believe in God? No. But throughout my life, I have tried to subscribe to the so-called Golden Rule, of Matthew 7, verse 12: 'So in everything, do to others what you would have them do to you.' I believe Mandela and the way he lived his life subscribed to this basic teaching, because he treated everyone, even his enemies, with respect and was willing to offer forgiveness. It is a lesson I believe the priest who turned away my mother momentarily forgot. It is one we should all learn.

–4–

In Search of Happiness

MY WIFE CATHERINE had never been to Jamaica before, yet in some ways it was a bit of a homecoming. She is of Irish stock and there has always been an affinity between the Irish and Jamaicans, a bond. The saying goes that if Ireland was England's first oppressed colony, Jamaica was the second.

Cromwell's New Model Army brutally occupied Ireland from 1652, while the same fella seized Jamaica from the Spanish three years later. After he brutally put down the Irish rebellion, he forcibly transported thousands of boys and girls to Jamaica as indentured servants. Many ended up alongside black African slaves, working in terrible conditions on plantations. It is weird to think that my ancestors might even have got to know Catherine's forefathers on her dad Joseph's side.

Jamaica's first prime minister after independence from the British, two years before I was born in 1962, was Sir Alexander Bustamante. He used to boast that he was 50 per cent Irish and 50 per cent Jamaican. Today Irish is the second most claimed ethnic origin, after African, on the island, and for many years the only Guinness brewery outside Ireland was in Jamaica's capital, Kingston. Generations of Jamaicans after the war grew up loving Guinness. My dad was no exception, with the black liquid a staple of his famous Jamaican Guinness punch. Add one egg, mix, add a bit of sugar and orange juice. Gorgeous.

And don't get me started on the influence of reggae on my wife! Along with her sister Winifred, they both bunked off convent school on the day of Catherine's French 'O' Level exam, getting the coach from Dorset to London, to see Bob Marley and the Wailers on their final 1980 tour at the Crystal Palace Bowl. It was only a few months before Bob died of cancer. Cath never regretted bunking off the exam, until we moved to Paris in 2007 when I was made the BBC's Europe correspondent, and she had to brush up on her French, struggling to get the gas and internet connected in our new apartment.

I first visited Jamaica in 1975. I was eleven years old and found the whole experience awful. It was the first time I had ever been on an aeroplane, and I felt terribly airsick there and back. I am pretty sure I must have used one of those sickbags, which are bizarrely made of paper. That flight to Kingston coloured the whole trip. I was hot and bothered most of the time, as I could not acclimatise to the tropical heat after a life raised in a cold, blustery Bolton. I missed my school friends badly, too. It was summertime when we went away, and as Bolton baked in the sun, I would normally have been playing out in the back street behind our house with my school pals.

In Jamaica, I was also constantly bitten by mosquitoes, which gloried in sucking my blood. I was so fed up with it, itching the whole time, with my arms and legs sore and bruised. Then there were the cross-country journeys to see a seemingly endless list of aunties and uncles, cousins, and more cousins and yet more cousins, all over the island. We travelled by car on bumpy bush roads that only fuelled more nausea. I just felt sick the whole time.

We made one cross-country trip from Kingston to Westmoreland, and I recall thinking that I was finally going to see Savanna-la-Mar, or Sav-la-Mar as my parents used to call it, a place whose name appeared on a very large number of the envelopes my mum and dad would get us kids to leave at the local post office in Bolton, to wind their way to the Caribbean.

Savanna-la-Mar is the capital of Westmoreland Parish and was an important fortress town on the coast during the time of the Spanish occupation, before Cromwell's troops arrived. We did not hang around in Sav though, only long enough to catch a glimpse of the ruins of the eighteenth-century fort in the town that was supposed to provide protection against pirates, and then we headed out to the homestead that belonged to my Grandad Clarence and Grandma Mavis. They had a plot of land growing corn, peas and sweet potatoes. They had chickens, too.

I remember that once there was an old hen sitting in the loo above the cistern. It had escaped the coop outside. Very still and quiet, it was not going to budge. I tried shooing it away. But nope, it was not going to go. I needed to use the loo, but I was worried that the old hen might jump up and peck away at my bum. I could not wait for the old bird to shift, so I gingerly dropped my pants, all the while looking into the beady eyes of the plump fowl. I have never been so nervous going to the loo in my life. But clearly the hen had seen it all before and while we stared each other out, it did not stir, feeling no need to leap forward and have a bite.

What I failed to appreciate fully at the time was that this journey to Jamaica was an important trip for my mum, along with my brother Garfield, and younger sister, Sonia. It was my mum's first time returning to the island after leaving in 1962. It was a huge visit for her, and all I could do was whine. I apologise for that. It must have been a difficult journey, revisiting the places and the people she had left behind, though at the same time a joyful trip too, reacquainting herself with her mother and father.

I was also meeting other members of *my* family for the first time, the line of Myries and Burnets (my mother's maiden name) that led down to me. This momentous occasion was lost on my eleven-year-old self. These were people to whom I could now put faces, having seen their names on hundreds of aerogramme envelopes over the years, the white ones with the funny little blue planes on, signifying the letter was going abroad. Inside would be postal orders of money, the fruits of my mum and dad's labour winging their way to Jamaica to help the rest of the family.

My parents did that every month when I was growing up. It was the emigration dividend, the justification for years of separation, the financial reward for putting up with not seeing your own mum or dad, or sisters and brothers, for years and years. The remittances were the hope invested in my mum's BA flight from Jamaica to the UK back in 1962, and my dad's ship fare from Kingston to Southampton the year before. But money can never compensate for the loss of those years of real contact, face-to-face love and friendship. The emigrant in search of happiness forever has a hole in their heart, the loss of precious time that can never be regained.

* * *

We hear a lot about 'perilous journeys' and the heartbreaking attempts made by migrants and asylum seekers to find their pot of gold in a new land, either via the Mediterranean, the English Channel, or the Mexico/US border. Some of course never make it, cruelly exploited by people traffickers extracting thousands of dollars for a one-way trip, sometimes to oblivion, on unseaworthy vessels. The loss of life and human potential is truly awful, and whenever I read or see a news story about a migrant boat capsizing in the Channel and people dying, I think about all that, and the hopes submerged beneath the water.

These were people just like my parents and the Windrush Generation, hoping to send back home little envelopes once they had got on their own two feet in an adopted land. It is a story as old as human history. I see the faces of those Iraqis and Afghans and Kurds and Ethiopians, Nigerians and Somalis, and I always think of my own family.

Yes, my parents were different in that they had been invited to make a fresh start in the UK, they were British citizens. But the desire to live anew and reinvent themselves was the same as for today's migrants. Or for the Italians who made their way on ship after ship to America at the turn of the twentieth century, or the Ten Pound Poms who headed to Australia and New Zealand after the war. Hope burns in the heart of every human being to live a happy life, to try to build a future. To find the funds to feed and help clothe and nurture those close to them, wherever they may be.

In 2015, I went to Italy to report on the growing numbers of people using traffickers to sail from Libya to reach southern Europe. Many were escaping war zones and authoritarian regimes. For others it was poverty and deprivation, the result of appalling kleptocratic governments who had bled their treasuries dry, leaders who had lined their pockets and those of their cronies. On the day I arrived in the Sicilian port city of Catania, we got word that a ship carrying migrants and asylum seekers had capsized and hundreds of people were thought to have drowned.

I visited a graveyard near the harbour, where I met Donatus Igyeye laying fresh flowers by the headstone of his late wife, Annetta. A few months before, both had set sail on a migrant ship from Libya with hundreds of others, and the overloaded vessel had capsized. Donatus, who was in his late twenties, told me that Annetta was clinging on to him as they both tried to stay afloat, but she could not hold on. She was screaming and screaming and exhausted, finally lost her grip on his sodden shirt. Donatus felt her weight suddenly vanish as she sank beneath the water, never to resurface, until the Italian coastguard recovered her body.

Clearly traumatised and looking off into the middle distance as we spoke, a hot Mediterranean sun beating down on the graveyard, Donatus said he felt guilty he could not save his wife, that they were forced to try to reach Europe because there was nothing for them back in Nigeria. No job, no hope. They wanted to have children together and send back money to their home village to help the rest of the family. Just like my mum and dad, they were searching for happiness.

* * *

Over the years I grew to love Jamaica and visited several times in the 1990s. So after Catherine and I were married, I was look- ing forward to showing her my family's homeland. We had met in 1992 in London, when she worked as a commissioning editor for a publishing house called Pavilion. She was launch- ing a book on Swiss cheeses and her colleague, who was an old friend of mine, invited me to the launch party. That is where the old Jamaican/Irish-Afro/Celtic connection kicked straight in, over little squares of cheese impaled on thin wooden sticks, washed down with warm wine.

We finally got the chance to visit Jamaica together in 2006 and decided to stay first in Montego Bay, a stunning, lush and quiet part of Jamaica's north shoreline, with pristine beaches and palm trees, then we headed south to the bustling capital, Kingston.

My first trip to Jamaica in 1975 was also the first time I met my wonderful Aunty Maizie. She was my mum's sister and seemed so glamorous, a very successful businesswoman, who had risen to become one of the most senior officials in the Civil Service, as the island's Commissioner for Income Tax. After that she was running her own real estate company. She was forever jetting off to Florida to close some big deal or other, according to my mum.

Her home in Red Hills, a well-to-do suburb of Kingston, was big and spacious, all white with cooling marbled floors and modern American furniture. Ceiling fans whirred above in every room drawing in the breeze. She had a huge garden, where lively little lizards would scurry from time to time, with the whole area big enough for several coconut trees to tower over. I picked up a big, heavy specimen that had fallen to the ground, at the behest of Aunty. 'You need to try this,' she said. So she went into the house and produced a giant machete and with the coconut in her left hand and the machete in her right, expertly swung the blade with precision, slicing off just the right amount of the top.

'Here, don't spill it now, bwoy, tek di husk and drink.' I raised the coconut up to my lips and out poured the clear juice that was not unpleasant, but did not exactly set my world alight. 'Now you're a true Jamaican,' she told me, as the liquid dribbled down my chin.

I will never forget my eyes popping when I noticed in the driveway a gleaming, green-coloured Cadillac saloon car, its elongated front and sharp-edged rear so very different to British cars, which were by comparison small and not very exciting. Growing up in Bolton, Mum told us that Aunty had bought a new car and it was a Cadillac. So I looked up what a Cadillac was and read that it was 'a car that could not be improved. The next generation of luxury car.' It looked wonderful to me in the flesh.

Every Christmas I would call Aunty Maizie in Jamaica and wish her festive greetings. A few times after becoming a journalist, I returned to the island on filming trips, and I would pop in to say hi and stay over. The Cadillac, by now a vintage car and it must be said looking a little worn, still sat in the driveway. The coconut tree I first clapped eyes on in 1975 was also going strong, and I still struggled to stop the juice dribbling down my chin on raising a giant husk to my lips, having been sliced with the machete by Aunty Maizie, now well into her seventies. My 2006 visit with Catherine to see her and my grandmother was poignant, as it would be the last time I saw both of them alive.

Aunty was now caring for grandma, at her home in Red Hills, after she had developed vascular dementia. Maizie was retired now and I was looking forward to catching up, as it had been a good few years since we last met. Aunty knew that we were coming and we would be staying for a few days. I know she mentioned this to my grandmother, but it probably did not register. Alzheimer's had cruelly taken away any notion she might have had about who I was. She had never met Catherine. Grandma only ever visited the UK once, in the mid-1980s, before I met my wife.

We had decided to fly to Kingston and not drive, the nausea-inducing cross-country journeys of my first visit to Jamaica still in my mind. We arrived at Norman Manley International Airport, and Aunty Maizie had organised a car to pick us up. Forty minutes or so later we arrived at her home. I gave a big hug to Aunty, and she hugged Catherine, whom she was meeting for the first time. Then I hugged my grandma, but I could see that she clearly had no clue who I was, or this white woman, Catherine, standing next to me. We sat down and my grandma looked perplexed and agitated.

'Are you okay, grandma?' I said.

All of a sudden, she responded to me in Spanish: '*Casa yu boca!*'

I had not the faintest idea what she was saying or why she was speaking Spanish. She said the phrase again. '*Casa yu boca!*' which in English means, 'Shut your mouth!' She then got up and turning to me, declared, 'I'm not your slave,' and left the room.

'What was that about?' I asked Aunty Maizie.

'Oh, don't mind,' she said. 'Mama's confused. Every now and again she reaches back to her childhood growing up in Panama where she learned to speak Spanish. It's the dementia.'

'Panama!' I said incredulously. 'Granny grew up in Panama?'

'Yes, bwoy, you neva know?'

'No, I didn't, and what was the slave thing?'

'Oh, it's because she saw Catherine, who's white, and wasn't sure what was happening. She's confused, it's very sad. The dementia has robbed her of her senses.'

I looked at Catherine and she understood what was going on, but was really worried she was causing grandma distress.

It was then that I found out that my great-grandfather, my grandma's dad, was one of tens of thousands of Caribbeans who, like my mother and father, had left Jamaica and other islands in the West Indies, to earn some money abroad. He went to South America, to help build the mighty Panama Canal. My grandma was around seven or eight when she made the journey to the Canal Zone, the vast area designated for the great waterway, with the land being the property of America, handed over by the Panamanian Government. My mind drifted off to what it must have been like for her, as alien as Jamaica was to me on my first visit. No doubt she missed her friends too and playing in the backyard as the sun sat high.

The West Indian migration narrative, that search for happiness, tends to begin with the *Empire Windrush* and the journey to England in 1948. But there is a much earlier and much larger history of foreign exploration, to the swamps of South America. It was the post-emancipation generation of the 1850s who travelled to seek their fortune, and it is a history only recently given the prominence it deserves.

For much of the twentieth century, the focus had been on America's role in the building of the canal. Wall Street and President Teddy Roosevelt bankrolled the project, and his engineers came up with a design that overcame the topographical challenges of cutting across the mountain range that sat proud above the isthmus of Panama. American physicians also conquered the scourge of mosquitoes and disease, which had forced the French to abandon their attempt to build a canal in the late nineteenth century, using mainly Caribbean workers.

But all America's money and know-how would have meant little without a ready labour force, and the West Indies was again the provider, digging the channel for the giant waterway. Untold numbers lost their lives or limbs in landslides and explosions during the construction. They were also treated as second-class citizens by the Americans, who took lock, stock and barrel their ideas of white racial superiority, honed through the segregation practices of the South, down with them to Panama.

Black workers were fed inferior food in separate dining halls with no seating, while white workers had table linen and fine china. Black workers were rarely given roles of responsibility, but white workers were mainly foremen or supervisors. Black workers were paid in silver dollars, and white workers were paid in gold, worth four times as much. In fact, black workers were referred to as 'Silvermen', working on the 'Silver Roll'. American racism was transnational and hemispheric, an export heaping more shame on the land of Lincoln.

With few opportunities for decently paid work at home in Jamaica, my grandmother's father, Eugene Graham, decided to take his family to Panama, after American recruiters came calling. As with my own father moving to industrial Lancashire from rural Jamaica in 1961, so it must have been a dramatic contrast for my great-grandfather leaving pastoral Westmoreland for the Panama construction site, a place of brutal modernisation with digging machines and railroad tracks taking away the spoil and rubble of the mountainside, and explosions at every turn as dynamite was used to blast away at the rock.

It was hard work for the migrant West Indians and, not having any idea what they were letting themselves in for, many regretted ever setting foot on South American soil. They chafed at the long hours, discrimination and segregation. My great-grandfather should never have gone to Panama. He had a heart condition, not helped by the hard physical labour.

It would have been at school in the Canal Zone that my grandmother learned to speak Spanish. Education was segregated, of course, and what black boys and girls were taught would have been rudimentary compared to the white children. But the Spanish my grandma Mavis learned stayed with her, despite rarely getting a chance to be aired after she

returned to Jamaica, until that day in 2006, when her grand-
son and his white wife came calling. My grandma was the
oldest of six children, including a set of twins, and when her
father died in Panama of his heart condition, she had to
return to her grandparents in Jamaica, leaving her father
behind, buried in Monkey Hill Cemetery, later known as
Mount Hope.

'It's really sad, though,' said Aunty Maizie after Granny
broke out in Spanish, 'because grandma's also been railing –
as if she found out only yesterday – that on her return to
Jamaica, after her father passed, the little piece of land back
in Jamaica that was her birthright and that he'd left her in his
will, was stolen by distant family members while she was
away. The dementia has brought back all the hurt.'

It made me realise that while the immigrant reshapes the
landscape of a new land, they also distort what is left behind.
The absence brings its own challenges.

The next morning at breakfast, grandma repeated the
Spanish phrase, '*Casa yu boca!*', but laughed as she said it and
we all laughed too. Then she gave Catherine a gentle smile.

My grandmother passed away not long after that. Aunty
Maizie remained active in her local church, Coke Memorial
Methodist, in Kingston, but she too slowly developed dementia, and gradually became withdrawn, retreating into a cloak
of darkness and silence. She died in the summer of 2022.

–5–

The Paper Chase

ALL FIRST-GENERATION IMMIGRANT parents want their children to be happy, of course, but it would also be nice if they grew up to be lawyers, dentists or accountants! Engaged in 'proper' jobs. My decision to become a journalist was at first a let-down for Mum and Dad. Though they might not admit it, I know they felt they had not given up everything they knew in Jamaica to fly 6,000 miles halfway round the world for their children to become bums.

The prize was so close for them too, in achieving their dream for me. I studied law at university and I won a place at the Middle Temple in London to become a barrister. As far as my parents were concerned, the stars seemed aligned: I had the ball at my feet and I was bearing down on the goal. I had rounded the keeper and the net was empty, yawning, willing me to bang the ball right down its throat, and maybe one day become a QC (or KC now).

Growing up as a teenager in the 1970s and 80s, it was television and watching Alan Whicker and Sir Trevor McDonald that influenced my ultimate career choice to become a jour-nalist. But it was also television that nudged me towards the idea of possibly becoming a lawyer, as there was no history of legal practice in my family.

I loved John Mortimer's brilliant *Rumpole of the Bailey*, with Leo McKern, touching, serious and funny all at the same time. In the afternoons, ITV used to show a drama series called *Crown Court*, which was very clever. Set exclusively in a courtroom, lawyers for the defence and prosecution – all played by actors – would go through a fictional case. The witnesses and defendant and judge were also actors, but the jury was made up of members of the public, who were picked from the electoral register and were eligible for real jury service. They alone decided guilt or innocence.

I used to watch the show if I happened to be off school because I was ill, or had popped home for lunch. I would pretend I was in the jury, having weighed up all the evidence on both sides, and I would guess the final verdict. I remember shouting at the TV with my mum, 'That's rubbish, the jury's never going to believe that!' or 'Why isn't that defence lawyer more aggressive, he's plainly innocent!' The opening theme music, the fourth movement of Janacek's *Sinfonietta*, always takes me back to those days watching the show.

But it was the American drama, *The Paper Chase*, that really made me think the law might be the way forward. It was broadcast in the late 1970s, so I would have been aged around thirteen or fourteen, and it centred on a group of students at Harvard Law School, ruled over by an overbearing but kindly professor named Kingsfield, played by John Houseman. He famously declares in the very first episode to a lecture hall full of terrified first years: 'I [will] train your mind. You come in here with a skull full of mush, and if you survive . . . I'll send you out thinking like a lawyer.'

Would they survive the rigours of Harvard, the exacting Kingsfield, and the tough discipline of law? Their trials and tribulations, their growing pains, their love lives and friendships were so well drawn and interesting, meaningful and fun. Harvard looked beautiful, the actors were beautiful, and I wanted to be one of those students.

The Paper Chase, or the dash for the final degree certificate, was about young people starting out, beginning life's journey, just like me. Lawyers on TV came across as noble and courageous, defenders of the innocent, pursuers of the guilty. They seemed to be in the business of helping people and I found that very attractive. So there was no question that when it came time to go to university, the subject I would study was the law.

I applied to Sussex, not only because I loved the campus, ranged across acres of beautiful rolling fields in the village of Falmer just outside Brighton, but because it was a university that employed the 'major/minor' system of course work. I could 'major' in law, but to satisfy my journalistic urges, my 'minor' was literature in the School of English and American Studies. I was trying to have my cake and eat it. But ultimately, I would have to make a choice. My head was telling me go for the law, while my heart was fixated on telling stories, on travelling the world and becoming a journalist. So, a year after graduation, I would join the BBC.

* * *

In the spring of 1982, I visited the University of Sussex campus on an open day, to check out if it might be the place where I would want to spend the next three years working for my degree. After going around the university at Falmer, I went into Brighton and I will never forget seeing the promenade for the first time, bustling with people enjoying the sun. The weather was glorious and the sea was a calm and wonderful, bold dark blue. Everything was a direct contrast to the grey of Bolton, and Brighton's stunning Regency and Georgian terraces, coloured magnolia and white, were picture-perfect, marzipan and icing-encrusted buildings bathed in glorious soft yellow light, architecture that I fell in love with.

As a seventeen-year-old I was wild eyed, intoxicated by the clean fresh air and sense of freedom that lay within my grasp if I attained the right A levels. Bolton suddenly felt claustrophobic and limiting. I wanted new experiences, to explore first-hand some of the worlds that television had tantalisingly opened.

I went for a stroll in the main shopping area of Brighton called 'The Lanes', full of gorgeous shops set along a narrow, winding path that weaved one way, then another, like a maze in which it was easy to get lost. Some stores were selling fancy clothes, others antiques, there were lovely bookshops and cafés and restaurants. Many of the people in and around the Lanes were young students, checking out the second-hand clothing and record stores. It was a vibrant milieu, and there was a sense of energy, that the place was alive. I was instantly smitten.

Right at the heart of the Lanes was a little square with shops around the edge and seating in the middle. I wandered into a record store, and as I checked out what they had to offer, a man walked in dressed rather unusually, I thought.

He was clearly a man because he sported a beard, but he was wearing white stiletto high heels, tight white trousers, and a white shirt. A white shawl was over his shoulders. In his right hand was a dog lead at the end of which was a white poodle.

I had never seen anything like that in my life. I am from Bolton and I was transfixed, looking on in amazement as this gentleman walked up to the counter to chat with the sales assistant, whom he clearly knew. After a few minutes he left, tottering along on his heels, click-clacking out of the store, with his poodle following behind. No one else in the shop batted an eyelid, for such a sight was clearly a normal every-day occurrence in this town.

Believe it or not, I had no clue on that first visit to Brighton that this glorious place was a gay mecca. I was straight as far as I could tell at the age of seventeen, but I felt a sense of belonging after that trip and knew I wanted to study at Sussex, despite offers from other universities closer to Bolton. You see, as a northern lad in a southern town hundreds of miles away from what I knew, I did not feel, as a black man, like an outsider. I got a sense I would be accepted here, because *everyone* was accepted.

The LGBTQ community had been established since the early nineteenth century in Brighton, and compassion and love for all human beings is what I felt on that first visit to the town. Yet being gay was still not fully accepted in wider mainstream society. In 1987, the first two gay characters appeared in the most popular TV programme at the time, *EastEnders*, and I will never forget the *Sun*'s headline that read, 'EastBenders'. An editorial also suggested it was irresponsible of the programme to promote underage sex, as one of the characters was under twenty-one, then the legal age of consent.

My university years were some of the happiest of my life. My closest friends at the time, Martin Evans, now a well-respected professor at Sussex University, and Neil Bullock, a successful barrister in London, are still my closest friends and both were my best men at my wedding to Catherine. Neil, Martin and I lived through the horror of the AIDS epidemic in the early 1980s, which was a terrible blow to the local community in Brighton and saw us lose friends and acquaintances.

So it was a special moment for me, much later in the mid-1990s as the BBC's Los Angeles correspondent, when I reported on the first successful trials anywhere in the world of a special combination therapy cocktail of antiretroviral drugs, which were capable of stopping the HIV virus from replicating in the body, limiting the damage to the immune system caused by HIV, and slowing down the development of AIDS. I thought of the friends I had known who could have benefitted, but for whom the breakthrough came too late.

It was also a special moment attending Neil's civil ceremony to his partner as British society and attitudes to the LGBTQ community transformed for ever, when same sex marriage became legal in 2014. No more 'EastBenders'.

While Bolton is where I grew up, Brighton and Sussex University is where I came of age, gaining in confidence and self-belief, finally to realise that the law was not what I wanted, despite my family's hopes. I realised it had to be journalism that I should pursue as a career, and that to be truly fulfilled in life, I had to follow my heart. All the roads I have travelled since lead back to that splendid resort by the sea.

* * *

We all know the ability of work or a career to empower us, to give meaning to our lives, and with a decent wage, allow us to do the things we want to do. In October 2022, for Black History Month, I was asked by the *Sun* (yes, the very same newspaper that thirty-five years earlier had so much trouble coping with gay characters in *EastEnders*) to write a piece on a figure who had inspired me, and I thought instantly of Roy Hackett. He had died in August that year at the grand old age of ninety-three, secure in the knowledge that because of his efforts and those of his colleagues at the Bristol Bus Depot in the 1960s, he left this world a better place.

After leaving university and joining the BBC, my first full-time job was in the wonderful city of Bristol, where Roy Hackett was a legend. It was there that he stood in the middle of Fishponds Road in 1963 on a rather fresh spring day, rubbing his hands and blowing warm breaths into cupped fingers to ward off an icy wind, as he began blocking the entrance to the main bus station. Along with other Windrush Generation activists, he was protesting the Bristol Omnibus Company's refusal to employ black and Asian people as conductors and drivers. Bristol had a centuries-old black population, because of the local port's involvement in the transatlantic slave trade.

Roy had arrived in Britain in 1952, from the Trench Town area of Kingston in Jamaica. There he had tried various jobs, including working in a chemist shop, on a coffee plantation and selling insurance, but he could not make a decent living. So he emigrated to Britain, arriving in Liverpool by ship. However, things were not much better on the work front, in fact he said he lived a 'dog's life', because he could not find a job, and so many landlords refused to offer rooms to him and other black tenants.

A decade before my parents arrived, Roy found a country that in many respects was as racist as segregated America, or apartheid South Africa. The owners of shops and other commercial premises, pubs, restaurants and workplaces, could legally ban non-white customers from certain rooms or facilities.

There were colour bars in some professions as well as in housing, and newly discovered documents unearthed in 2021 show that courtiers at Buckingham Palace had a policy of banning 'coloured immigrants or foreigners' from serving in clerical roles in the Royal Household. It is an indelible stain on the Transport and General Workers Union, that it rigidly wanted to enforce the Bristol Bus Company's colour bar, as the union said, in order to protect jobs for 'local' people.

After a while Roy Hackett left Liverpool for Wolverhampton, then tried his hand in London, getting bits and pieces of labouring work here and there, before gradually drifting westwards to south Wales, where he was employed on building sites. On one construction project, he spent time with a soon-to-be-famous pop star called Tom Jones, who according to Roy, greatly irritated him with his constant singing.

Roy then headed for Bristol, where a succession of landlords refused him a room, causing him to spend his first night in the city sleeping in a doorway. But he later found his feet, befriending local black activists, and on hearing that black people were being refused jobs as bus conductors, he helped to force the hand of the bus company to end its colour bar.

That fight for justice is credited with helping to persuade the then Labour government to introduce the first piece of anti-racist legislation in Britain, the Race Relations Act of 1965, which outlawed discrimination on the 'grounds of colour, race, or ethnic or national origins' in public places in Great Britain. The new law made sense on so many levels. Not only was racism and bigotry morally reprehensible, but the country needed committed workers in all sectors of society, to contribute to the economy.

As I wrote in the *Sun*, when I learned of Roy Hackett's death, I felt a deep sadness at the passing of a national hero. I never had the pleasure of meeting him or speaking with him, yet he had a direct impact on the course of my life and that of millions of other Britons. Roy fought at great personal expense for my right to be treated fairly as a black Briton, and to be allowed to work where I was capable, without being disqualified simply because of the colour of my skin.

Roy's obituary, which appeared in the *Guardian*, described him as a 'humble man', who in later life remained committed to supporting the black community in Bristol, joking that 'a lot of young people ask me if I can help them, and I always say yes – as long as I can sit in the shade.'

* * *

Quiet revolutionaries like Roy Hackett have fascinated me my whole working life, the people who just get on with things, seemingly without ego, changing the world for the better. I am reminded of Rosa Parks, a woman I described as a quiet revolutionary in my report on her funeral for the *BBC News at Ten*. She was a black seamstress, who in an unassuming show of defiance, helped change the course of history.

It was late at night when I saw the line of mourners grow and multiply along Detroit's Seven Mile Road, on the eve of her funeral service, in October 2005. Thousands of people, black, white, old and young were happy to queue well into the early hours and far beyond, as the dead of night became the very pale blue of dawn, then the bright blue of mid-afternoon, when the commemorations would begin. One man told me he was waiting in line because Rosa gave a voice to oppressed people all over the world that it was important to stand up and do what you know to be right. A woman remarked that Rosa changed a nation, simply because she was tired of moving to the back of the bus.

Riding public transport in the segregated South was a daily reminder of race hate, as it was for black people like Roy Hackett in Bristol. 'Omnibus' translated from Latin means 'for all', yet that was an oxymoron. Buses incubated attitudes of separation on both sides of the Atlantic, and in America white people sat at the front with easy access to the door, while black people were forced to clamber to the back.

In 1955 in Alabama, Rosa Parks decided that the daily humiliation must end, and she refused to give up her seat at the front to a white passenger. She was arrested and thrown in jail, but in protest, African Americans in the city of

Montgomery, the state capital of Alabama, boycotted the entire bus system, causing severe financial losses for the bus company. Eventually, after a court ruling, segregated buses were ruled to be unconstitutional, and a nascent civil rights movement led by Dr Martin Luther King was galvanised to fight for the outlawing of all segregation policies right across the South. Rosa Parks was an unfussy and unassuming woman, gently radicalised over time by the injustice of segregation, groomed to rebel by a society morally unmoored.

On that October day in 2005, the Greater Grace Temple Church was the setting for her funeral service, where her open casket lay. Three thousand people took up their seats to pay their respects, including Bill and Hillary Clinton. In his address, the former president spoke of Rosa's act of simple defiance, showing all of us every day what it means to be free. I was myself in awe of Rosa, and her strength to take on a system that had crushed so many in its unfairness. Would I have had the will and strength to do what she did? To refuse to adhere to an indefensible code that required her, because of the colour of her skin, to bow to a white person every day?

The dignity in her defiance to stay put and be arrested was earth-shaking, and standing in front of her coffin I felt a deep sense of failure, that perhaps I would not have had the strength and courage to do what she did. I felt inadequate and suddenly unsure of myself. I was a successful journalist; I was providing for my family, but was I changing anything? What did my fancy education really add up to? Had I made a mistake in not becoming a lawyer, where I could tangibly be helping people every day I went to work. '

The Windrush Generation, my parents included, were quiet revolutionaries too, transforming Britain: our bus and council services, the rail network, helping to build our towns and cities brick by brick, and staffing the NHS. So many black Caribbeans after the war ended up working in the public sector, helping to knit communities together and improving the lives of millions of ordinary people.

My older sister Judith became a lecturer; my younger brother Garfield is in PR and has worked for the Unison trade union and a black non-profit organisation; Sonia, my younger sister, is a teacher; and my youngest sister Lorna works as a carer. My nephew Lewis even became a doctor in the NHS, driven by his own battle with sickle cell anaemia, a blood condition that particularly affects black people. He wanted to help alleviate the pain of others.

As for me? Well, having thwarted my mum's dreams, first by being born and secondly by becoming a reporter, I suppose I am the family outcast when it comes to public service. But I do think journalism can make a difference in all our lives for the better, even if it is simply by shining a light on those who help us all; the quiet revolutionaries in the background, who deserve the centre stage.

* * *

I had a paper round as a young teenager growing up in Bolton in the 1970s, and I devoured the copies of *The Times*, the *Sunday Times* and *Guardian* that I would get for free. To this day, my sisters and brothers tease me about the fact that I used to pretend I was reading the news on television, around the age of twelve or thirteen, reading out loud the front pages, looking up from the text and addressing an imaginary camera in front of me, mimicking the famous newsreaders of the day like Kenneth Kendall, Reginald Bosanquet, Gordon Honeycombe or Alastair Burnet. My print heroes were Harry Evans and the Insight team at the *Sunday Times*, and John Pilger at the *Daily Mirror*.

On television I particularly loved Alan Whicker, a man whose range of wonderful tales spanned the globe, from profiling geisha girls in Kyoto, to interviewing Francois 'Papa Doc' Duvalier in Haiti, the murderous dictator who made opponents and critics disappear using his fearsome secret police, the Tonton Macoute. They were the thugs and henchmen immortalised in Graham Greene's novel about Haiti, *The Comedians*. I will never forget Duvalier telling Whicker with an air of nonchalance that 'democracy is only a word'.

The first time I heard of the concept of plastic surgery, the idea that fit and healthy human beings would go into hospital to have a doctor cut and pull their faces to make them apparently look younger, was in a 1970s edition of Alan's brilliant info/travel series, *Whicker's World*. I was sitting in our living room watching the TV as a kid and seeing these strange people in Los Angeles, a very odd-looking place on the other side of the globe. I was utterly fascinated.

I had never heard of such a thing – altering your appearance to make yourself look younger! It was all a bit mad and I was transfixed. It was one of the moments in my early teens that made me realise I wanted to tell similar stories of the lives of others. To paint a picture of our world: the good, the bad, the weird, the delightful and the ugly.

But would this be possible? I was not sure, so I resolved that in case I did not make it as a journalist, I would follow my family's wishes and become a barrister or solicitor, which is why I ended up studying law at university. The sad truth is there was no one on television in those days who looked remotely like me or sounded like me. Alan Whicker, born in British-controlled Egypt, had a cut-glass accent forged at a public school in the Home Counties. He wore thick glasses and was also, of course, as white as a sheet.

Then one day I turned on the TV and I saw another journalist wearing glasses who seemed to be speaking directly and only to me. His tone was soft yet firm, his diction crystal clear. Funnily enough he sounded a little bit like my mum when she used to speak on the phone, someone smoothing out the natural patois of their usual voice into received pronunciation. The accent of the man on the telly was closer to how Alan Whicker sounded. It was again the early 1970s, and the man I was watching in rapt concentration was black.

Trevor McDonald was born in Trinidad and worked for ITN, the news service for commercial television. He inspired a whole generation of black people in the 1970s and 80s to believe they could achieve anything. Years later I interviewed the comedian and actor Lenny Henry, himself an inspiration to many, and he recounted tales from his own childhood of how everyone in his household would drop whatever they were doing to gather around the TV to watch Trevor when he was on.

My family did the same and I suspect there were many others up and down the country. First- and second-generation black immigrants, desperate for heroes. For them the sight of

Trevor McDonald on TV suggested that the new improved life they hoped for, far away from the Caribbean, *was* possible and the sacrifices might be worth it. The trauma of the racism they were experiencing today could morph into the triumph of success tomorrow. I too came to believe that someone like me could make a career in television journalism.

Later in 1994 or 1995, on a summer's day at Television Centre in West London, I was a young BBC network news journalist, and talk turned to deciding who would be the reporter assigned to cover the Notting Hill Carnival that was coming up in a couple of weeks. I prayed I would not get the assignment. I resented the possibility that viewers might think I was only covering the carnival because I was black, and I was not capable of covering other stories.

I was in the newsroom, sitting with others on what was called the 'taxi rank', where we so-called 'pool' reporters waited to be 'hailed' by the news editor to go off and report on some item of breaking news. I did not want to go to Notting Hill. In fact, I did not want anything to do with a story on British soil involving black people. I wanted to cover all kinds of stories all over the world, like my heroes Alan Whicker and Trevor McDonald, and not to be pigeonholed. For viewers to think, there's Clive Myrie on the TV, and not, there's that black man on the TV.

It had been difficult for women to be taken seriously in TV newsrooms when I first became a journalist. It was only in the 1980s and 90s that female correspondents in British broadcasting were given assignments deemed to be 'challenging'. While print journalism had its war heroines, trailblazers like Clare Hollingworth, Martha Gellhorn, Lee Miller and

Marie Colvin, broadcasting was very late to the diversity party, with Kate Adie, the BBC's chief news correspondent from 1989–2003, paving the way for the likes of Orla Guerin, Lindsey Hilsum and Lyse Doucet.

Similarly, I did not want to be put in a box, and so it was that I came to have a meeting in 1995 with the BBC's Foreign Editor, Vin Ray. I had been a network news reporter for three years after joining the BBC on a trainee scheme, and having worked in local radio and regional television in Bristol. I was categorical in my meeting with Vin that I did not want to be framed as a 'black journalist, who only did black stories'. I was quite militant about this at the time. I was at the start of my career covering national and international news, and I wanted to be defined by my work, not my colour.

Vin was a man who liked a sharp suit, as I recall. A natty dresser, he favoured the relaxed Armani look of the mid-90s. I may be completely wrong on that, but I do know that he had a gentle air that made him approachable; not like the usual BBC manager, who was generally fiercely intelligent, but uncomfortable around people and unable to truly engage with them. In conversation, they normally looked at the floor.

Vin was different. As well as being highly intelligent, he was a thoroughly likeable bloke. A man who had 'been there, done that' as a frontline field producer working on the BBC's coverage of the first Gulf War, the coup against Mikhail Gorbachev in 1991 and the Bosnian War, among many other major stories. Now he was the BBC's Foreign Editor, and I wanted to report abroad.

'I am not a black reporter, I'm a reporter who just happens to be black,' I emphasised.

'I get it, I understand,' came the reply, or words to that effect. It was shortly afterwards that Vin got back to me to say he was sending me to Japan.

Of course, I was channelling my own insecurities in all this. Should I have cared what some members of the public might have thought, about a black man covering the Notting Hill Carnival? Of course not. But I was young and more importantly I did not want the BBC to be gripped by lazy thinking, 'Oh, it's a "black" story, send Clive.' I kicked against that possibility as hard as I could. However, as I grew in confidence in journalism, I felt the need to tell *more* not *fewer* black stories. I am proud, for instance, of the work of the BBC TV series *Black Britain*, which looked at the lives and issues surrounding the Caribbean community in the mid-1990s. I am now the *first* to raise my hand to cover a so-called 'black' story.

Over the years I have met Sir Trevor McDonald on many occasions, and I am sure he is fed up to the back teeth of me going on about how he inspired me to become a reporter. He was gracious enough, now in his eighties, to find the time to present me with a Special Award from the Television and Radio Industry Club in 2022. But in 2018, I interviewed him on stage about *his* life and career, at the University Women's Club in central London, in front of a packed audience. As he spoke, I was transported back again to my family living room in the 1970s and 80s and his profound influence on a young kid whom he had never met.

During our conversation, he revealed that more than forty years earlier, as a young ITN reporter, he had also sat down with *his* bosses and had the same conversation that I had with Vin Ray. Explaining to them that he was not a black journalist, but a journalist who just happened to be black, and he wanted to be treated as such and not steered towards so-called 'black' stories. How curious, I thought, that we had both felt the same way, twenty years apart, and perhaps had survived an often ruthless industry because we managed to define our own careers, and to develop our own voices, from the very beginning.

–6–

My Cute English Accent

IT IS A quirk of fate that I do not speak with an American accent, something my colleagues at ABC News in California could not quite fathom. I was the BBC's Los Angeles correspondent in the late 1990s and working out of ABC News's West Coast Bureau in the city. A black producer and cameraman, who became good friends, simply could not believe when they first met me that I was speaking in their words 'like the Queen of England!' The only accent they had ever heard come out of the mouth of a black person was the sound and inflection of African Americans, and they had little idea there was a black British community in the UK.

'Oh, your accent is so cute,' is a phrase I wish I had received a dime for every time it was uttered while I lived in America. I was in LA at the time of Princess Diana's death, and some white American colleagues were very troubled. 'I'm so sorry for your loss,' one person told me, as if I personally knew the Princess of Wales, because we both had English accents.

One day I was driving down Sunset Boulevard in the baking hot sun, the windows down to catch a rush of cooling air, and I came to a junction and stopped. In America, they drive on the right and motorists are allowed to turn right on a red signal, most of the time. Sometimes, however, it is not allowed, and signage should point this out. That day I turned right on a red, missing the sign saying it was not allowed, and after driving for a few seconds, I could see the blue flashing light of a police car in the rear-view mirror.

I suddenly began to sweat, wondering what the hell I had done wrong, and being a black man, images naturally crowded into my head of cops and guns and trouble. I pulled over and was very careful to keep my hands visible the whole time for the officer as she approached my car. I tried to assess what mood she might be in through my side mirror, and I saw the gun on her hip.

'Licence and registration, please,' she said, very courteously. Her manner calmed a rising anxiety and I leaned over and grabbed my wallet on the passenger seat and produced my licence. The registration was in the glove box.

'Sorry, officer, I'm not sure what I've done wrong.'

'Oh, you're British,' she said, rather startled.

'Yes, I am, I'm a reporter with the BBC, working over on the ABC News lot in Silverlake.'

'Ah ha!' she said, as if she had just been struck by a bolt of lightning, explaining my poor driving. 'Well, what you did was turn right when you shouldn't have and I know there are different traffic laws in the UK. I was there last summer visiting some friends. You Brits jaywalk all the time over there! Anyway, welcome to America, I won't cite you this time, but just be careful on our roads.'

And with that she gave me back my licence and registration papers and returned to her colleague in their squad car. The flashing blue light was switched off and it drove off past me. I felt guilty thinking there might be trouble with the officer, as I had feared the worst of her. But I also thought, thank God I speak the Queen's English!

The discombobulation of Americans every time I opened my mouth was interesting, because I could so easily have been an African American. My ancestors as slaves could have been taken from west or southern Africa to a cotton or tobacco plantation in the southern United States, leaving me centuries later with an American accent. Instead, they were chained and stowed away with millions of other poor souls, below deck in the hold a slave ship, which ended up in the warm waters of the Caribbean. It is not quite as simple as that, but you know what I mean. For the entire time I worked in America, I did think about that sliding doors moment, of two slave ships, and how my life could have been so different.

In 1995, I was sent to the southern African country of Angola by BBC Radio 4's *Today* programme. I was reporting on one of the intermittent lulls in years of fighting between two former anti-colonial guerrilla movements, the communist People's Movement for the Liberation of Angola or MPLA, and the anti-communist National Union for the Total Independence of Angola, or UNITA.

Hundreds of thousands of people had already died in the civil war. UN peacekeepers were now trying to monitor a deal between the warring parties, which they hoped would end the fighting and start a process of national reconciliation. I spoke with leading figures in the MPLA about the prospects for a lasting peace, and I visited the city of Huambo, around 330 miles south-east of the capital Luanda, and the scene of the infamous and brutal 55 Day War, where around 11,000 people were killed in an orgy of bloodletting in early 1993.

There were claims of civilian massacres on both sides, and bodies being dumped in the local Cunene River.

All this was harrowing, the terrible by-product of one of the Cold War's proxy battles between the Soviet Union and America, and frightening in its intensity since the fall of the Berlin Wall. But what touched me about Angola, was the surreal sense of calm I felt travelling through the country, despite everything. There was a part of me that felt somehow at home, as if I had returned to the source of my being. It is hard to put into words, but there was a sense of comfort and belonging, which made the gruesome details of the war even more difficult for me to process.

Of course, all this was purely psychological. I had never even been to Angola before, but a voice inside my head said that perhaps I was actually *from* Angola, or that part of southern Africa, that this was the place where my ancestors came from.

My dad tells me that 'Myrie' is a Cuban name. But Cuba was a Spanish possession during colonial times, while Angola belonged to the Portuguese. So Angolan slaves are more likely to have ended up in the Portuguese territory of Brazil, rather than Cuba. There was, of course, migration over the last two hundred years from South America across the Caribbean and amongst the islands of the West Indies themselves. My ancestors could well have been taken as slaves from the port of Benguela on Angola's coast and shipped to Brazil. Then at some point after emancipation, the descendants of those slaves might have moved to Cuba, and then on to Jamaica.

My dad says that in the early twentieth century, his father disappeared off to Cuba before he was born, to lie low for a while, after siring several children and trying to avoid their mothers. He must clearly have had a few connections in the bigger island to the north.

* * *

Back in America, one of my first visits there was for a friend's book launch in 1992. I landed in New York, making my way from JFK International Airport into the city, and I will never forget looking up in awe at the skyscrapers of Manhattan as they came into view. Nothing in the UK at that time rivalled such a vista. It was summertime, hot and muggy: T-shirts, sodas and slush puppies were the order of the day. Everything was cheap compared to Britain – food, clothes, music – and I loved going to jazz and nightclubs, because Americans seemed to know how to have fun.

There was also a cheek-by-jowl quality to New York that I liked. Everyone looked to be muddling along together, black and white, rich and poor; a place where apparently everyone could dream, and *maybe* have those dreams come true. America's possibilities appeared as infinite as the sky above the gleaming towers, because of its wealth and industrious- ness and never-ending capacity to reinvent itself.

As well as Los Angeles, I was also the BBC's Washington correspondent in the mid-2000s, and they were both stints living in the country that I cherish. In fact, on and off I have lived and worked in America for over a quarter of a century. I have many friends there, and on so many levels there is much to like and admire. But it is a troubled place and as a black man I thank my lucky stars I was not born and had to grow up there; a country so sadly awash with guns, where a bullet can end any quarrel or argument. But also, a country defined by race, in a way I have never wanted to be. I am glad my slave ship steered south.

At night on that first visit in 1992, I noticed that black workers would take certain trains to leave the city to go home, and the white workers would take different trains. The level of integration I had grown up with in the UK was simply not there in America. White and black were on parallel roads after dark, literally living on different sides of the street, their lives only really intersecting from 9 to 5. Rarely did I see mixed-race couples, black and white never prayed together, and they hardly ever ate together, except perhaps at work.

One time I was shopping with Catherine in LA and as we approached the check-out, the lady behind the till barked at me to step back, that it was one customer at a time. I replied that we were together, and for good measure added, 'She's my wife.' The lady at the till was more than a bit rattled. This separation, the lack of true connectivity as if black and white were strangers, did not make any sense to me; after all, they built America together and its constitution shouts: 'All men are created equal'. But it is the country's contradictions that make it an endlessly fascinating place for a reporter. The gap between the rhetoric and the reality. The distance between the promise and the lived experience.

By the time I got to New York in the 1990s, things should have been a whole lot different when it came to race. The same year I was born, 1964, the American Civil Rights Act had codified the demands and acknowledged the sacrifices of the Civil Rights Movement, outlawing discrimination based on race, colour, religion, sex and national origin. Only two months before, Sidney Poitier had become the first African American to win the Oscar for Best Actor, for his role as a construction worker who helps build a chapel in *Lilies of the Field*. Dr Martin Luther King Jr once said, 'The arc of the moral universe is long, but it bends toward justice.' It felt as if America was moving from slavery to segregation to integration.

This was the same year in the UK that the Conservative candidate for Smethwick in the 1964 General Election, who had failed to repudiate that campaign slogan, 'If you want a nigger for a neighbour, vote Labour', won the seat! It seemed that America was going forwards and Britain was going backwards.

In 1964, a British branch of the Ku Klux Klan was formed, with some black and ethnic minority residents in the area having burning crosses put through their letterboxes. The firebrand American civil rights leader, Malcolm X, even felt compelled to visit Smethwick from the United States the following year, to show solidarity with local black and Asian communities. After years of battling the worst examples of racism in America, even *he* was appalled by what he found in sleepy old Smethwick.

Apparently as he walked down one street in the centre of the town, people jeered at Malcolm X, with shouts of, 'We don't want any more black people here!' and 'What's your business here?' He came up against British 'colour bar' rules too, preventing or discouraging black and Asian people from using pubs, restaurants, barbers and other public places in Smethwick. It was all so shocking to him, and a far cry from the perception of some African Americans about Britain and the British.

Yes, it had ruled an empire made rich by slavery, but it outlawed the practice more than three decades before America. Britain professed to be a place infused with ideas of fair play, equality and decency. During America's Revolutionary War, some 20,000 black slaves even left their plantations to fight for the British in a special Black Pioneers loyalist regiment, far more than fought for the Patriots, because King George III had promised them freedom.

So what went wrong on race in America, after the optimism that outshone Britain for a time in the 1960s? Plenty it turns out, but to my mind the sense of white racial superiority that the entrenched slave system coded and stamped on the American psyche has been difficult to wash away. That is primarily because those feelings are buried very deep, and there has been little desire to confront those attitudes on the part of the most crucial constituency on these matters, white people.

I have always held the view that racism and bigotry and 'othering' of whatever despicable stripe is a reflection not of the victim – the black person, the Jewish person, or the person who is LGBTQ or disabled – but a reflection of the bigot themselves. So in 2016, a good friend of mine, Jacky Martens, the series producer on a new BBC Two current affairs programme *This Week's World*, approached me asking if I wanted to make a film for the show, and said I could choose any topic under the sun.

'Okay,' I said, 'I'd like to make a film on race in America, and only talk to white people!'

'Brilliant idea,' came the reply.

Jacky understood my train of thought instinctively. She is a white South African, whom I first met back in 2000 in the BBC's Johannesburg Bureau, when I was the Corporation's Africa correspondent. Jacky grew up under apartheid and saw the corrosive effects of white supremacy first-hand. She knew exactly where I was coming from.

The mini-documentary was called *Inside the Mind of White America*, and it was revelatory. I wanted to focus on the issue of race in America because that year Donald Trump had won the Republican Party nomination to run for president, against Hillary Clinton. His rhetoric around Mexicans and immigration – whether he meant it to or not – gave the far right and white supremacists the space and oxygen to feel very comfortable making their views heard. Such dark forces have always been a part of the fabric of American society. Now they were able to break cover with impunity, leaving many African Americans feeling deeply concerned. I had also read that record levels of hate crime were being reported to law enforcement agencies, according to the FBI that year, stoked by Trump supporters.

So, to make a film on race in America was timely, given that unlike most presidential candidates, Trump sought to win by dividing America, not uniting America, and he would do this using race. It was the most divisive US election I could remember, and I had covered every election for the White House since Bill Clinton defeated Bob Dole in 1996.

I chose the Midwestern city of Milwaukee as the location for my conversation with white America. It was reputed to be the most segregated urban area in the US, and it was here that one could see how easy it is, for the majority white population living in a bubble of privilege, to ignore the black minority.

I visited the Washington Highlands area, the kind of suburb that says you have arrived. The lawns are immaculate: manicured green parcels bordering big, square-jawed houses, with each home a hotchpotch of architectural styles. Clearly, most owners built the dwelling of their dreams themselves. Birdsong mingled with the gentle sound of garden sprinkler systems firing into life. Non-existent was the noise of traffic, belching out fumes. All I heard was the sound of affluence.

They were having their annual rummage sale in the neighbourhood on the fine summer's day in June when I turned up. Different homes with household goods spread over their front lawns. From old electrical appliances like irons and lawnmowers, to records and books and CDs. I noticed a lot of old 1980s music, Huey Lewis and the News, Hall and Oates, and a 12-inch copy of the single 'A Night To Remember' by Shalamar that I used to love hearing on the radio back in the day.

Most Americans are courteous and welcoming, and while some of those standing around checking out the old woodworking tools and other bric-a-brac were not willing to go on camera, others were happy to speak to me. I was up front about what I was trying to do. I was making a documentary on race in America, and I was only going to interview white people. The conversations, initially a little sterile, became more candid and part of the appeal in talking to me, a black Brit with a funny accent, was the fact that I was an outsider, almost like a neutral priest. The interviewees could confess all, and there would be no comeback from 6,000 miles away in Britain.

'I'm part of the problem,' Charles Wilkie told me, his red baseball hat shading a look of resignation. A retired businessman, he said it was easy for him to avoid so-called 'black

America' and ignore their privations and struggles. 'I don't know how to solve the problem, so what do I do, I ignore it, and yes, a lot of people do that. It's a lousy excuse and a poor answer. It's much easier not to know.'

The Washington Heights district of Milwaukee, where Charles lives, has 99 per cent white occupancy, yet a few blocks up the street are black neighbourhoods where lawns are not manicured, shops are boarded up, many houses have repossession notices slapped on their front doors, and the air is one of decay and poverty. The separation of black and white in Milwaukee is replicated in big cities right across the US, and separation breeds a lack of empathy.

Paula Kieferndorf, a teacher in the public school system, was candid. 'We're on 68th Street, but if you go down to 49th Street – especially through the summer – you can hear gunshots a couple of blocks further down. Bam, bam, bam, bam, bam,' she said. 'The next day the news will come on, and sure enough, there was a shooting of some young black man, or a girl caught in crossfire. There's a lot of tragic things going on down there.'

I asked Becky Zrinsky, in her mid-thirties, for her perception of the African Americans living a few blocks away. 'It's based purely on what I see on the news,' she said, 'and it's mostly negative. I'd like more information.'

'So what you know about black people isn't based on personal contact?'

'Sadly not,' she admitted.

All the comments I heard that day disheartened me. Despite countless high-profile deaths of young black men at the hands of the police, nearly half of white Americans, according to a

Pew Research Center survey published the year I visited Milwaukee, said they did not believe racism was a big problem in the US.

What planet were white Americans living on? Half of black Americans who are born poor stay poor. Black students attend the worst schools. About 1.6 million men aged twenty-four to fifty-four have disappeared from civic life because they have died or are in prison. If you are black in Milwaukee, and earning $100,000, you will be rejected for a mortgage as often as white people who are earning $20,000 are rejected. A black person with a college degree has less chance of finding a high-paying job than a white college dropout.

The socio-economic data is damning, so is white America blind, or as I wrote in an accompanying article in the *Guardian* at the time, is it playing dumb? It seemed to me that race was an intractable problem in America, in a way not replicated in any other modern democracy, and too many white people did not care enough to solve this problem, as Charles Wilkie admitted, because their lives were not touched by it.

Attitudes were similar in the 1960s and meant that the moment of hope for African Americans with the passing of the Civil Rights Act was brief. A Gallup poll from 1963 showed that 66 per cent of whites believed that black people were treated equally when it came to housing, education and employment. Another poll, from the year before, showed that 85 per cent of white people believed that black children had the same chances of a good education as white children. So even in the age of lynchings, Jim Crow segregation, bus boycotts, sit-ins and civil rights marches, most white people believed Martin Luther King was simply a dangerous

communist preaching revolution, rather than a man committed to arresting America's betrayal of its promise.

More than half a century after I was born, it seemed as if
the arc of the moral universe was getting longer and longer,
and was not bending towards justice, but doubling back on
itself, towards injustice.

There was another reason I chose to make a documentary
on race in the summer of 2016, after Jacky had tapped me up
for a film. Two years earlier I had finished a late shift in the
newsroom at the BBC's New Broadcasting House studios off
Oxford Street, in London, and as I waited for my taxi, I turned
on the TV to see a report on CNN and a video that I will never
forget. It involved several New York City police officers
pinning a black man to the ground. His name was Eric Garner
and he had been accused in Staten Island of selling 'loosies',
or single cigarettes, which is illegal.

He said he was innocent, but when officers went to arrest
him, he raised his hand and that is when four officers rushed
him, with one putting his arm around his neck, pulling him
to the ground. A bystander captured on his cell phone what
happened next. At that moment, my own phone pinged in
the newsroom, and it was a message from my taxi driver, all
jolly and welcoming. 'I'm here outside, take your time whenever you're ready.' I switched off the phone a little irritated
and continued watching the video, which had me transfixed.
Why are so many officers holding this man down, I wonder?

My eyes were glued to the TV and my mind wandered back
to Los Angeles and the video of the beating in 1991 of Rodney
King, the black man hit multiple times with police batons
while prostrate on the ground and seemingly defenceless.

Walloped over and over again. Now on the TV in front of me, somewhere beneath the crush of police bodies on top of him, Mr Garner can be heard trying to say, 'I can't breathe,' and he says it repeatedly, eleven times in fact, before losing consciousness. The video ends and the news anchor reports that Mr Garner was eventually taken to the hospital, where he was pronounced dead an hour later.

My eyes were filled with tears and writing this now makes me well up again. I had seen a fellow human being killed right in front of me. To all intents and purposes, it was a snuff movie. I felt sick and angry. My taxi was still waiting, but there and then I composed an email to the editor of the *Panorama* programme, describing what I had just seen, and that I had to make a film about the state of race relations in America.

I also thought again about those slave ships long ago. If the one carrying my ancestors had docked in Charleston, South Carolina, and not Kingston, Jamaica, maybe at some point down the line, I could have been another dead black man, killed at the hands of the police.

My mum Lynne looking lovely in the 1970s. I'm pretty sure she made that dress. She was a brilliant dressmaker, turning her hand to the craft when her dream of teaching in Britain couldn't be realised.

My dad, Norris. I don't think he ever adjusted to life in the UK after moving from Jamaica. The grey leaden skies of the north-west were a jolt from the vibrant colours of the Caribbean. He longed to go home.

From L-R: My sister Judith, brother Garfield and me. The picture was taken not that long after she'd arrived from Jamaica. It was a tough adjustment for her and I'm sorry I didn't understand just how hard it was when we were kids.

Check the suit and the hair! Newsreader in the making. I was a shy kid, which I know is hard to believe now.

The family all gathered in our living room. From L-R, back row: me, mum and Judith. In the front: younger sisters Sonia and Lorna, with Garfield. We were only allowed in the front room on special occasions. This was one of them. My parents had hired a photographer to capture the moment. Again mum made all those dresses and our shirts.

Bolton in the 1970s. It was my uncle Cecil, who'd been in the RAF, who suggested to my dad that he relocate here from Jamaica. I don't know a single member of the Windrush Generation who, when they came to Britain, thought it a good-looking place. But I have many happy memories of growing up in the former mill town.

My great-grandfather, my grandma's dad, was one of tens of thousands of men who left Jamaica and other islands in the West Indies, to help build the mighty Panama Canal. The work was dirty and dangerous and many died. Their contribution to one of the greatest feats of engineering the world had ever seen has only recently been recognised.

My great-uncle, William Runners, was one of nearly 16,000 men from across the Caribbean who signed up to fight for King and Country in the Great War. Two-thirds came from Jamaica. Notice the rifles of these three young men, old stock. They weren't allowed newer weapons.

My mum (right) was a primary school teacher at the time of Queen Elizabeth's visit to Jamaica in 1953.

Norman Washington Manley was a veteran of World War I, just like my great-uncle. He was Jamaica's Chief Minister, then Premier, in the last days of British colonial rule and helped to negotiate the country's independence. His meeting with JFK in 1961 marked a huge turning point for the country. Jamaica would become an independent state, remaining firmly in America's orbit, not the Soviet Union's.

Apart from my father, these two men, Alan Whicker (top left, interviewing Francois 'Papa Doc' Duvalier in Haiti) and Sir Trevor McDonald (right), have been the most influential in my life. Watching them on television as a teenager in the 1970s and 80s convinced me that a life of travel and journalism was what I wanted.

I have been lucky enough to meet Sir Trevor many times as an adult. I'm sure he's fed up of me telling him what an inspiration he was to me.

My dad loved cricket and watching the West Indies beat England was always cause for celebration in our house, especially in the Test series of 1976. Here Michael Holding (right) has smashed the England captain, Tony Greig's stumps. Greig said before the series that England would make the West Indies 'grovel'. Look at the delight on Holding's face.

We also watched sitcoms like *Mind Your Language*, set in an adult education college in London where different people from around the world are trying to learn English. The show was littered with stereotypes and notions of British superiority over other nations and was cancelled after three seasons. We did laugh though, not knowing any better.

Watching the 1976 Notting Hill Riots unfold made me realise that I did not have to travel far to find the ill-treatment and othering of people who looked just like me, that I saw around the world on the TV news.

As a student at university, I was intensely moved by *The Autobiography of Malcolm X*. Malcom X visited Smethwick in the West Midlands in 1965 and was horrified by the racism he encountered there.

Roy Hackett, who, alongside his colleagues, protested the Bristol Omnibus Company's refusal to employ black and Asian people as conductors and drivers, was also a huge inspiration to me. Roy fought at great personal expense for my right to be treated fairly as a black Briton, and to be allowed to work where I was capable.

7

Kim Choi Kar

If you prick us, do we not bleed?
If you tickle us, do we not laugh?
If you poison us, do we not die?
And if you wrong us, shall we not revenge?
If we are like you in the rest, we will resemble you in that.
Act 3, Scene 1, *The Merchant of Venice*

HAVING LIVED ALL over the world, there is little question that Singapore is one of the strangest places in which I have ever set up home. Clean, ordered and very rich, on the surface it is the ideal place for an expat, with great childcare and schools. It is very safe and you can walk the streets at night with absolutely no fear. It has a wonderful transport network and geographically it sits right at the heart of Asia, ideal for getting around the continent with Changi Airport being one of the finest air hubs in the world, slick, hi-tech and efficient.

Singapore, because of its investment in great infrastructure, is also not crippled by the intensity of the tropical weather, the way Kuala Lumpur, Jakarta or Manila are often disabled by heavy monsoon rains causing waist-high flooding. And for everyone desperate to stay cool, air-conditioning is seen as a vital national asset.

In fact, the country's founding father, Lee Kuan Yew, whom I interviewed during my time in the country, said air-con changed the nature of civilisation by making development possible in the tropics. Without the powerful box units, big and small, mounted in almost every room in every private house and in every public building across the country, life could not function efficiently in conditions of more than 90 per cent humidity. (The effect on the planet's climate of all this air-con is now, of course, a huge issue.)

The first time I walked Singapore's streets, it felt like I was strolling through clouds of water vapour. Indeed, the first thing Lee said he did on becoming Prime Minister in 1959 was to 'install air-conditioners in buildings where the Civil Service worked. This was key to public efficiency.' It meant work 'wasn't restricted to the cool early-morning hours or at dusk.' All the above, along with the nation's hard work and industry, allowed Lee to turbo-charge the country's GDP by 100 per cent per capita between 1960 and 2011.

But there is a darker side to the success. Lee was at best a benign dictator, at worst an authoritarian, who veneered Singapore to look like a democracy. He banned critical media and often used defamation lawsuits to shut down opponents. Speakers Corner was supposed to be modelled on the version at Hyde Park in London, where you can speak on any subject you choose. It was an expression of freedom, and crucially free speech. But Singapore's had a twist. You had to register the subject you wanted to talk about with the authorities ahead of time.

The judicial system he designed still uses the death penalty, often for drugs offences, and corporal punishment involving the rotan or cane applies to a wide range of crimes. Prison officers are specially trained to use their entire body weight to lean into every single stroke to ensure the maximum amount of pain. A few lashes on bare buttocks have been described as excruciating, like being burnt with hot coals. Singapore is also supposed to be tolerant of other races and cultures, but beneath the surface of society sits a rigid caste system, where under different circumstances, I am sure I would have been at the bottom.

Catherine and I arrived in Singapore in 2001, desperate to live in what was called a 'shophouse', and some of the finest examples were in the Little India area of the island. As the name suggests, mainly south Asians lived in this enclave; there were few Chinese Singaporeans.

Shophouses were as distinctive as Georgian terraces in Bath or Brighton, and the best examples are just as magnificent. Rows of beautifully coloured or tiled buildings with a veranda at the front forming a continuous and covered passage from house to house. The resulting arcades or colonnades were ideal for any kind of retail enterprise at ground level, allowing family members to live on the floors above, hence the name, shophouse. Many were spectacularly ornamented, and the examples that we saw in Little India during our search for a new home were covered in beautiful, intricately patterned, pink, white and green ceramic tiles, and to our delight, one property was up for rent.

The house was ranged over four storeys and dated from the early 1900s, with green louvered shutters on the outside of every window. Through the double front doors, as you walked in, you were greeted by a giant atrium at the heart of the building rising the full four floors up to the roof, with all the rooms off to the sides. At the foot of the atrium was a giant fishpond, full of exotic Singaporean carp, with the gentle sound of a small mechanical pump humming away, oxygenating the water. It was all so calm and soothing. Outside, the row of shophouses faced an open green, with buildings way across on the other side and off to the right. It was an impressive view, despite being right in the heart of a heavily built-up area.

The street was called Petain Road, and you reached the little lane that ran in front of the residencies off the busy Serangoon Road, so there was very little to trouble one's ears once you had reached the shophouses; it felt like a little oasis. But how come rental costs in the area were so cheap? Trust me, the BBC allowance was not huge. One of the three brilliant BBC cameramen based in Singapore, Joe Phua, took it upon himself to show me and Catherine why. A Chinese Singaporean, he was not only a wonderful shooter, but also one of the kindest men I have ever met, with a cracking sense of humour, and he was genuinely worried for our wellbeing.

'Clive, listen, you and Catherine need to come back to this area at the weekend.'

'Eh?'

'No, seriously, you and Catherine come back at the weekend, then decide if this is where you want to live.'

Joe told us to be at the shophouse in Petain Road for 12 noon. The golden light of a Singaporean dawn seemed particularly intense that day as the heat rose and rose to more than 30° by lunchtime. Thank God there is great air-conditioning in the house, I thought, as we made our way along Jalan Besar running parallel to Serangoon, then turned right into Petain Road, the opposite way we had entered the street on our initial visit. The shiny surfaces of the multi-coloured tiles adorning what we hoped would be our new home glistened and shimmered in the light. I could hear crows squawking high above, periodically swooping down to find tit-bits of food discarded from the local restaurants.

That was the other thing about the Little India area that was so attractive. The food. Gorgeous cuisine from right across Asia, made by people from those regions: Chinese, Japanese, Vietnamese, but principally from South Asia, India, Bangladesh and Pakistan. All this right on our door-step. Fragrant curries served on bamboo leaves for a hand-ful of Singaporean dollars, washed down with local Tiger Beer. From the 1960s onwards, the area developed beside what was called a vegetable cultivation zone, and so earned the nickname 'kim chio kar', or 'foot of the banana' in Hokkien, the southern Chinese language spoken by many Singaporeans, whose ancestors originally came from that region. Eating good-quality food was in the blood of the area.

We rounded the corner and up ahead was our dream home, but to our right a line of men came into view, a queue that got longer and longer, an orderly line of mainly young South Asian men, waiting patiently for something. They were smok-ing or reading newspapers, chatting on phones, but there was no interaction between any of them. The closer we got to the shophouse, we could see the front of the queue snake round and down into a back alley before disappearing to the right across the path that ran in front of the verdant verandas of the shophouses.

'Erm, what's down the alley?' I asked Joe, a little hesitantly.

'Well, it's a brothel.'

'A brothel!' said Catherine.

'Yep, your dream shophouse is right in front of one of Singapore's busiest streets of entertainment!'

Now we knew why the rent was so affordable. The queue shuffled along, flip-flops and sandals scraping the ground, when a truck turned up with about a dozen men sitting in the open wagon at the back. All of them, again South Asians, jumped out and joined the queue. What was interesting was that they were very patient, waiting their turn, and some of them were dressed quite smartly, many in white shirts and formal trousers in the baking heat. Down the alley were several low-rise buildings where women had rooms and could ply their trade. Most were peasant girls from rural China, others from Burma and Vietnam and Singapore itself. It must have been hard for them, earning a living in this way, servicing an endless conveyor belt of men.

Yes, Catherine and I loved the shophouse; we had been dreaming about finding one for months, but I could not leave her home alone in such an environment potentially for weeks on end while I was away reporting. So we contacted the letting agent, and very sadly, said no. What we had not appreciated was that the Singaporean Government strictly controlled how the city state's brothels were run. Prostitution was legal, the women were taxed on their earnings, and had to have regular health checks. Police cars periodically visited the area, making sure all was well, and because of this, Petain Road was actually situated in one of the safest areas of on the whole island.

Licensed brothels were seen by the authorities as a pressure valve for the thousands of migrant workers who were vital to the economy. They did so much of the back-breaking work in the country, in construction, road-building and maintenance, and there was a sense that allowing them the opportunity to 'let off a little steam', as it were, was an acceptable thing to do. The Government also argued that tightly regulating the sex industry helped to stop human trafficking and kept organised crime and triad gangs at bay. Criminalisation would only have forced sex workers underground, as was the case in so many of the other countries in the region.

But it was all still a bit weird to me, because of the kinds of things that Singapore *did* outlaw. Chewing gum, for instance, was officially banned and selling it could land you a fine of $100,000 US dollars, or a prison sentence of up to two years. The fines for littering were $500–1000 US for a first offence, and $2000 US for repeat offenders. Urinating in a lift carried a heavy penalty, too. But WHO WOULD DO THAT?

The cost of cleaning up gum off the pavements and dealing with litter was expensive, but there was a much more important reason for the heavy fines in a nanny state gone mad, which was to do with the very 'idea' of Singapore. The island was supposed to be a civilised haven of stability and good manners, a shining example of what Asia could and should be: a Switzerland of Asia.

Singapore could not be allowed to look shabby and dirty. Its survival depended on projecting the image of a modern, forward-looking society, where foreign investors could happily come and build their businesses. A clean and tidy environment, with very low tax rates, high incomes, and little regulation (unless you chewed gum,) and a place free of corruption. Lee believed that if he paid civil servants good salaries, they would be less likely to steal from the public purse, and today Singapore is one of the least corrupt countries in the world. All this in the service of making the city state an attractive proposition to the outside world.

Catherine and I kept kicking ourselves on passing up the opportunity to live in Petain Road. So for the next year we kept in touch with letting agents, and when No. 36 came up for grabs, we seized it with both hands.

Lee Kuan Yew had created a slightly odd, but fascinating world, which functioned incredibly well and had become – as he desired – the envy of Asia. The success was down to his vision and pragmatism, and included the importance he placed on promoting tolerance among the country's different ethnic groups – the Chinese majority, along with the sizeable Indian and Malay minorities. He knew co-existence would be vital, a view that hardened after he witnessed race riots in 1964 between Muslim Malays and the local Chinese population, when Singapore was still part of Malaysia.

The riots ended up helping the cause of independence, and Singapore's new constitution emphasised the need to adopt non-discriminatory policies based on race and religion. Nevertheless, Lee did work hard to maintain a Chinese Singaporean majority on the island, encouraging young people to go out and procreate, with financial incentives and love hotels paid for by the Government. Malays were sometimes penalised if they had too many children, and they were not necessarily offered the best government housing. But for Lee striking the right ethnic balance was vital, and there was no repeat of the intercommunal enmity and bloody riots of the past once he took control.

Everyday attitudes are sometimes difficult to change, however, and some Chinese Singaporeans maintained the sense in their mind that they were superior to others living on the same island. Lee knew this, and that is where his pragmatism kicked in once again. When we lived in Petain Road, I was staggered to find out that the pay of a domestic helper or maid depended on his or her nationality. So a maid from the Philippines could be paid more than someone from Indonesia. Below them are Sri Lankans and bottom of the pile are maids from Myanmar or Burma. They all could be doing the same work, but the pay was legally variable. I dread to think what a black maid might have been able to earn.

Chinese Singaporeans can be rather blunt and direct in conversation. One night I was returning to Petain Road and hailed a taxi downtown.

'Where you go?' said the driver 'Kim chio kar,' I replied.

'Ooooooh,' was the response. Taxi drivers would either say 'ooooh' or there would be silence, and I knew what they were thinking.

I got into the cab and true to form, he said, 'So, you look for goodtime, eh?' suggesting I was heading to the back alley to look for prostitutes.

'No, I live in Petain Road in one of the shophouses,' I said firmly.

'Umm, how much you pay?' – as in what's the rental cost?

'It's affordable,' I replied.

'Where you from in Africa?'

'No, I'm not from Africa.'

'You American?'

'No,' and before I could say I was from Britain working for the BBC, he said, 'We need foreigners to make our country grow, very important, bring money, but not people like you.' With that I reached my destination, paid the driver, and slammed his door. Now imagine where a black maid in Singapore might sit in the pay league.

Despite the sometimes unpleasantness beneath the surface of life, diversity worked for Singapore and Lee's vision of a tolerant society, welcoming to all its communities, was undoubtedly the right one. It is a winning formula that saw the island's transformation from a tropical swamp at the tip of the Malay Peninsula into one of the wealthiest nations in the world per head of population.

That tolerance was not replicated in other parts of Asia. The enmity of different ethnic groups characterised much of my reporting at the time. The power of the region's leaders often rested in their tribal allegiances, leading on several occasions to very brutal and bloody politics.

* * *

The second of the trinity of genius cameramen in Singapore was Jone Cheung, a wise soul, who worked a camera with the skill of an artist painting on a canvas. Then there was Darren Conway, or DC, a wonderful Aussie whose eye for the visual could so easily have seen him shoot *Lawrence of Arabia* for David Lean in another time and in another life. His work has a magisterial, filmic quality, often shooting close-ups using a wide-angle lens that created a kind of CinemaScope for television. I made some of the best work of my entire career with Joe Phua, Jone and DC.

I learned so much from them about the craft of telling stories with pictures, and it was the Aussie from Brisbane and Jone who were in the office the day we decided to follow up reports that a particularly nasty ethnic conflict had flared up again in Kalimantan, the Indonesian portion of the giant rugged island of Borneo. This was a place famous for three things – a stunning biodiverse rainforest, its orangutans, and a capacity for savage violence that took the form of beheadings with machetes. Legend also had it that fighters would rip out the hearts of their enemies, extricating the still warm organ dripping blood from the chest cavity, in order to 'drain' their foes of their power.

Along with the producer Peter Leng, a Brit who understood the grammar of television news better than most, we flew to Kalimantan and headed for one of the villages where we understood the worst of the ethnic violence had been taking place.

I had learned over the years reporting in Asia that there was no point taking big bags of luggage on an assignment. For a week or so, better to take only three or four shirts and wash them out in the sink of the hotel, and in the heat they dry in minutes. On this trip to Borneo, I packed three polo shirts, blue, green and red. We landed in the capital of Central Kalimantan, Palangka Raya, and found our fixer, who would help us with the language and direct us to the best place to tell the story of what was going on. But what *was* going on? It all seemed mind-boggling.

In a nutshell, there had been inter-ethnic violence between the indigenous Dayak people and the Madurese, who had originally come from the Indonesian island of Madura and had lived in Kalimantan for several generations. What lay at the heart of the conflict was a mixture of resentment and jealousy. The Madurese, who are Muslims, had worked hard, dominating low-level sectors of the economy, affecting the job prospects of the non-Muslim Dayaks. New laws had also allowed the Madurese in certain regions to control many commercial industries, including logging, mining and plantations.

Rightly or wrongly, the Dayaks felt shut out of their own country and there were claims on both sides about how the violence began. A brawl between students of the two differ-ent races at the same school was one suggestion, another theory was the Dayaks claiming the Madurese were behind an arson attack on a house.

We endeavoured to travel only while the sun was still up for fear of encountering a night-time checkpoint manned by one of the armed groups. But it was growing late on our arrival as we made our way to our hotel. The sun was getting lower and lower, fading to a flicker on the horizon, releasing a golden glow as it said goodbye. I was beginning to feel uneasy as the dimming light slowly blackened, with the only illumination coming from the headlamps of our 4x4, lighting a lonely road ahead. No other traffic competed for space, for no other drivers were dumb enough to be out after dark.

We were all exhausted after the flight from Singapore and I began to doze off in the back, when Peter Leng noticed something moving up ahead, and the flickering flames from fires came into view. The driver slowed down and as I blinked into life, we could see there was a checkpoint further along the road. I was suddenly very awake. A log had been fashioned as a barrier across the track, placed on top of two oil drums at either end, and there were two chairs on the left of the road.

Then three figures appeared, two had white markings on their faces, illuminated by the headlamps of our car, a white line across the forehead and a line on both cheeks. They were carrying long spears with a red ribbon tied at the end of the shaft before the blade. The other man had a long machete in his right hand and a red bandana tied around his head. Our vehicle slowed right down and stopped just before the log.

Our fixer wound down his window and spoke with the man wearing the red bandana, who seemed a little unsteady on his feet, as he had clearly been drinking or taking drugs. The other two men with the markings on their faces slumped back onto the two chairs by the road. All three were drunk, not what you want at a checkpoint in the middle of Borneo at night, as an ethnic battle rages! But before long we were on our way, the men at the checkpoint too inebriated even to check our press passes.

'Tuak,' explained our fixer. 'They've been drinking rice wine since late afternoon,' he laughed, 'so they were in a good mood.' Tuak is strong stuff and deeply rooted in Dayak culture. I had not realised it, but the men we encountered were some of the head-hunters of Borneo.

The next day we set off early from the hotel to film every-thing we needed, to avoid another night-time encounter. As we made our way in our 4x4 along a dusty road, deep into the heart of central Kalimantan, the heat began to rise and the vehicle's air-con worked overtime. I was in the back collecting my thoughts on the day's filming ahead, deciding how to tell this brutal story as vividly as I could to convey the sense of menace and dread that permeated the forest.

I was reminded of another example of intercommunal violence, the Rosewood Massacre, in rural Levy County in Florida in 1923. Among the many stains on the American conscience when it comes to the treatment of black people, what happened in Rosewood represents one of the worst. The town was prosperous and took its name from the reddish colour of cut cedar wood that fuelled the timber industry upon which people lived. Jim Crow segregation laws meant most residents were black people, and they made a huge success of their little village.

Around 350 inhabitants lived a good life, earned from logging and turpentine mills. The village had two-storey wooden plank homes, small two-room houses, and several small unoccupied plank farm and storage structures. Some families owned pianos, organs, and other symbols of middle-class prosperity. There were three churches, a school, a large Masonic Hall, the turpentine mill, sugarcane mill and two general stores. It even had a baseball team, the Rosewood Stars.

The neighbouring village of Sumner was predominantly white, and one night, several men decided to lynch a black Rosewood resident, following accusations that a black drifter had assaulted a white woman. A mob of several hundred white people combed the countryside hunting for black people and set alight pretty much every structure in Rosewood, with the settlement razed to the ground. Estimates of the dead range from two dozen to 150. Survivors hid in nearby swamps until they were evacuated to larger towns by train and car. No arrests were ever made and the village was abandoned by its former residents, which was exactly what the white racists had wanted. Rosewood ceased to exist.

It was as if the black success that the whites resented had never happened, as if the sense of inferiority the rednecks felt at their lack of industry and purpose, their absence of drive, ingenuity and resourcefulness, could now be wiped away. They could go back to their mundane lives living in a cocoon of superiority, because there was no one else around to remind them how unremarkable they really were. They were not God's elect, not the chosen people, and deep down they knew it, but they could not face the truth.

Was this what the Dayaks were trying to do too? Erase the existence of the Madurese in this part of Kalimantan to erase their own inadequacies?

We drove further into the forest, the landscape thick, green and lush, ploughing on deeper into the wretched guts of this current tragedy. We were heading for the logging town of Sampit, where we heard some of the worst violence had taken place. Our fixer told us there would be more roadblocks along the way, then said, 'You ought to know the Dayak colours are red, as you saw last night, so if we're stopped at a Madurese checkpoint and they see one of us wearing red, they may become suspicious.'

I could not believe it. Bloody hell! I had chosen to wear the RED polo shirt I had packed back in Petain Road, and on my wrist I had one of those thin, red string bracelets, part of the whole Kabbalah craze, a talisman to ward off misfortune. It never once crossed my mind as I showered and put on the shirt at the hotel that morning, that the bloody colour would be relevant. In the back of the 4x4 I yanked off the strands of red string from around my left wrist. But what to do about my shirt? I started to feel queasy and kept wiping my sweaty palms on my trousers.

Oh my God, do I take off my shirt and parade around the jungle topless? I could not believe I was in such a mess. I had a green neckerchief I was using to mop the sweat off my brow from time to time in the heat, and I took it out of my pocket and tied it around my neck, hoping it might draw attention away from the red polo shirt. Surely a Madurese fighter would not think I was a Dayak. I don't look like a Dayak, I consoled myself, I'm black. Yes, there won't be a problem. Thank God I'm black.

I looked out of the front window and up ahead looming on the horizon was a checkpoint. DC and Peter were calm, and I gave the impression I was too. As our vehicle drew closer to the barrier, I fumbled for my press pass. We could see four men, all holding very large, long machetes. One of them waved us down and our 4x4 came to a halt.

Our fixer in the passenger seat rolled down the window and a blast of hot sweaty air suddenly filled the vehicle. He spoke in the Dayak dialect and then gestured to us to produce our press passes. DC and Peter handed theirs over, while I wanted to shrink down behind the passenger seat so that the man with the machete could not see me. I handed over the pass and he looked at it, then peered inside the vehicle, having gazed at my photo.

Our eyes locked and he glanced down at the photo again. Then he stared at my shirt. I suddenly could not breathe as our eyes locked once more, and I held my breath. He gestured to one of the other men and they both looked at the passes, then began walking towards the back door where I was seated, inspecting me through the window. I was expecting them to suddenly make a grab for the door handle, yank it and drag me out.

My palms were sweating more and more, but I did not want to make any sudden moves, so I kept them down by my side as the men stared at me. I felt utterly helpless. They suddenly began walking back to the front of the car. One of them reached into the vehicle to give back the passes. The fixer spoke to them again, and then we were free to go. As we drove on through the checkpoint, I kept thinking, thank God I'm black!

'We need to go to the local football pitch,' the fixer said, 'because that's where some of the killings took place,' so we drove on further into the rainforest. We saw burnt-out cars along the road and pulled over. DC got his camera ready and we walked towards one of the vehicles. It was completely charred and the fire would have been intense, causing the petrol tank to explode. Inside, we could see the figures of two people, incinerated by the heat.

We pushed on towards the football pitch, which was a muddy, open stretch of land. Recent monsoon rains had left pools of water by the goalposts. DC started to film and in the middle of the pitch, we found discarded photographs of men, women and children. Some passport-style, others group family photos. We did not know their names or where they lived. What we did know, was that they were all dead. An eyewitness told us most were killed by spears, the women and the children. The men had their heads chopped off, while the babies were slashed with machetes. I pictured the chaos and carnage in my mind and I could hear the screams: the pleas for mercy, 'Spare the children!', the exhortations to Allah, and the cries of anguish.

We found a child's yellow romper suit in the mud; it had a bear on the front surrounded by pink balloons. We found a thick pile of long, matted black hair, as if someone had tried to scalp the victim, and also a slashed belt; the cut was neat and straight, sliced by a machete that would have ripped open the belly of the person wearing it. All the victims were Madurese people, butchered by Dayak gangs who had raided their village and frog-marched well over a hundred of them to the football pitch. As the victims left their homes for the last time, they had grabbed the family photos.

Madurese villages were being systematically destroyed by gangs of Dayak men, and makeshift refugee camps were springing up everywhere for the survivors. Some were heavily bandaged after being attacked, their wounds healing, while others with their stitches visible had clearly been sliced by machetes. The dead on the football pitch had been removed by the time we arrived, but the site of another massacre was still fresh and the bodies littered the street. Corpses were putrefying in the baking hot sun; the stench was overwhelming.

There was no dignity in how they died, and no dignity in

death either. We saw bodies piled high outside the hospital, dumped in carts or lining the side of the road. Most were headless, and some had severe chest wounds, suggesting that perhaps the legend that hearts were ripped out might be true. Further up the road as we drove on, we saw what looked like boulders from a distance, but as we got closer, we could see they were severed heads placed by the side of the road, carefully arranged. They were clearly a warning to the Madurese.

I could not believe what my own eyes were seeing. I felt a mixture of revulsion, but bizarrely, also excitement. I was at the heart of an incredible story, there was a rush that I felt deep down. Alan Whicker would have been proud to report on a story like this. But at the same time, it was a tragedy beyond compare.

I am often asked if I have ever suffered post-traumatic stress after thirty-odd years of reporting wars and other terrible events. The simple and complicated answer is I don't know. I suspect I have, but it has not been diagnosed. I have never *not* been able to function in my work because of a past experience, but every now and again, usually triggered by an extreme example of pain and suffering that I witness on the TV or in a film, or while reporting, I will get intensely emotional and it lasts for a few seconds. My eyes will well up with tears and I will weep, and then as suddenly as it starts, it stops.

This began happening to me after my encounters in Borneo, and I can pinpoint the exact cause. It was meeting a Madurese woman called Hyatti. She was wandering around aimlessly in a large refugee camp when I came across her. Hyatti, who was in her late twenties, her black hair scraped back in a ponytail, with her red patterned dress tired and torn, was nine months pregnant and inconsolable. Crying, her tears flowed with an urgency that seemed to me to sum up the suffering of all the Madurese people, as well as anyone that I have seen in pain ever since.

In Afghanistan and Iraq, the mothers of young boys stabbed on London's streets, the families of those killed in mass shootings in America, and the loved ones of victims of police brutality everywhere. The survivors of the zealotry of the suicide bomber, or those living through the unconscionable war in Ukraine. It is not the dead I feel sorry for, they are at peace, their trauma is over. It is the pain of the living that always gets me. Whenever I see that pain, I think of Hyatti, and it is the image of her face, imprinted on my mind, that makes me weep and crowds my nightmares.

I wonder about the child she was carrying when I came across her. They would be a teenager by now, that is if they are alive. Hyatti had lost her husband, her other children, her mother and father, and both grandparents. They were all murdered in the football pitch massacre, and she was alone in the world, save for the child that was yet to be born. What I cling on to is the fact that Hyatti *did* survive the massacre, and that her new baby might bring a measure of solace and consolation. I think it is that realisation, on the deepest of levels, that snaps me out of the torment, when for a brief few seconds I sink into a quagmire of despair.

I don't know how to explain the carnage of what happened in Borneo, or the myriad tragedies concocted by men everywhere. The mentality to despise a fellow human being so utterly to the point where you kill and dismember them, I will never understand. Part of the trick is not to see the victims as humans, but animals. The Dayaks often referred to the Madurese as monkeys, just as American whites thought of black people living in Rosewood, and as some Russians view Ukrainians. It is so much easier and more comfortable to swing a machete or string up and lynch or fire a missile at a tower block full of men, women and children, if you think the victim is nothing like you. If you deny their humanity, and deny your own.

It is common sense that underpins the Jew Shylock's quote in *Merchant of Venice*, asking are we not all 'warmed and cooled by the same winter and summer?' In Borneo and the tragedies of extreme 'othering' everywhere, it is always the absence of common sense that prefaces disaster.

Back in Singapore, having seen it first hand, intercommunal violence drove Lee Kuan Yew to work for peaceful co-existence of communities, and he succeeded. His vision for the country had diversity at its very heart, no matter how imperfect, and his tiny nation, half the size of London, was the better for it. On 23 March 2015, it was announced that he had died at the age of ninety-one. Lying in state during a week of national mourning, it is estimated that 1.7 million Singaporean residents, Malay and Indian, as well as Chinese, filed past his coffin.

8

Conscience and War

Only Fit to Die, Not to Live

I REALLY WISH I had met my great-uncle, William Runners. He sounds like one hell of a guy. First, he was a successful businessman and a pillar of the community in the market town of Green Island, in western Jamaica, where my father grew up. Secondly, turn up at his chemist or 'doctor's shop' as they called them in 1930s Jamaica, and he would diagnose your aches and pains, and sort out the remedy. Thirdly, and this is pretty cool, he could also solve crimes. He was a police detective in the Jamaica Constabulary Force.

Murders were thankfully a rare thing in early twentieth-century Jamaica, so there are no real comparisons between his work and the cases featured in *Death in Paradise*, the BBC drama set on a fictional Caribbean island. But I have to say that whenever the actor Don Warrington appears in the show as Commissioner of Police Selwyn Patterson, I always think of my great-uncle.

As if all that was not enough, William Runners was also a war hero, according to my dad, a veteran of the trenches, injured in the leg on the Western Front in the First World War, which left him walking with a limp for the rest of his life. He sounds like an amazing man, with perhaps his biggest achievement being to help advance the claims for representative government, and ultimately the cause of Jamaican independence, by risking his own life in battle, along with thousands of other brave Jamaican men and women.

At the outbreak of the First World War, every fourth person on Earth owed allegiance to the British Crown, with the thread of Empire weaving its way around roughly a quarter of the Earth's surface. For those in the Motherland, it was a benign silken thread, gentle, soft and amiable, almost caressing as it laced around its dominions. The view in the clubs of Pall Mall and the offices of the colonial mandarins in Whitehall continued to be that Britain was doing the poor savages a favour, by guiding the shining light of civilisation upon them, a paternal hand for millions of people who needed salvation.

However, for many of the colonial subjects themselves, including my family in Jamaica, the thread was chafing and rough, not silken at all. It was a tight, strangling girdle of coarse rope, choking a national identity and freedom.

By the time of the Festival of Empire at Crystal Palace in 1911, the cord of whatever stripe that bound Jamaica to Britain since the seventeenth century was perhaps at its tightest and most secure. The festival was part of the celebrations marking the coronation of King George V, and according to the official brochure, the aim was to promote the British Empire to the British public as a 'Social Gathering of the British Family', and to encourage the 'firmer welding of those invisible bonds which hold together the greatest empire the world has ever known.' Depending on your point of view, 1911 marked either the zenith or nadir of British imperialism.

My family and other Jamaicans would never see the depiction of the colonies and the depiction of them as colonised people represented at the festival, but they could have guessed at the kind of portrayal. Human models were arranged into 'visual narratives' apparently representative of their ethnic traits, reinforcing ideas that black- and brown-skinned people were primitives and cannibals, who were being saved by colonisation. Those visiting the festival were encouraged to 'compare themselves with the peoples on display', and as Britain was now their overlord, 'note their progress from the relatively lowly states of the human race'.

Yet only three years after the celebratory gorging on the perception of how great colonialism was and the cast-iron logic of white supremacy, the Empire came calling on places like Jamaica for help to keep the Empire intact. Britain was at war with Germany and it was all hands on deck, including black and brown hands. But what the colonial authorities and the British Army knew full well was that the call to arms might fire the consciousness of some in the Caribbean about who and what they were going to be fighting for. Was it for the King and the perpetuation of inferiority, or was it for themselves and the cause of freedom?

Good cable communications meant the news that Britain had declared war reached the dominions not long after the people of Doncaster, Birmingham or Leeds found out, and Jamaicans were soon voicing their desire to enlist, with my great-uncle having a lot of thinking to do. He was educated, he had business interests and a good job as a detective. Birth records, we think, suggest he was slightly older than most of the young men who pushed to join the British Army. Most were between nineteen and twenty-five; William would have been over thirty, and there were others well into their forties.

So why risk everything to volunteer to go to the front? There is no doubt many of the young men who signed up wanted adventure. They would have been kicking their heels in Jamaica, a poor country where the job prospects were thin. Unemployment was high and wages were low. Cutting cane paid a derisory nine pence a day. Joining the war effort would have given them substantially higher earnings, and who knows, possibly a longer-term future in the British Army or Royal Navy if they wanted it.

There were others who were undoubtedly patriotic, who saw it as their duty to fight for the King. My great-uncle was himself a member of the establishment, part of the apparatus of Empire enforcing British laws as a police officer, and so perhaps his decision to go to war was an obvious one. But for him and others, showing willingness to fight for Britain might also be rewarded at the end of hostilities with more political representation, and greater social rights for all Jamaicans.

It was in the autumn of 1915, in the heart of the capital, Kingston, when the Empire asked those in its realm with no voice, to make their voices heard in the conflagration that was engulfing Europe. Outside Hibbert House, the seat of the colonial legislature, the authorities had built a high platform with a rail upon which four giant Union flags were draped. Several lengths of red, white and blue bunting fluttered in the breeze, while a line of fresh-faced boy scouts, black and white, fidgeted, their neckerchiefs freshly tied and uniforms pressed, as they formed an honour guard. It was here that

Jamaicans were able to sign up to go to war, with colonial officials looking on.

It was the first recruiting day held for the newly created British West Indian Regiment, and my great-uncle wanted to be part of the fighting force. Eventually, recruiting meetings were held in every parish across the country, and public calls to duty were listed in the newspapers. William Runners was one of nearly 16,000 men who signed up during the war from across the Caribbean, with two-thirds coming from Jamaica.

They were fit and healthy, reared on sunshine and fresh food, as opposed to the many Englishmen who were rejected for service on the grounds of poor health. But so pervasive were the ideas encapsulated in the Festival of Empire exhibition, of the inferiority of black and brown people, that during the war the British military establishment decided men from the colonies were not fit to engage a white enemy on equal terms, or fight alongside white comrades shoulder to shoulder. Black and brown troops were only permitted to take on an adversary of equal standing, and so most Caribbean soldiers allowed to engage in combat were sent to Africa and the Middle East.

For the rest, that meant the Western Front in France and Flanders and service largely behind the front lines, in what were called 'labour battalions'. Black soldiers, including my great-uncle, were barred from holding ranks above sergeant, confined to logistics teams, moving supplies and munitions. If they were issued with weapons at all, and few were, they were old and out-of-date rifles. For many, it was a humiliation.

For the top brass, maintaining the edifice of white supremacy was paramount, amid the fear of what they believed would be the 'racial degeneration' and adverse psychological response of many white men, if there were black soldiers fighting alongside them. They believed white troops might be influenced by ideas of racial equality and fairness after seeing fellow soldiers in combat fighting and dying on the same side. There may be feelings of sympathy and kinship, threatening the notions that underpinned the existence of the Empire that Britain was fighting to protect.

'They wouldn't give him a gun,' my father tells me of William Runners. 'Black people were only fit to die, not fit to live. It meant he couldn't fight back. They had him working up in France, but there was no rifle or bullets. He got hit. Many black people were hit by shells and were hurt, but they were second-class soldiers.'

It was one of the more bizarre episodes of the war. Even as Britain was struggling in 1915, the mindset of Empire suggested the German enemy that was trying to kill British soldiers was superior to the black men who were trying to keep British troops alive by carrying their supplies. If you want a supreme example of how dumb racism is, there you have it.

I feel a deep sorrow at the treatment of those black men such as my great-uncle. He would have carefully considered the prospect of death in battle, leaving behind his wife who was a teacher, and two sons. Yet in the eyes of his superior officers, he was worth very little. Imagine facing the possibility of dying, knowing your own comrades saw you as worthless, because as the shells rained down and the enemy advanced, you were not allowed bullets to defend yourself? You were the ultimate sacrificial lamb on the altar of Empire and the notion that white is right. My dad is very proud to talk about my great-uncle's contribution to the war. I can hear it in his voice. But there is also regret that William Runners could not be the man he really wanted to be.

After returning home to Jamaica, my great-uncle remained prominent in the community of Green Island. My dad says he was a bit of a local 'wise head', intervening in neighbourly disputes and helping steer young guys on the straight and narrow with fatherly chats, those destined for a spell of trouble with the law if they did not buck up their ideas. It was on William's visits to see his sister, my father's mum, that my dad got to know him a little. My father is keen to point out that *he* was not one of those young men who needed a stern talking-to.

Throughout the later years of his life, my great-uncle would have cheered on one of his Jamaican comrades in the British Army, a man called Norman Washington Manley. A handsome, aquiline-jawed Rhodes scholar, he had read law at Oxford having moved to England on the death of his mixed-race parents, and enlisted with the Royal Field Artillery in Deptford in 1915 to fight in the war. Racism was rife in the ranks, according to Manley's memoir, and taking a demotion he switched to join the Royal Garrison Artillery, where he was a gunner, fighting at the Somme and Passchendaele.

He had a feel for the concerns of the common man, despite his smart English education. He admired the bricklayers, engineers, farmers, carpenters, clerks, blacksmiths, tailors, printers, waiters and grooms, all the ordinary folk with whom he shared a trench, a laugh or a cigarette. The memory of his fallen comrades was seared in his mind for ever after the

Third Battle of Ypres and seeing 'a lot of dead people, three-parts buried by mud, you spotted them by an emerging hand or foot, or even a head. It was indescribable.'

After the war and winning a military medal for bravery, Manley returned to Jamaica to work as a lawyer and became active in politics and social justice, along with other ex-servicemen. The fears of the colonial authorities were justified in thinking that participation in the war might fuel the cause of those who wanted to throw off the yoke of empire. Many troops who served in the British West Indies Regiment became left-wing activists on returning home, fired up by their wartime experiences of racism and discrimination.

Then when the Great Depression hit Jamaica particularly hard, causing sugar prices to slump in 1929, economic stagnation led to widespread discontent. Wages were low, prices were high and poor living conditions led to social unrest in the 1930s. There were uprisings, which began on the Frome Sugar Estate in Westmoreland, that my great-uncle William would have witnessed. Those quickly spread east to Kingston, with Jamaica setting the pace for the Caribbean region in its demands for economic development from British colonial rule.

In 1938, Manley founded the People's National Party, the PNP, supporting the trade union movement and demanding universal adult suffrage. When that dream became a reality, Manley was eventually elected to office, later becoming Chief Minister, then Premier, in the last days of British colonial rule and helping to negotiate Jamaica's independence. He was proud of the democratic Jamaica he fought for – literally – in risking his life in the mud of Flanders' fields, just like my great-uncle.

Do Not Desert the Old Land

The experience of war can psychologically alter and redefine. It can lift us closer to the truth of our lives, who we are and what we want to be. In this regard, war is almost cleansing, helping to wash away doubts and uncertainties, helping focus minds on what is important to us. That belief can be instructive if it means that lessons are learned after battle, but the notion can drive belligerents *into* battle in the first place, a sense that a jolly good conflict will clear the air, as some believed before the First World War, or perhaps Vladimir Putin believed before his disastrous invasion of Ukraine.

For Norman Manley, it was the lesson he learned during and after the conflict that was so instructive, as his son Michael told me in an interview I conducted with him in Jamaica in 1996, not long before he died. He said he understood what drove his father to set up the People's National Party, the only broad-based political organisation in Jamaica at the time. It was a duty he felt to the ordinary people of Jamaica, to help create a society fit for all, no matter their class or breeding. Michael told me that from an early age he took a keen interest in his father's political movement, becoming Jamaican prime minister himself for the PNP, espousing his father's ethos of self-reliance and promoting a Jamaica where everyone could share fairly in its fruits.

Michael Manley served in the Royal Canadian Airforce during the waning days of the battle against Hitler, having studied at McGill University in Toronto, and that is where the experience of war comes closer to me. My uncle Cecil and uncle Rennie both served in the RAF. Rennie was with maintenance crews and Cecil was a munitions driver, delivering all manner of bombs and weaponry around the country, not unlike the labour battalions my great-uncle William served in during the First World War.

My dad would have been a teenager when his older brother Cecil left Jamaica to join up as war raged in Europe. After regular communication in the first few months away from home, calming the nerves and anxieties of his family, there was a period of about a year when nothing was heard from Cecil. Was he dead, injured? The fear was that perhaps he had been caught in an air raid at the wheel of his truck loaded with high explosive shells, during the Blitz. My uncle did tell the family his instructions were that while he was out in his truck, if he heard an air-raid siren, or the hum and buzz of the engine of a doodlebug, he had to slam on the brakes and dive for cover, in case his cargo of munitions got hit and went up like a box of fireworks, taking him to the Pearly Gates.

Eventually, Cecil sent back word to Jamaica that he was fine, but our family has never got to the bottom of the year-long silence. Maybe he was simply having too good a time in England to write back home. It was after he was demobbed at the end of the war, and had been living in the UK for more than a decade, that Cecil suggested to my father that he move to Britain. This is how my parents joined the Windrush Generation and how I came into being. War had caused Cecil to leave his birthplace, and peace saw him create a new home. Clearly, he *did* love being in Britain, unlike my dad. Cecil died in the mid-1990s, leaving behind an English wife and two grown-up children.

Something often overlooked when discussing the Windrush Generation is the fact that many were ex-British forces.

Aboard the *Empire Windrush* were hundreds of veterans of the Second World War. These brave men and women were part of more than 10,000 who had volunteered to leave home and join the fight against Hitler, with thousands more serving as merchant seamen. West Indian women served with the Auxiliary Territorial Service and the Women's Auxiliary Air Force, while the RAF gained more recruits from the Caribbean than any other part of the British Empire, with around 400 flying as air crew and 6,000 working as ground staff, including my Uncles Cecil and Rennie. They had fought not only for the old Britain, but for a new inclusive Britain, of which they were encouraged to be a part.

They were now also crucially filling the places of white workers who had left Britain after the war. Winston Churchill called them 'rats leaving a sinking ship'. Two million white Britons abandoned the country, escaping the rationing and Blitz-battered buildings, in the years after Hitler's demise. Canada, Australia, New Zealand, South Africa and Rhodesia-Nyasaland were the destinations of choice. Around forty years earlier, during the Festival of Empire, Britons were being encouraged to emigrate and cement the roots of empire around the globe. Now Churchill was trying to stop a mass exodus, seeing his plans for a post-war economic recovery disappear with every ship of white British migrants that sailed away over the horizon.

They cannot be blamed for wanting to find their Eldorado. The urge is within all of us to do what has to be done to make our lives worth living. But Churchill was angry and he turned to the BBC to issue an appeal: 'I say to those that wish to leave our country, "Stay here and fight it out. If we work together with brains and courage, as we did in days not long ago, we can make our country fit for all our people. Do not desert the old land."' But they did in their droves, leaving our bus and train services short of workers, towns and cities needing to be rebuilt, and a National Health Service and Welfare State to be staffed. As it was in war, so it was in peace, West Indians came to Britain's aid, despite the often hostile and grudging reception.

After the war, it would be almost forty years before all the branches of the British Armed Forces were again engaged in combat together, and this time it would be a new generation going to war, my generation.

* * *

At the age of seventeen, I had never had cause to think about death or dying. I was in good health and no one close to me in our family had died. Although I did have a school friend in the fourth form at Hayward Grammar School in Bolton, whose father died suddenly of cancer, and it hit him hard. I was upset for him and that year my schoolwork was badly affected. It was the closest I had come to the idea of what death means. The absence and sorrow.

I used to pretend I liked drinking pints of warm beer as a fifteen- and sixteen-year-old, but I did not really, it was all part of the act of looking grown-up with my mates. There was a young woman in our sixth form about the same age as me also doing her A levels, who was very proud of the fact that she had a boyfriend who was in the army. That trumped my attempts with glasses of warm beer to look mature. She had a fella, and he was old enough to die in combat.

Of course, death was the last thing on his or her mind, despite his line of work. True, British soldiers were engaged in a complex affair called the Troubles in Northern Ireland, and it seemed like a scary place, never off the TV news. In fact, the previous month the IRA had killed three British soldiers in a gun attack in west Belfast, and it was believed an M60 machine gun was used. I knew about those weapons because my Action Man had a silver one, when I was a kid. But death and thoughts of mortality were far from the minds of all of us as we approached adulthood. Life's journey was just beginning and I was only thinking about the future and university.

Then a place very far away, which it seemed no one had ever heard of, suddenly started dominating the news. It was the Falkland Islands, way off in the South Atlantic, and apparently it was British territory that Mrs Thatcher wanted to rescue, because the Argentinians were trying to steal it. It was the first time in my life that I really began to think about death and dying. All the talk was that Britain had to fight; the newspapers were baying for blood, and the pressure was on to show the Argies who was boss. Britannia ruled the waves, no tin-pot Argie dictator was going to show us up! We were going to war, and I was convinced I was going to war too.

All my friends had visions of the call-up, of uniforms and shiny boots and M60s. It is odd to think of it now, but we were really scared of being conscripted and having to sail away to this place beyond the sea we had never heard of, never to return. Conscription ended in the British Armed Forces in the 1960s, but needs must. The Argentinians were using young conscripts barely out of school, who I am sure liked snogging girls and were already shaving and drinking beer. They were young men like me and my mates, so maybe like them, we would have to fight too. Those in society who came out against a possible war were talking about there being more sheep than people on the Falklands, that the islands did not belong to Britain and should have been given up long ago to Argentina.

Those lands seemed so far away to me, and I was not sure why I should have to die for them. I could not get Kate Bush's song 'Army Dreamers', out of my head, released two years earlier, and the lyrics took on a whole new significance, because now she seemed to be singing about me.

> *What could he do?*
> *Should have been a rock star*
> But he didn't have the money for a guitar
> *What could he do?*
> *Should have been a politician*
> But he never had a proper education
> *What could he do?*
> *Should have been a father*
> But he never even made it to his twenties
> What a waste,
> Army dreamers
> Oh, what a waste of
> Army dreamers

I did not get my call-up papers, a new uniform, shiny boots or an M60 rifle. But Jason Burt did. A native of Hackney in East London, not far from where I live today, he signed up to join the

Parachute Regiment straight from school. Tragically, he was killed in action in the battle for Mount Longdon in the Falklands, hit by a 50-calibre machine gun round. He died on 12 June 1982, still not old enough to vote, a boy of seventeen, the same age as me. Among those members of 3 Para who fought on Mount Longdon, ten were aged seventeen, and forty-two just eighteen. Jason was one of the youngest soldiers to die for his country. That summer, as I was preparing to go to university, his parents were preparing to greet his coffin on its return home.

In 2007, I went to the Falkland Islands to report on the twenty-fifth anniversary of the war. The landscape was barren and treeless, tortured by ferocious winds. I was reminded of rural Scotland or Wales, and indeed the nineteenth-century settlers whose descendants are now the Falkland Islanders were mainly Scots and Welsh. Land Rovers, red phone boxes and traditional English-looking pubs in the capital, Stanley, gave the place an air of being stuck in time: a 1950s England. Yet it was changing from a mainly farming community to mass tourism and fishing.

I went to a party in Stanley with my BBC producer, Stuart Hughes, and cameraman John Landy, and the woman who had invited us, in her mid-twenties, was leaving the local paper where she had a job in sales, I think. She was bored and restless and wanted new opportunities, of which there were none in the Falklands. So, she was heading off to New Zealand to find work. Smart, educated young people like her were to become the beneficiaries of Britain's renewed interest in the Falklands at the end of the war.

When Britain took back the islands, London had to make sure the sacrifices of people like Jason Burt were not in vain.

It could not be business as usual, leaving the islands to continue to rot, neglected and abandoned, so a major effort was made to create jobs and prevent more young people leaving. Now there is a rapidly growing population, with immigrants arriving from around the world in search of opportunity.

Some of the soldiers who fought in the Falklands did wonder what they were fighting for, after seeing the barren scraps of land upon which they could fall, as the freezing wind howled about them. Yes, it was for territory and the Falklands remain a corner of the south Atlantic that is forever England, though it could be argued that the war was also for the promise that the territory held for future generations. But for the week or so I was in the Falklands, I could not stop thinking about all the young men on both sides, around my age at the time of the war, sixteen, seventeen and eighteen, who died. What about their futures, and their promise, sacrificed for others?

It would be twenty years after the conflict in the South Atlantic, before I finally went to war with an enemy happy to see me dead.

Thank You, Mr Bush, Thank You, Mr Blair, Now Go

It was the weirdest of circumstances in which I received my call-up papers. It was January 2003, and I was at the MTV Asia Awards in Singapore when my phone buzzed in my pocket. It was Malcolm Downing, one of the foreign duty editors at the BBC in London.

'Clive, we're wondering if you want to be embedded with one of the British military units going into Iraq. You don't have to say yes, it could be very dangerous, it's totally up to you.'

In front of me, the rapper Missy Elliott and her dancers were gyrating on stage. War was the furthest thing from anyone's mind as the music pumped.

That same month, one of the most senior officers in the unit that I ended up being embedded with, 40 Commando Royal Marines, was being given a secret briefing in San Diego by America's top generals. It had only recently become clear behind the scenes that the UK military would be involved in an invasion of Iraq, which by then the Americans had decided was going to happen, no matter what the situation politically. The briefing was startling. The marines would be tasked with securing Iraq's southern oilfields, an area that would be heavily defended.

The region in the Al-Faw peninsula saw intense fighting during the Iran–Iraq War and so there would be fortifications and defences. On the sea approaches the beaches would be mined, and that meant the marines could not use landing craft; they would have to approach in helicopters. That in turn meant flying in the dead of night and landing on top of enemy targets, rather than approaching steadily in daylight as conventional military doctrine dictates. In short, it was a nightmare mission that was being offered up and if I had known all this ahead of time, I might well have decided not to go.

The 40 Commando Commanding Officer was Gordon Messenger, a man who understood the mission perfectly and what would be required of his men, but he also had regard for the families of his marines. He took the decision, precisely because of the danger, that it would be important to have journalists tag along, to ensure the families back home were receiving regular updates about how their loved ones were getting on.

It was a master stroke of compassion and transparency that saw me and cameraman DC, along with Tom Newton Dunn of the *Daily Mirror* and his photographer, clamber on board a Chinook helicopter as darkness cloaked the makeshift airstrip in the Kuwaiti desert in the early hours of 20 March 2003, ready for the night-time assault. As embedded journalists we had been given the title of Captain, the highest rank a Myrie had achieved in the British military, and yet I was the only Myrie not actually engaged in combat or handling weaponry.

On board the Chinook as we headed into Iraq, none of the marines we were with spoke a word. It was a twenty-minute journey and we were all lost in our thoughts. The previous day, I noticed that some marines had written letters to their loved ones back home in the UK, which were only to be posted if they did not return. I did not write one myself, fearing it might tempt fate. On the flight I thought to myself, what the hell am I doing here? We were flying low to sneak beneath Iraqi radar, making us sitting ducks for anyone with a decent rifle, and we were going to land right on top of the intended target, the main southern Iraqi oil installation on the Al-Faw peninsula.

Military manuals call it a 'vertical envelopment manoeuvre', and it is very high risk. For sure, it is the last thing the Iraqis or any army would expect, so an attacking force has certainly seized the element of surprise. The Iraqis had little night vision capability and would not see us descending vertically until it was too late. On the flight I prayed along with everyone else that US Special Forces had done their job. Navy SEALs had flown in less than an hour before us. They had to identify Iraqi troop positions and guide in coalition artillery fire and aerial bombardments to make our landing a little less rocky.

As it turned out for the Chinook ahead of us, it was a less than smooth touchdown. Our own vertical descent was delayed by ten, maybe fifteen minutes. We had to hover while Royal Marines beneath us were in the middle of a firefight. This was the beginning of the ground war for Iraq; the marines were the first regular coalition troops on Iraqi soil, and I was there with them.

The plan all along was to prevent the Iraqis blowing up the oil infrastructure and setting fire to the oil wells, thereby destroying the country's wealth. An ecological disaster would also be averted. By the early morning, Royal Marines had fanned out across the area. There were skirmishes and while intelligence reports suggested there were around 1,300 Iraqi troops on Al-Faw, up against 900 or so British commandos, it was clear Saddam's forces were poorly trained and ill-equipped. Their bunker positions, once located, were attacked. In one instance, despite a warning to surrender, the Iraqis refused to budge; in fact they fired back. The British called in a mortar attack and the bunker was mercilessly shelled.

When it was deemed safe, we went to look at the damage. There were bodies everywhere. I counted six and one man dying on the ground. Royal Marine medics rushed over and tried to save him. His right arm had pretty much been blown off, he had shrapnel wounds to his leg and chest, and I could hear him groaning. The medics tried to stem the bleeding and inserted a drip to keep him hydrated. As a civilian watching all this, it was a strange sight, because minutes earlier the marines had been trying to kill him. Later I heard that the wounded soldier had died.

Over the next few days, the marines advanced north towards the southern city of Basra; the oilfields had been secured, and Baghdad had fallen to American troops. We had been sleeping in disused buildings, schoolyards and open ground on the approach to Iraq's second largest city, and when we arrived in Basra, I felt a huge sense of relief that we had all made it safely. 40 Commando did not lose a single marine. There were injuries, several after one night-time attack on a heavily defended building, but DC, Tom and I were never in the position of having to report to the families back home that one of theirs had fallen.

Basra was also the place that offered up real food, usurping the military rations we had been eating out of plastic bags for weeks – condensed meals that were bland and tasteless, requiring lashings of Tabasco sauce to make them palatable. In the old city we found bread and tins of dolma, grape leaves stuffed with rice and onion. I will never forget that first taste of proper food after eating baby food for so long. I thought I was in heaven.

The people of the city thought they were in heaven too. The war seemed to be over, and word had reached them that Saddam Hussein's statue in the centre of Baghdad had been toppled. The hated leader, whose secret police had murdered and tortured and drained the country's vast oil wealth into the pockets of his family and cronies, was on the run. Southern Iraq and Basra were home to mainly Shia Iraqis, and Saddam was from the Sunni branch of Islam. I remember the chill I felt going into the police headquarters in the city and finding below-ground torture chambers.

In one room, hooks were embedded in the ceiling, from which victims dangled as they were beaten. Two thick rubber vehicle tyres were on the floor next to a long electric cable. The speculation was that while a torturer stood on the tyres, water would be poured on the floor, and the electricity cable would be pushed into the water, giving electric shocks to the barefoot prisoner.

It was no surprise to me when the next morning, we wandered into the centre of the city to find looting. We saw one of the big hotels being systematically stripped. People were throwing the contents out of the windows to be scooped up later. Blankets and sheets, pillows, mattresses, beds, TVs, lamps, mirrors: anything that was not nailed down was swiped. Saddam had filled his pockets for years and these people were at last getting something for themselves. I understood their frustration and rage and relief. It was their turn to loot the country.

When the US Defense Secretary, Donald Rumsfeld, heard what was happening in Basra, he famously quipped, 'Stuff happens.' He denied that coalition forces only had a plan for the war and not the peace. But that was the sad truth, with Rumsfeld being one of the chief architects of the failure of the Iraq War. He helped drive the push to topple Saddam without sending in enough troops to stabilise the country once the war was over, and he along with Dick Cheney, the US vice president, helped to push the narrative that the best way to deal with Iraq's supposed WMDs was by going to war, not using the United Nations, and weapons inspectors.

Rumsfeld had become drunk on US global hegemony, which caused a staggering level of hubris in the Bush administration that America was invincible and could do anything. I recall a British tank commander talking to an Iraqi official in Basra about what should happen next in the country. The official was blunt. 'Thank you, Mr Bush, thank you, Mr Blair, now go, your troops must go.' The Shia were now in charge, and they would be calling the shots. Rumsfeld did not have the troop numbers to suggest otherwise.

In the years after the war, I attended the regimental reunions at 40 Commando's base in Taunton, commemorating the tenth and twentieth anniversaries of the conflict. They have been wonderful opportunities to catch up with the guys who went into battle believing they were helping rid Iraq of weapons of mass destruction. So now, understanding that there were no WMD in the country, it has been hard. There is a sense among the men that they were lied to and put their lives on the line for nothing. They had done their job in securing the oilfields, why had the war planners not done theirs in properly establishing whether Saddam had WMDs?

My great-uncle fought in the First World War, two of my uncles were involved in the Second World War, and I saw the guts of the conflict in Iraq. I pray no future member of the Myrie family has to experience what war really means.

–9–

The Cricket Test

THERE WERE NOT many things in life that made my father happy in Britain, but watching the West Indies cricket team beat the pants off the English was always a cause for mirth in our home when I was growing up. It was the way the team played the game. Swashbuckling, adventurous, exciting. The forward defensive was anathema to Caribbean cricketers, unless absolutely necessary. The aim was to entertain, with sweeps and pulls and hooks and drives, manipulating the bat as if it was a fly swat.

I never saw the batsman Viv Richards wear a helmet, only the claret red of a West Indies team cap, so confident was he that no bowler could ever get near his handsome face as he flashed the willow. As for the West Indies bowlers, they were fast, very fast, four of them bowling relentlessly in a row, sometimes five, affording no let-up for opposition batsmen, who had to contend with deliveries of over 90 miles an hour, over after over after over. It was exhausting for the opposing team.

The West Indies' success in the 1970s and 80s was enough to banish the frustrations of immigrant life, one over and one boundary at a time. The players provided summer bounties of hope to the Windrush Generation in England, and recognition that the Caribbean had something special to offer the world. Cricket was a pursuit where the English bowed down to the West Indies, not the other way round. Led with magisterial ease by the captain Clive Lloyd, the team's success was a high-water mark in the desire of British Caribbean immigrants to stick two fingers up to the racism they encountered in the UK.

It was a full-throated riposte to notions of inferiority. Yes, while some of Britain's white working class also drove buses, swept the streets and collected rubbish, worked in factories, cleaned offices and populated the lower tier jobs of the NHS and British Rail, it was the majority of the black population that filled these positions.

So where was *my* allegiance going to be as the son of Jamaican parents but born in Britain? With England's cricketers or with the Windies, as the team was affectionately known? Some believed the extent to which my parents had integrated into British life could be gauged by what side they supported in international cricket matches. A bizarre idea and one that clearly failed to acknowledge the sacrifices already made by many in the Windrush Generation, in fighting for King and Country in the Second World War. One would have thought being willing to lay down one's life would be enough of a guide to loyalty.

My family failed the so-called 'cricket test,' as it later became known, and I am afraid I failed it too. I will take a Gordon Greenidge hook shot over Geoffrey Boycott endlessly prodding forward defensives, any day of the week. However, those who believed in the cockamamie theory of the 'cricket test' were driving at a deeper point: that Britain's post-war

Caribbean immigrants must assimilate into British culture and assume the host nation's characteristics, rather than hold true to their own cultures and identities. The idea that Britain could or should become a multicultural nation, a patchwork of ideas that together created a new nation, was not going to fly. Britain was fine as it was, it was the immigrants who must change.

Their argument was that I could never call myself British or English unless I conformed to *their* idea of what that meant. And why would West Indians now living in Britain along with their children not want that too? After all, as that ardent believer in British imperialism, Cecil Rhodes, famously said, 'to be born English is to win first prize in the lottery of life.'

The summer of 1976 was a bad year for proponents of the 'cricket test'. It was one of the hottest on record for the UK in the whole of the twentieth century. The gum that held the sole of my gym shoes to the uppers became so weak, it melted in the heat. Tarmac roads became sticky as they changed consistency in the more than 30° temperatures, and they were bouncy to walk on; it was the strangest feeling. The first time I heard the idea of rationing water was in that parched, breeze-stifled year. The word 'drought' was all over the news too, not in relation to some far-off place in Africa, but closer to home in Gloucestershire and Dorset.

I was eleven years old in 1976. I had a Raleigh Chopper bike, a great circle of school friends and by and large I loved the summer heat. So did my dad and he was in a good mood from May to August. That is because Caribbean people were beating the English at their own game: cricket. Just as my ears would prick up on hearing the high-pitched tinkly tune that heralded the arrival of an ice-cream van, laden with 99s and Strawberry Mivvis – a particular favourite of mine – my dad's ears would prick up and his eyes widen turning on the TV in those summer months to hear the theme tune to the BBC's Test Match coverage. Booker T and the MG's 'Soul Limbo', the soundtrack of summer. And what a summer it was.

Sport has an amazing ability to transcend its boundaries, to become something more revelatory, a magnifying glass on hidden truths, and I believe it was the Test series that summer that helped to create a modern Britain. England had drawn the most recent encounter with the West Indies two years earlier, away in the Caribbean, so the English were confident they could win on home soil in 1976. In fact, the England captain, Tony Greig, who was South African-born and qualified to play for England because his dad was Scottish, made it clear on camera that he believed the West Indies would be made to 'grovel'.

Black men made to grovel to white men, the sorry story of the history of black and white relations down the centuries, and this coming from the lips of a white South African! My dad, like every West Indian in Britain, was riled up. Honour was at stake and the pride of a proud people. The tone had been set for a battle royal between the former master and former slave, coloniser and colonised, oppressor and oppressed. The winner could indirectly chart the course of race relations in Britain for a generation.

Black Caribbeans in Britain were looking for heroes, and that summer there were eleven of them. As I played in the back street behind our house with my friends, I would hear 'Soul Limbo' piped out of our television, as all the doors and windows were open to catch any hint of a breeze, with the sun higher in the sky and seeming to be more intense over Bolton than in Jamaica.

'YES!' I would hear my dad exclaim, as Viv Richards or Gordon Greenidge clattered the ball to the boundary for four or a mighty six. 'YES!' as Michael Holding, with the elegance and balance of Rudolph Nureyev, ran in over the wicket to fire down the ball and shatter the stumps of another hapless English batsman.

The biggest 'YES!' of all, of course, was reserved for the England captain, Tony Greig, whose stumps were destroyed by Michael Holding with a delivery straight and true. It was like a bowling ball smashing through the pins to the delight of the crowd, with many of the stands full of black people, massed at the Oval ground just up the road from Brixton in south London, the enclave that was a home from home for so many of the Windrush Generation. Some had their shirts off in the heat, white sun hats bobbing around the ground, dancing as if at a carnival in the Caribbean.

I watched Tony Greig's walk back to the pavilion having had his stumps skittled and I could read his mind, the sense of failure and resignation, the public humiliation that it was *he* who was grovelling. 'A very disappointed, disenchanted Tony Greig there,' was the commentary, as that walk of about 150 yards, I am sure, felt to Tony Greig like 150 miles.

There was only one team grovelling. The West Indies won the five-match series 3–0. Viv Richards scored 291 at the Oval, his highest Test score. My father's smile and laughter and whoops of joy filled the house, in scenes that were probably played out in every West Indian home across the land. The summer months of 1976 left a profound impression on me and so many young black kids. They showed us that we as a people were worth something in our own right. We were no longer simply appendages and adjuncts to the British and their empire. Looking back, I believe that year was seminal in the post-colonial life of Britain, helping to usher in an age of multiculturalism that has defined modern Britain and defined my life.

That year Bob Marley and the Wailers were on tour in the UK, cultivating that uniquely West Indian export of reggae, but selling it to the rest of the world. The following year his 'Exodus Tour', promoting the album of the same name, drove home the message to British fans that reggae was a cultural phenomenon that could sit happily next to home-grown rock and pop. Indeed, the precursor to reggae, Jamaican ska music, was later melded into a uniquely British sound by bands like The Specials, formed the year after the West Indies gave England a caning.

The band Madness was formed in 1976, The Beat in 1978 and The Selector in 1979, with the most successful ensemble to use reggae as the basis of their sound being The Police. They even called one of their albums *Reggatta de Blanc*, loosely translated from French as 'white reggae'. These bands and their sound filled my head as a teenager, the soundtrack of my youth.

In 1976 Cindy Breakspeare became the first Jamaican to win Miss World, a title at the time coveted round the globe, and a win made even more newsworthy when she and Bob

Marley became lovers. It was also the year when I first became conscious of the inequities of life for black people in South Africa, with the terrible images on television of the Soweto Uprising – the series of protests and demonstrations led by black school children in South Africa in response to the introduction of Afrikaans as the language used by teachers in classrooms. Thousands of pupils took part in the protests and were met with astonishing brutality, with estimates of the dead, shot, or those attacked by police dogs ranging from 176 to over 700.

As an eleven-year-old, I read about the massacre in the newspapers I was delivering on my paper round, and I saw the shocking photograph of the lifeless body of Hector Pieterson, only twelve years old, being carried away from the line of police fire. He had been shot and killed. The world could no longer ignore the rights of the black majority in South Africa. Little did I know that while the struggle would be long and difficult, publication of that terrible image was the beginning of the end of apartheid.

Worlds were colliding in my head. International affairs, Jamaican music, British rock and pop. I was also playing the violin at school and beginning a lifelong love affair with classical music and opera. This was *my* multicultural Britain, and it was wonderful.

Then in August 1976 came the Notting Hill Carnival and the kind of trouble those warning against multiculturalism believed was inevitable. A show of strength exhibited by the Metropolitan Police, suspicious of large gatherings of black people, resulted in heavy-handed tactics leading to the worst rioting, public disorder, and most protracted street battles on mainland Britain for forty years. New laws had been introduced, giving the police the powers to stop and search suspects, and they were being used over-zealously to take young black men off the streets.

So in that tumultuous year of 1976, I did not have to travel to Africa to find a drought or to find the ill-treatment and othering of people who looked just like me. It was all on my own doorstep. Natural disasters and those man-made. No matter how wonderful I believed multiculturalism was, there would always be others who despised it, a reaction I simply could not rationalise and understand.

* * *

While my family and I luxuriated in the dominance of the West Indies and their cricketing prowess, one of my other sporting loves was tennis. I was obsessed as a teenager with Bjorn Borg, the Swedish maestro. I used to feel sick and have butterflies in my stomach every year he appeared in a Wimbledon final, praying he would win. My bedroom was plastered with pictures of tennis stars.

Cheekily, I used to ring up big sportswear manufacturers and ask them to send me posters of the players they endorsed wearing their products, claiming they would be put to good use gracing the walls of the youth club I was pretending to represent. Then I would get the giant posters of McEnroe or Arthur Ashe or Borg wearing Nike or Diadora or Adidas, and they would line the walls of my room.

On the tennis courts up the road from our house, I used to mimic Bjorn Borg's famous whipped double-handed, cross-court backhand. 'Oh, I say!' I would comment as the ball looped over the net, hit with 'venomous' top spin then dipping 'viciously', giving my opponent little chance of getting to it in time, as the ball bounced like a dead cat. These were familiar words and phrases that peppered the television commentary of the great Dan Maskell, during the BBC's coverage of Wimbledon fortnight.

I would map out many of the years of my youth according to the Grand Slam tournaments, the crème de la crème of world tennis. The French Open signified spring, played at Roland Garros some time in May; Wimbledon of course meant summer; the US Open marked the onrush of autumn in September; and the Australian Open, usually in January, meant freezing cold mid-winter.

British male tennis stars were thin on the ground in the 1970s and early 80s. On the women's side, Sue Barker won the French Open in 1976 and Virginia Wade famously won Wimbledon the following year during the Queen's Silver Jubilee. But on the men's side success in major singles tournaments was non-existent. Our best hope of a top international title came in the Davis Cup, the international team competition involving singles and doubles matches.

It was in Palm Springs in Florida in 1978 that a British team finally had the chance to restore a little national pride, getting to the final of the Davis Cup against the United States. I loved the way a brash, left-handed, serve-volley genius from New York by the name of John McEnroe played the game. A powerful server, he had a great baseline game using all kinds of spin, but it was at the net where he really excelled, with a deft and delicate touch.

I was rooting for the Brits to win, of course (I passed the tennis test!), and it was upon the shoulders of a young man called Buster Mottram that our Davis Cup dreams rested. I would cheer him on every year on the grass at Wimbledon, but he was a hard surface and clay-court player, so was never likely to win in SW19. Nevertheless, every year I hoped for the best.

Then, sometime in the late 1970s, while I was playing wall tennis with a friend at the back of our house, in the middle of one of those hot summers when we did not have to worry about going to school the next day, my friend told me something rather disturbing. We pretended to be famous players walking out onto the grass at Wimbledon about to contest the final. I would use a tennis racquet to measure the proper height of the net and, with a piece of chalk, to draw a white line at that height across the width of the wall.

On this particular day, I said I would be Arthur Ashe and my friend could be Buster Mottram.

'Ugh,' he said, 'no chance, he doesn't like brown people.' (My friend was of Pakistani heritage.) He went on, 'And he'd send you back home on a banana boat.'

'What?'

'Yes, he supports the NF [National Front].'

It turned out that Buster had rather right-wing views and believed Enoch Powell was right to warn of the dangers of migration from Britain's former colonies. I admit it was a shock, and I was very sad that someone I admired, whom I cheered on at Wimbledon from the family living room every summer, felt this way. He believed post-war immigration to Britain from her colonies was a mistake.

Mottram was thrashed in three sets by John McEnroe in his match decider at the 1978 Davis Cup, 6–2, 6–2, 6–1. McEnroe, of course, being the progeny of that great wave of Irish migration to America at the turn of the twentieth century.

* * *

The multiculturalism Mottram did not want is now part of who we are as a nation, but rather than adapt, some still fight it. In October 2017, I was despatched to Las Vegas to cover the worst mass shooting by an individual in modern American history. The flight was long, Vegas was hot, and I was tired and frankly pissed off by the time I had to appear on air, live on the *BBC News at Six*. I was incensed at the meaningless slaughter, yet again. Sixty people dead, almost 900 wounded, some in the crush to escape as the shooter rained down more than a thousand bullets into a crowd of people enjoying a music festival on the Las Vegas Strip.

I filmed a report on the madness of the carnage that took place. To this day, no motive has been established for why the killer, a 64-year-old man called Stephen Paddock, pointed a succession of weapons out of the 32nd floor window of his hotel and sprayed bullets down on the people below. On the face of it, Paddock committed mass murder simply because he could.

My report was being broadcast and I was standing by waiting to be interviewed live by George Alagiah back in the studio in London. I felt I had somehow to get across my astonishment at what had happened and my anger at the

American people. *They* had allowed this slaughter to take place, *they* were obsessed with guns, *they* were in the dock to my mind, as much as Paddock. I had never felt more British in my life than at that moment. I was proud we did not have guns on our streets, and we had not subscribed as a society to the twisted notion that they make society safer. I was proud that our average bobby on the beat did not routinely carry a weapon, and firearms made most Brits recoil in horror.

George asked me a question about the investigation, and I said that as yet detectives had no motive, the killer was found dead in his hotel room from a self-inflicted gunshot wound, and he had specially adapted his weapons with so-called 'bump stocks', which allowed them to fire repeatedly like automatic rifles, used by armies in war.

Then I said, 'As an Englishman, I cannot fathom America's love affair with guns. It boggles the mind and has resulted in another mass shooting tragedy, and mindless slaughter.'

Little did I know that a 66-year-old white man, sitting watching the *News at Six* at home in Leeds, was taking umbrage at the idea that I, a black man, was calling myself 'English'. He was not offended or disgusted by the story I was reporting on, the deaths of innocent people enjoying a music festival. He was not appalled by the lives ruined and futures lost. He was simply incensed I had the cheek to claim I was his equal, that I was as English as he was.

Over the years as a BBC correspondent and presenter I have received letters, emails and messages from bigots and racists. There was one stage in the 1990s when someone took to sending faeces in the post to a number of ethnic minority

BBC reporters and presenters, including myself. However, the abuse has become more frequent in recent years.

Where I might have been targeted occasionally over many years, now it is two or three times a year. During the early days of the COVID-19 pandemic in 2020 during the first lockdown, when I was reporting from the Royal London Hospital, I received one email to be applauded at least for its brevity.

'Fuck off, you black cunt.'

I have received a card with a gorilla on the front and the message: 'We don't want people like you on our TV screens.'

One woman in an email with the subject line, 'Why are you dressed like a pimp?', intoned: 'Love the "I don't give a fuck" approach to presenting, but tonight you looked like a badly dressed pimp. Perhaps [it's] time to look for a new role outside the BBC!' This person later remarked that: 'as a License Holder . . . I feel I have every right to comment . . . As a person in public life, it goes with the territory being critiqued by the public.'

Another comedian, clearly not very happy with my reporting from Ukraine, went to all the trouble of writing a note, popping it in an envelope, licking a stamp (1st class), then putting it in the post. It read: 'To Clive. It's KIEV not KEEV you token twat, woke warrior. If you were white you'd probably not be on TV.'

But the gentleman in Leeds, watching the *News at Six* as I reported live from Las Vegas, apparently wanted to go a step further than simply abuse me with words. He wanted to kill me. In November of 2017, a month after I had been in America, I received an email from the BBC's in-house security department. They had seen a number of troubling messages received by BBC Audience Services, the platform that allows members of the public to leave comments about BBC programmes they have been watching.

This man had left messages and threats to kill me, according to a BBC investigator. The messages had been left between 4 and 30 October.

> 04.10.17: Well Myrie best stay in Vegas because just guess who has gone to the top of the list and he is much easier.
> 07.10.17: Have you told Myrie he's for the chop?

The investigator said the above comment was at the end of a paragraph which contained the word 'nigger' and 'coon' in the context of the message.

> 30.10.17: . . . the nigger Myrie . . . still on my list . . . and does he know not to call himself an Englishman and does he know he's at the top of my list of BBC niggers for being the recipient of a .303 round sometime soon? If I can't get him then some other BBC nigger will do . . .

I was shaken when I read the messages. Surely, it is just banter from a sad racist, I said to the investigator.

'They cannot be dismissed as banter or just having a laugh,' he told me. 'They are serious claims to want to do you harm.'

I was a little apprehensive walking home for the next few days. Violent racism was alive and well in the UK and it was knocking on my door. However, I was going to get on with my life and not allow the threats to frighten me. I would not let him win.

Then the following month in December, the BBC investigator got in touch with me again to say that the man who had threatened to kill me had been arrested in Leeds for sending twenty-seven malicious communications via the BBC's complaints website between 2015 and 2017. But there was more. Over a thousand child sexual abuse images had also been found on electronic devices in his home.

'Do you want to go to court and testify against him?' the investigator asked.

'No,' I replied. I did not want to see this person or to have all the attendant publicity that would surround me turning up at court in Leeds. On the first day of his trial he pleaded guilty to two counts of sending malicious communications, and one count of possession of indecent images. It also transpired that he had been jailed in 2007, after firearms were found at his home when he was arrested for posting a menu with 'racist words' written on it through the letterbox of an Indian restaurant.

Some of his malicious communications involved a Formula 1 presenter on Radio 5 Live, Jack Nicholls, targeted because he described Lewis Hamilton as 'English'. His messages also included what were described as 'disturbing references' to the murder of the BBC journalist Jill Dando, shot dead outside her home in south-west London in 1999.

The man who threatened to kill me had accessed firearms in the past. I could not believe it. He had issued terrible threats and used the worst racist language, so ultimately, what was he planning to do?

I will never know.

* * *

In July 2005, I was in my office in the BBC's Washington Bureau watching the latest developments on TV after the coordinated attacks of four suicide bombers in central London. They killed fifty-two people and hundreds of others were injured. It was the worst terrorist atrocity on British soil. Three of the four killers were British-born, second-generation immigrants like me, with their parents from Pakistan.

One was born in Jamaica, but moved to the UK when he was only a year old. I felt overwhelming anger towards the four men. My wife Catherine worked with one of the innocent victims who died. Miriam Hyman came to our wedding and the beautiful pottery she gave us as a present twenty-five years ago still sits in our home. Miriam was on the double-decker bus in Tavistock Square, not far from King's Cross, when it was blown up by one of the suicide bombers sitting on the upper deck.

I was angry at the senselessness of it all, the lives blighted for ever, furious at the bombers for what they had done. But I was also angry at their failure to have bought into the idea of a multicultural Britain, their failure as brown people to buy into the values of tolerance and freedom that underpin liberal democracy. The bombers did not see themselves as British Pakistanis or as British Caribbean. They had been unable to assume the dual identity I wore so lightly, along with many millions of other second-generation immigrants, who were proud to call Britain their home.

The 7/7 bombings confirmed the suspicions and fundamental antipathy to multiculturalism of the man who coined the phrase 'the cricket test'. Norman Tebbit, the former Conservative Party politician, was speaking to the *Los Angeles Times* in 1990 when he said a large proportion of Britain's

Asian population fail the test: which side do they cheer for? In a separate interview, he said, 'Some of them insist on sticking to their own culture, like the Muslims in Bradford . . . and they are extremely dangerous.'

His test was not a very good gauge of loyalty or assimilation, and I told him this when I interviewed him myself in 1990. I had left BBC local radio and joined the news service Independent Radio News, which worked with Britain's commercial radio stations providing news and current affairs. I was interviewing him down the line, so he could not see that I was black, and I must admit I half expected him to say that of course his test was crude and hardly scientific, and he meant it as a bit of a joke.

But no, he maintained that those immigrants who supported their native countries rather than England at cricket were not assimilated enough into the UK, and that could lead to conflict further down the line. He did not accept my contention that for most people, integration was about more than a game of cricket. That it was about accepting the values of the host country, and this could be done in a multicultural setting, allowing for a richer, more diverse and interesting society.

Mr Tebbit was having none of this, and the 7/7 bombings fifteen years later only confirmed him in his view. Speaking to a politics website, he is quoted as saying that the attacks could have been prevented, if more of an effort had been made to integrate Britain's migrants to assimilate. He said that multiculturalism was now in danger of undermining British society, and he warned that London was 'sinking into the same abyss that Londonderry and Belfast sank into.'

In my view, that was completely missing the point. Multiculturalism is about shared values, not modes of prayer or dress, food, the colour of one's skin, or which cricket team we support. Shared values of right and wrong, of equality and fairness, outweigh culture. What the bombers lacked was a belief in the worth and equality of us all as human beings. Their values were skewed. I have faith that for most Britons our shared values endure.

–10–

Obama

IN 1989, WITH the fall of the Berlin Wall, America had won a monumental battle of ideas. The moment was described as the 'end of history' by the American political scientist, Francis Fukuyama. Power and influence, projected across the globe – politically, economically, culturally and militarily – meant the United States was now the most powerful nation the world had ever known. And yet Washington DC, the capital and beating heart of this big beast, is quite a sleepy little place compared to most other capital cities, with a population at its core of barely over 700,000.

The BBC's Washington Bureau is situated on M Street, in the Georgetown area of the city. I adored walking the leafy thoroughfares and avenues in the area, adorned with handsome row houses in the Georgian and Federal style, especially in the spring and autumn months as budding shoots blossomed into canopies of green, then transformed into all shades of browns, oranges, yellows and reds.

Catherine and I lived on Dent Street, a 15–20 minute walk from the office. John F. Kennedy was reputed to have lived on the same road, but every neighbourhood in DC claimed to have had him as a resident at one time or another. I would often think of him as I headed to the office. There is no

145

question that American politics in his day was bare knuckle. Rambunctious, noisy discourse, even unseemly and indecorous at times, showed the vibrancy of the democratic process since the founding of the Republic, with little quarter given to the opposite side of the aisle.

But in his day, I believe most people signed up to a core set of values and aims, which everyone championed as being good for the overall prosperity of the nation: work hard and you could make it, your children will be better off than you are when they come of age, the issue of race is unfinished business, the rights of the individual are as vital as the rights of the corporations, and the rule of law applies to everyone and must be respected. Those core values meant common ground could be found more often than not between Republicans and Democrats – you give a little here on what you believe, take a little there. Finding consensus was possible on the big issues.

In the early 2000s, however, I lived and worked in a nation where absolutely no quarter was given, where there was a fatal irreconcilability to politics. America felt to me like a place where the governing class bowed down to special interests and big business, the influential and mighty. It was a place where consensual politics was for wussies. The aim of the game was to beat your opponent, show them up, diminish them, get what you want and damn the many millions on the other side.

Aided and abetted by loudmouths on talk radio and opinion TV, this led to an America that was an unhappy place, fractured, splintered and divided. Politically, nothing got done, and gridlock was the name of the game if you could not have it all your own way. The public simply did not matter. There seemed to be no politician who could cut through the division. No one seemed even willing to try.

In Georgetown, there appeared to me to be a clear divide between the lives of black people and the lives of whites. African Americans and Latinos worked in the grocery stores and were the valet parkers, the refuse collectors and postal workers. White people worked in the offices and legal firms, were political operatives, lobbyists and advertising execs. It was a divide I found uncomfortable and it spoke volumes about America's blind spot on race. To date, in the entire history of the United States, there have been only eleven black senators.

Barack Obama was the fifth, elected from the state of Illinois in November 2004, the same year I left Singapore to become the BBC's Washington correspondent. We became Washingtonians together, though of course he did not know me from Adam, and few outside Illinois knew who he was either.

If you come out of the BBC's office on M Street and turn left heading into the centre of Georgetown, you reach a bridge that crosses the Potomac River. Keep heading west and you will hit the Ritz Carlton Hotel. Very posh and swanky, it had a wonderful gym. Lucky for me the BBC had a preferential rate for membership, which was a godsend, as the premises were equidistant from work and home. Of course, being the Ritz Carlton, anybody who was anybody would stay there and use the facilities.

One day I turned up and the tour bus of the rapper 50 Cent was parked outside, while he was inside pumping weights.

On another day, Israel's prime minister, Ehud Olmert, was bench-pressing, with two very burly close protection officers standing either side of his barbells with their jackets on, earpieces visible, as the man they were keeping an eye on had sweat pouring off him.

One summer's day, Catherine had finished a session in the gym and was on her way back to the changing rooms for a shower when Oprah Winfrey walked by. 'Nice abs,' she remarked on seeing my wife's toned belly, leaving Cath to reply meekly, 'Thank you,' on recognising one of the most famous faces in the world.

I tended to use the pool more often than the gym. It was usually quieter in office hours, so I had the whole place to myself much of the time. The door had a small porthole window through which visitors could see who was splashing around. Usually Cath would walk by, look through the window, push the door and shout a quick hello. I would look up, wave and smile and return to my lengths.

One day Catherine looked through the window and saw a very focused black man with his head in the water, long arms pushing a front crawl. Catherine pushed the door and shouted hello as usual, and the figure looked up. It was not me, it was Barack Obama.

* * *

My first ever trip to Washington was in the chill mid-winter of 1997, helping out the bureau while some staff were on leave. Imagine my sense of awe reporting from the White House for the first time. Bill Clinton was in residence and what struck me was how small the building is, given the global scope of American power and influence. It is a white wedding cake of a property, all porticoed and perfectly proportioned, a tastefully elegant HQ for the free world. All foreign policy roads lead to the front door, and I would spend much of the rest of my US working life there, trying to divine the mind of whomever was parked behind the Resolute Desk in the Oval office, from Clinton to Bush, Obama, Trump and Biden.

I had experienced my first presidential election the year before, covering the race for the White House in California, a safe Democrat state where Bill Clinton cleaned up against the Republican Second World War veteran, but unimpressive campaigner, Bob Dole. So it was an uneventful first foray into American politics.

My second presidential race, however, between George W. Bush and Al Gore in 2000, was very different, full of controversy, acrimony and cross words. It was also a race that high-lighted some of the strengths, but also many of the weaknesses of the American electoral system. There was no clear winner on election night, so the Electoral College votes of the state of Florida were going to decide. But it was so close there, state law required a recount. That led to sharp-suited and equally sharp-elbowed lawyers being drafted in on both sides, while I was in Austin, Texas, where Bush was headquartered.

In a nutshell, the Democrat candidate, Bill Clinton's vice president, Al Gore, wanted a lengthier recount over a wider area, but Bush's team wanted a more limited county-based recount. In the end, the Supreme Court made the final ruling 5–4, stopping the recounts in their tracks and leaving Bush the winner. The split decision in the highest court in the land was along partisan lines, with the conservative majority siding with Bush, and the liberal dissenters siding with Gore.

I had covered numerous elections in other parts of the world, where force of arms in a contested race would often decide the winner. But not a single shot was fired and no blood was spilt in America, although the flaws in the system were plain for the world to see. With the controversial result settled, I was then reporting on who might or might not be in George W. Bush's first cabinet, an administration that would oversee the response to the 9/11 terror attacks along with retribution in Afghanistan, as well as prosecuting America's disastrous war of choice in Iraq.

Before a bomb was dropped, at an anti-war rally in Chicago, a fairly anonymous state lawmaker, Barack Obama, described the upcoming conflict as a 'dumb war'. Words spoken on the same day the resolution authorising the use of military force in Iraq was introduced in Congress, later to be passed and signed into law by President Bush.

Sadly, in both the 1996 and 2000 elections, I did not get the chance to experience that mother-of-all political get-togethers, the jamboree that is the American nomination convention. I had not experienced the fanfare, the balloons, flags and button pins, the tubthumping and breast-beating declarations of love for the Republican or Democratic parties, along with the anointing of a candidate who would go forward to contest the most powerful job in the world, that of President of the United States.

I finally got my chance in the race for the White House in 2004. However, the Republican Convention at Madison

Square Garden in New York was always likely to be a less than riveting affair. George W. Bush ran unopposed, engaged as he was in his 'War on Terror' after 9/11, and no one was willing to step forward to say they would do a better job taking on international terrorism. That meant no primaries, caucuses or Super Tuesday – when several states declare on the same day who they want to go forward to run for the presidency. This despite the situation in Iraq turning difficult and the conflict in Afghanistan still left unfinished. So, there was little sense of anticipation when he took to the stage to deliver his acceptance speech and said he would be honoured to run again.

The Democratic National Convention in Boston earlier that year was a very different beast. I could feel the excitement, in a corner of America that was Democrat blue in its blood, as I turned up at the Fleet Center Sports Arena in Boston, for four days of BBC coverage. The polls were neck and neck, an extraordinary situation given that George W. Bush was effectively a wartime president, and Americans usually rallied behind the Commander in Chief in perilous times.

The Democrats were anxious to show America they had picked a candidate in John Kerry, the junior senator from the local state of Massachusetts, who understood the War on Terror and could keep America safe. A decorated veteran, he had guided missile frigates and swift boats on the Mekong Delta during the Vietnam War and was awarded two Purple Hearts. His military service contrasted well for the Democrats with George W. Bush, who had been dogged by allegations that he dodged the draft by exploiting family connections.

The day John Kerry was due to give his acceptance speech at the convention, I spoke with his younger sister Diana, who was confident her brother could beat Bush. She was a teacher and bizarrely we ended up talking more about that profession than politics, as I mentioned my mother was a teacher in Jamaica and my two sisters were also teachers. She was nervous for her older brother and his big moment that night. How he came across on prime-time television to millions of voters, who knew him only in passing, could help set the course for the presidential race.

I was in the press box that night, the evening of 29 July, and John Kerry was introduced from the stage as a man 'ready to answer this nation's call'. He then entered the hall walking through a sea of flags and outstretched hands hoping to be touched, and the thousands of people on the floor held aloft tall thin, white cardboard signs on sticks bearing his name, and as the mass waved those signs, they looked like giant corn stalks swaying in the wind in a farmer's field.

The deafening applause and cheers and the Bruce Springsteen track 'No Surrender' filled the arena. 'KER-RY!', 'KER-RY!', the crowd shouted, tens of thousands corralled into the cavernous arena, delirious and seemingly convinced their man had the right stuff to retake the White House. I was delirious too, as I was finally experiencing a slice of Americana that I had only ever seen before on television.

Then came John Kerry's first words when he finally reached the stage, having soaked up all the applause and adulation after the cheering finally died down, words I will never forget. 'I'm John Kerry, reporting for duty.' And with that he saluted the crowd, which then went absolutely nuts.

Given the context of the War on Terror, which America looked in danger of losing, as well as Kerry's war record compared to George W. Bush, American anxiety and fears about Islamic extremism, and the creeping fear of many that the 'American Century' of supremacy and global superiority was coming to an end, Kerry positioned himself as a saviour. Everyone got to their feet.

It was the most dramatic beginning to a nomination acceptance speech in recent times. Pure theatre, and I was there. The little kid from Bolton, standing on the shoulders of my heroes, Alan Whicker and Trevor McDonald, no longer with my face pushed up against the window of history, but actually experiencing those moments as they were happening. I was living them.

But the euphoria of that night for Democrats died during the election, after an 'October Surprise', one of those unforeseen events that scatter everyone's calculations to the wind about how the presidential election the following month might play out. Four days before the polls opened, I was in Washington when Al Jazeera broadcast a videotape from Osama bin Laden, in which he accepted responsibility for the 9/11 attacks, and condemned the Bush administration's response in launching the War on Terror.

Watching the tape, I saw this 'bogey man' in his white turban and robes play with the minds and emotions of the American people, speaking directly to camera from his diabolical lair, like a grotesque Bond villain. All that was missing was the fluffy, purring white cat. I knew what the effect of the tape would be. I had covered the wars in Afghanistan and Iraq, and I had seen how America was fighting bin Laden and his followers. The mass mobilisation of American troops was engaged in a 'just' war in Bush's mind, but for bin Laden on the other side, it was glorious holy war.

The problem was that by calling it a 'war', that gave bin Laden and his zealous supporters a certain nobility, a status. He saw himself as a warrior commander defending the faith, rather than merely being a grubby terrorist. This belief was burnished by his miraculous escape in 2001 from the might of US forces in the peaks of the Tora Bora mountain range, in eastern Afghanistan. For several days in the run-up to Christmas that year, I watched and reported on giant American bombers pounding the area close to the border with Pakistan, hoping to flush out bin Laden and his loyal fighters.

US Special Forces Green Berets, Army Rangers, the elite Delta Force, British Special Boat Service Commandoes and other British Special Forces troops, as well as Afghan tribesmen and militias, were all engaged in the battle. And yet bin Laden escaped them all, first to Jalalabad, then on horseback to the forested mountains of Kunar, where it has been written that he disappeared into a place so remote and obscure that it did not appear on any maps. Like a ghost, he simply disappeared.

In a widely read article in the *New York Times* magazine shortly before polling day, Kerry suggested he wanted to cut back the scale of the War on Terror. It would become a largely covert operation to target and take out the killers, using special forces and black ops. But that is not what the American people wanted. The pain of 9/11 necessitated a massive war of vengeance and retribution, where good would triumph over evil, and that was the view of the born-again Christian George W. Bush.

What bin Laden did in releasing the tape was to remind Americans of the horror of the September 11 attacks and put the issue of terrorism front and centre of the election, pushing it to the forefront of voters' minds. The exit polls later showed by a significant margin that the public believed Bush would better protect them than Kerry, and that they trusted the president would battle harder to defeat the likes of bin Laden and his acolytes. Voters ended up not casting their ballots with an eye on employment and jobs, the economy or the environment, but on who could best keep them safe. That is why bin Laden released his video. He wanted to keep waging Bush's war, to keep fighting and killing Americans. That was clear to everyone, and it was clear to me.

Kerry's defeat in the election that year could have rendered the 2004 Democratic Convention a complete failure, and largely it was, as the ultimate goal was to help put their nominee over the top and into the White House. But history now records one bright spot. Two days before the 'ready to serve' rallying cry and salute, there was another keynote speech, which marked the arrival of a new political superstar.

–11–

The Mere Distinction of Colour

I SPENT MUCH of the first half of 2008 disappointed and in a bit of a sulk, and truth be told, a little bit angry, most notably with Hillary Rodham Clinton. I was now based in Brussels as the BBC's Europe correspondent, and while you can take the reporter out of America, you can never take America out of the reporter. The race for the Democratic Party nomination that year was electric, and I was thousands of miles away, reporting on the inner workings of the European Commission. I knew where I would rather be.

The contest was a close one, very close indeed between Barack Obama and Hillary Clinton, in the race to decide who would take on the Republican nominee in the battle for the White House that November. I admired Hillary for many achievements in her life, but I felt a black man winning the nomination would be more ground-breaking than a white woman, given the tragic legacy in America of almost 250 years of slavery.

As a teenager, I had been intensely moved by the power of the book *The Autobiography of Malcolm X*. The minister and controversial civil rights activist's philosophy of black pride resonated with me and was reflected in my father's pride in black achievement, whether on the field of sport or seeing

Trevor McDonald on the TV; or my mum's insistence that all her children worked hard at school to become the best we could be, and to have pride in who we were as individuals and as a people. As a black man, it seemed Obama's success would somehow curiously be my success too.

But Hillary was not going to give up. She was dogged in her pursuit of the nomination, even when it became clear the odds of victory were getting longer and longer, not shorter and shorter. 'Just concede, Hillary, your time will come again,' my inner voice would wail as the contest dragged on and on. I was devouring the latest twists and turns of the race in all the major American newspapers online, and catching as much of the coverage as I could on CNN and BBC World on TV. The contest had begun in January, but by early June there was still not a clear winner.

It was dragging on much longer than usual, with Hillary in no mood to throw in the towel. And why should she? No woman had come as close as she had to securing the nomination of one of the two major political parties in a presidential race, and just as Obama and millions of African Americans felt history calling, so too did Hillary and millions of women around the world.

It was not until 3 June, six months after the race officially began, that Obama was able to claim he had secured the simple majority of delegates needed to win the nomination. But Hillary, even then, took another four days to concede. Man, I was tearing my hair out. 'Hillary, goddam it! Give it up, enough already!' boomed my inner voice, and when she finally did retire from the race, my excitement was off the chart. Barack had not messed up. In life it seemed to me, black people are rarely given second chances. You screw up, that is it. I believed that if Obama had not secured the nomination, it might have been a long time, perhaps even a generation, before another African American would have been allowed to come so close again.

Now he *had* to go on and win the White House, and it would not have mattered if he was a Republican and not a Democrat. The point is he was capable, and he was black.

* * *

When I lived in America as the BBC's Los Angeles and then Washington correspondent, I was fascinated by the question of race, and wanted to understand why America could not come to terms with its past and move on. Controversies surrounding race were still central to the American experience in the twenty-first century, much more deeply than in most Western democracies.

I realised that part of the problem was that the slave-owning states and territories, extending from Utah in the far west across to the deep south, and up the north-eastern seaboard hitting Maryland and Delaware, were never forced to atone for the crimes they perpetrated against humanity during the years of brutal human bondage. They lied to themselves about the horrors they were engaged in and were allowed to lie to everybody else at slavery's end. The 'Masters' called themselves Christians, and yet they had to rewrite the Bible to justify their crimes. Many euphemistically referred to slavery as the 'peculiar institution', unable to admit to themselves what it really was.

The Civil War in 1861 led to the Emancipation Proclamation and the freeing of the slaves, with the northern armies defeating the Confederacy, but that did not lead to a re-education of Southern minds. While President Lincoln fought the war to prevent the spread of slavery to the new territories in the west, all the death and bloodshed only served to harden attitudes in the South that their cause was just, even though they lost the war.

It has been said that history is written by the victors – well, the opposite happened in America. The notion perpetrated by the losers of the Civil War, the idea of the 'Lost Cause of the Confederacy', stubbornly persisted for a hundred years, and was only finally challenged by the Civil Rights Movement of the 1960s. The 'Lost Cause' claimed the Civil War was not actually about slavery and its cruelties. The conflict was really about the interference of outsiders in the lives of good people simply trying to live their lives. God-fearing honest people, bound by codes of honour and ethics, who were being told how best to run their states. (They also treated their slaves well, by the way.)

This view of the Civil War took hold pretty much as soon as the last shot was fired, a tapestry of lies that has infected the body politic of America like a cancer, and a romanticised view of events that was indulged by the North, to keep the United States together. Never mind the fact that this nonsense is underpinned by the idea of white supremacy, the rest of America turned a blind eye as black people were lynched, the Ku Klux Klan was lionised on film, and segregation was deemed lawful by the highest court in the land.

The legacy of the 'Lost Cause' is a modern America where inequality between the races is baked into the system, because not enough white people have wanted to flush it out of the system, and even now, those who do want to fight racist attitudes must prepare to be demonised as 'woke' or 'politically correct' if any attempt is finally made to affect white minds. The 'Lost Cause . . .' informs white attitudes in the belief that the Confederate flag is still something to be proud of and should still fly high, and it informs attitudes as to whether statues of Confederate generals or slave owners should remain high above mere mortals on plinths. It has made America seemingly its own lost cause when it comes to tackling the issue of race.

In 2005, I travelled to Milwaukee in Wisconsin to interview an extraordinary African American. James Cameron greeted me with a firm handshake. The skin of his right hand felt as soft as silk, his hair was old-aged white. He was ninety-one, wheelchair-bound and had been ill for the last year or so, but his eyes were still alert, his mind sharp. He had agreed to talk to me about a painful time in his life, the day seventy-five years earlier, when a racist mob of thousands tried to lynch him. I spent most of the interview shaking my head in disbelief at his incredible story, it was so shocking and brutal.

Back in 1930, on a hot August evening as crickets sounded and the flapping of fish jumping could be heard in the nearby lake, James was a sixteen-year-old accused with two other black teenagers of the murder of a white man, in the city of Marion in Indiana. All three were arrested and held in the local jail, and James told me he cried that night until there were no more tears to shed. Then a vengeful mob of thousands heard that the three had been caught and broke into the prison.

They murdered James's two friends, Tommy and Abe, beating them to death, then stringing up their bodies from two trees standing in the shadow of the courthouse where lawful justice was supposed to be dispensed. Then they went after James, who told me the crowd was chanting his name as if they were at a football game, cheering on a favourite player. 'We want Cameron! We want Cameron! We want Cameron!' He was shaking and shivering, cold at the thought of imminent death.

He was dragged from his jail cell and beaten all the way to the tree outside, where he could see the bodies of his two friends already hanging limp, twenty-five feet in the air, their necks broken and blood from the heavy beatings staining their clothes. A rope was then put around James's own neck and he began to pray. 'Lord have mercy on me and forgive my sins.'

A man started hoisting him up off the ground and the thick rope began to scorch his neck. Miraculously, someone suddenly shouted out from the crowd that he was not a murderer. Dazed and bewildered, James was lowered down and the noose was removed. The mob spared his life and he was led back to jail. At this point, I sat open-mouthed as I listened.

Rubbish and packing boxes were now piled under one of the bodies of his friends still hanging, and the debris set alight. The mob wanted to burn the corpse and leave the blackened, charred remains swinging in the breeze, as was often the case after a lynching, but the corpse was hanging too high for the flames to lick. Later that night, the local coroner wanted to take both bodies down, but the mob warned him they had to hang there till dawn, as a lesson to other blacks.

James had kept a macabre souvenir from that day, a piece of the rope used to hang one of his two friends. Lynchers often cut up the rope they used to commit murder and sold the pieces as 50-cent souvenirs. I did not want to see the rope, James's story was graphic enough, and I was moved by the dignity he showed in telling me his story. Softly spoken, he simply recounted calmly the events of that terrible day.

James Cameron died less than a year after I spoke with him in 2006. He did not live long enough to see America pass a law making lynching a federal offence. Down the years, seven presidents petitioned Congress to do something about the extrajudicial killings, but stonewalling mainly by southern senators meant no vote was ever taken on the issue, and so the states could continue to allow mob rule and murder if they so wished. Some 200 anti-lynching bills went before Congress, and all were effectively ignored. It was not until as late as 2022 that President Joe Biden finally signed into law the legislation that made lynching a federal hate crime.

Three years after I spoke with James, America would elect a black man to the White House. Did that momentous occasion prove the country had changed since the days when the 'Lost Cause . . .' held sway in the minds of many Americans, or was the arrival of Barack Obama the exception that proved the rule, that America had yet to change?

In the summer of 2008, once Barack Obama had won the Democratic Party nomination, I made up my mind that nothing was going to hold me back from reporting from America on election night. But I was not the BBC's Washington correspondent anymore, so how the hell was I going to get across the Atlantic? The Foreign News Department was not keen on turf wars, and correspondents were supposed to stay in their own lane, unless there was a story so big it needed many extra pairs of hands. In North America, the BBC already had more than enough correspondents to cover election night, but I *had* to be there, and so bombarded the foreign news editor with emails of ideas for stories I could do if he decided to deploy me. But there was no response.

In the meantime, completely out of the blue, the Controller of BBC Two had proposed I make a primetime documentary on Barack Obama to flesh out for British viewers exactly who this person was that might soon become the most powerful man on Earth.

It was a filming trip that lasted over a month, and I really wanted to get under the skin of the man. I flew to his birthplace of Hawaii and spoke to childhood friends and those close to his mother Anne, who had died in 1995. She sounded like a wonderful woman and reminded me in many ways of my own mother. Not afraid to speak her mind, strong-willed, and focused on instilling in her children a sense of pride about who they are; all designed to build an inner confidence that would help protect them against the inevitable racism and bigotry, which for black people goes with the territory of living in a white-dominated world.

I saw many parallels in Obama's life journey to my own: the distant father, the law degree, the mixing of two worlds, black and white, and the deep inner faith that if you work hard enough you can reach the very top of even the highest mountain. Crucially, we shared the early emphasis of a doting mother on education being the key to unlocking a life worth living.

I travelled to Harvard, where he had been the first African American to be elected president of the *Harvard Law Review*, the prestigious in-house legal journal, and I spoke with his influential law professor, Lawrence Tribe, about Obama's ability to bring people of differing views together on common ground. I also spent plenty of time in Chicago, where he cut his political teeth as a community organiser and state legislator, before finally becoming the junior senator for Illinois. That is when he started using the swimming pool at the Ritz Carlton in Washington, when my wife mistook him for me.

Keep On Pushin'

The first thing that had struck me when I saw Barack Obama walk out onto the stage at the Fleet Center in Boston to give his keynote speech at the 2004 Democratic Party Convention, was the swagger. The music he chose to accompany his entrance, booming out over the PA system, added a certain jauntiness in his stride. It was the soulful 'Keep On Pushin'' by the Impressions, featuring Curtis Mayfield's distinctive falsetto voice. Keep on pushin', reach higher, he effectively exhorted the crowd over the next seventeen minutes, with 2,297 words that changed him overnight into a potential future national leader.

His eloquence and vocal tone, the rising and falling cadences like a seasoned preacher in a Baptist church addressing his flock on a Sunday morning, caused a hush in the hall.

Everyone was silent, focusing on his words. He was preaching the Bible of inclusive politics, of finding common ground and understanding the opposing side's point of view, of consensus, collaboration and working together. He was preaching a politics sadly long gone from American life.

'We can make sure that every child in America has a decent shot at life, and that the doors of opportunity remain open to all . . . we can do better.'

The press box was silent too, no fidgeting and slurping of coffees. This man with a funny name held everyone in the palm of his hands. For me watching, it was the empathy in the speech that I found powerful, and which really got to me. This man had a value system that seemed to be the same as mine. And I knew where I got my values from, my mother. It was clear to me as I watched Barack Obama speak that he got his values from his mum too.

'If there is a child on the south side of Chicago who can't read, that matters to me, even if it's not my child. If there's a senior citizen somewhere who can't pay for their prescription drugs, and [has] to choose between medicine and the rent, that makes my life poorer, even if it's not my grandparent. If there's an Arab American family being rounded up without benefit of an attorney or due process, that threatens my civil liberties.'

This was my kind of politics. Not the slash and burn of the modern era in America, where the aim was to appeal to the party zealots, the special interests and the powerful. This was a speech about hope for *everyone*, without which we are all sunk. What I also liked about the speech was that Obama *knew* it was a good one. He knew he had struck a chord with everyone in the arena, and the millions of people watching on TV at home. Why? Because most Americans are decent people. Most human beings are empathetic if they are encouraged to be so. Most people can be good neighbours and want the best for others.

'Do we participate in a politics of cynicism, or do we participate in a politics of hope?' he asked the crowd. '. . . there is not a liberal America and a conservative America; there is the United States of America. There is not a Black America and a White America and Latino America and Asian America; there's the United States of America.'

The speech announced a man of substance, and a consequential political figure, and was hailed as an instant classic, drawing comparisons with Dr Martin Luther King, and John F. Kennedy. Four months later, Barack Obama would win the US Senate race for Illinois, and only four years after that, he would be running for the White House, and I *had* to be there!

Yes, We Can

Two weeks before the US presidential election of 2008, I was in Brussels thinking I was not going to make it to America in time. There had been no word from the foreign desk back in London, no response to my emails about ideas for the election coverage if I was deployed. Total radio silence. I thought about taking two weeks off and paying my own fare to fly to the US to be part of history.

Then the most extraordinary thing happened. With little over one week to go before polling day on 4 November, I received an email from the BBC's foreign editor saying that I was cleared to go to America to cover the election. My years as a Los Angeles and Washington correspondent had counted for something, I thought.

But there was also a sense, only realised by the BBC at the very last minute, that being a black man reporting on the first African American to have a good chance of winning the White House, I might bring an added texture to the coverage, and even a visceral understanding of the journey African Americans had made. Other broadcasters and news outlets had reached the same conclusion, that this could not be a story told solely by white correspondents. Now I would be there, and I would be heading for a very special place.

I had not been to Atlanta, Georgia, in over a decade. In 1996, I was flown there by CNN for a meeting about possibly leaving the BBC and becoming one of their correspondents. I could have been tempted, and the CNN boss said he would get back to me. But it took him four years and by then, despite the amazing offer he finally came up with, I was not in the mood to leave the BBC.

What I remembered about Atlanta, though, as I packed my bag to fly there again in late October 2008, was seeing and being among a large black urban middle class, all suited and booted going to their offices and places of work by day, the opera or theatre at night. They seemed to have power and agency, characteristics not ordinarily representative of the black experience in America. This was a version of the United States that I had not really seen before on any great scale, whether in Los Angeles, New York or Washington.

Atlanta seemed to belong to privileged African Americans who had earned their social status. So many of the white-collar folks in the city were black. The lawyers and judges, bankers and school principals, surgeons and doctors, and millionaire big business owners and insurance executives. Black residents had built their businesses and prosperity in the twentieth century, catering to their own during segregation and making a success of the hideousness of their enforced circumstances. That created a base of wealth that gave African Americans in the city clout.

Crucially too, those who ran local government, where political power resided, were black. Atlanta got its first African American mayor in the 1970s, a time when other cities like Los Angeles, Detroit and Cleveland were also elevating black officials to high office. But only in Atlanta did that political power seem to translate into widespread economic strength, with prosperous black suburbs and neighbourhoods becoming the norm, not the exception. Atlanta was now home to black entertainment moguls and even dubbed the 'Hollywood of the South', with film and TV studios and hip-hop impresarios in residence, alongside the long-established black-owned businesses.

There was something in the air about Atlanta, a confidence, a self-belief. Atlantans were easy in their black skin, there was no stigma in blackness here, no disapproval from whites, and I realised that came in part not merely from their wealth, but also from the city being the crucible of the civil rights movement and the birthplace of Dr Martin Luther King. There was a sense that they had worked hard and deserved their place in the world as a centre of black excellence. The perfect place then, twelve years after my first visit, from which to report live on election night on the 2008 presidential race.

My base was to be Morehouse, one of America's most famous historical black colleges, set in over sixty acres of beautiful rolling fields, with the main campus established in 1867, two years after the Civil War. The college would cater to freed slaves hungry for an education, hungry for a future. Its motto is *Et Facta Est Lux* – 'And There Was Light'. The Oscar-winning film director Spike Lee and actor Samuel L. Jackson are old boys, along with an assortment of Fulbright and Rhodes scholars, business leaders, diplomats and judges, and perhaps the most famous 'Morehouse Man' of them all, none other than Dr Martin Luther King.

He was a student when the influential Baptist minister Benjamin Mays was president of the college, the man credited with laying the intellectual foundations of the civil rights movement. He taught and mentored many of the most influential activists, including MLK. Mays' belief in black self-determination, social justice through nonviolence and civil resistance – the idea that if they worked together, ordinary people could defeat entrenched forces much bigger than themselves, created an atmosphere of defiance and hope at Morehouse that was infectious and helped to crystallise MLK's own political philosophy.

On the day of the election, our BBC team arrived in the mid-afternoon, on what was a beautiful, clear sunny day. I looked out onto the grounds surrounding one of the main halls where we would be setting up our equipment for the night's broadcasting, and all was still and quiet. But I imagined myself as a student there in the 1950s and 60s, surrounded by like-minded people committed to a cause so much bigger than themselves, and what that must have felt like: galvanising and energising.

To have been an agent of social change at a long-established seat of learning, one that existed not simply to maintain the status quo, but to be radical, bold and adventurous. To shake up a rotten system of white privilege and bigotry and to free millions of African Americans from what was effecitvely a life of mental servitude to an existing social order. But also to free many millions of white Americans from the oppressor status that only a minority wanted to cling on to. It must have been so intoxicating and exciting to have been part of such an important movement for change at that sunny campus in the South.

Journalists from all over the world began arriving, and I noticed the big American TV networks had also sent black correspondents. The night's watch party would take place in Frederick Douglass Hall in the centre of the campus, with giant TV screens erected that would beam in all the election programming as the major broadcasters battled to be the first to get the results on air. My job on the night was to report live into the BBC's *American Election Special* programme, hosted by David Dimbleby.

As day turned to night, more people began turning up. Faculty past and present, alumni revisiting the place that helped kick off their respective professional careers, and scores of current students, some of whom had themselves voted earlier in the day in another part of the campus in Archer Hall, casting their ballots for the man on the ticket who looked just like them. Many were first-time voters. African Americans had never in the history of the United

States had the opportunity to vote for a black person with a realistic shot of winning the presidency, despite their ancestors helping to build America and create its wealth and global pre-eminence. That day had finally come.

But there was another group of people slowly drifting into the hall that night. Old comrades involved in the civil rights struggle. Some in their eighties, a few in wheelchairs, the legs that once marched them to Selma and Little Rock, to protests and sit-ins, now less sure. All of them desperate to be part of history being made, and upon whose shoulders Obama would be standing, if he won. They were the ones who had defied the police dogs, baton charges and water cannon, and the abuse and filthy looks from white onlookers, to desegregate schools, buses and lunch counters, ignoring the signs that read WHITES ONLY, right across the South, side by side with Dr King. If Obama won, this would be as much *their* victory, as it would be his.

By around 6.00 p.m., Frederick Douglass Hall was filling up and I could sense a nervousness as the hour crept ever closer when the polls would close, and the vote counting would begin. I could feel the tension. Might John McCain, the Republican nominee, pull it out of the bag? He had not run the best of races. He was a foreign policy expert, well-respected on both sides of the aisle and a decorated Vietnam vet who had been captured and tortured by the Vietcong. He was a decent man too, honourable, unwilling to resort to the kind of dog-whistle racism and ad hominem attacks in a long campaign that we all know others would have resorted to. He did not want to appeal to the worst in voters, but to their better angels.

The election's big issue was the banking and financial crisis engulfing economies around the world, and McCain did not seem to have a plan to deal with the mess. But would the electorate trust his much younger challenger to sort things out, a one-term senator, and a black man to boot? *I* was beginning to get nervous! Was America ready to take this giant leap? It was clear that voters were energised, as turnout was the highest in history, long lines of people outside polling stations anxious to have their say on the state of the union, a nation battered by ongoing wars in Afghanistan and Iraq and now economically vulnerable too.

The clock struck 7.00 p.m. and the first races were called by the networks. Frederick Douglass Hall was now packed, and everyone was looking up at the TV screens. Kentucky went for McCain, Vermont for Obama, so far so predictable. At 7.30 p.m., it was West Virginia for McCain; 7.48 p.m., South Carolina for McCain; 8.00 p.m., Connecticut, Delaware and DC for Obama, again predictable, but the black guy with the funny name was holding his own. Then at 9.23 p.m., the 'bellwether' state of Ohio was called . . . for Obama. They had voted for George W. Bush in 2004, now the Democrat had flipped the state. Cheers went up around Frederick Douglass Hall.

It was then that I first believed, not just dared to hope, that he could do it. At 10.00 p.m., Iowa called for Obama, another state turning Democrat blue from the Republican red of four years before, and as more and more results came in, it was clear the public had wanted change. Ballots had been cast up and down the land for hope, and a reinvestment in the possibilities of America. Barack Hussein Obama embodied that hope for millions.

As the news networks on the giant TV screens counted up the Electoral College votes needed to put Obama over the top, the atmosphere inside Frederick Douglass Hall went from anxiety to relief to expectation, then finally to unalloyed joy, as around 11.00 p.m., the races were called in California and Washington – both for Obama, giving him more than the 270 Electoral College votes needed to become the President Elect of the United States.

What a moment! The junior senator from Illinois had done it. All around me people were on their feet cheering and singing, hugging and smiling. So many were also in tears as I stood next to the president of Morehouse, Robert M. Franklin, who was looking down in disbelief at what he had just witnessed – a black man had won the White House. At that moment our BBC producer, Mark Georgiou, heard the director of the election special in London call out to him in his headphones, saying they wanted me to come up on the line for a live interview with David.

I was happy, excited and elated that Obama had done it. This victory meant so much to me, and as I began to prepare what I was going to say, I thought of James Cameron, the man I interviewed in Milwaukee who survived being lynched. I thought of Emmett Till and Frederick Douglass, Harriet Tubman and Equiano, who wrote one of the most famous narratives of his time as a slave, and Rosa Parks, and all the others who marched and prayed for better times. I thought about all those black men and women whose names we do not know, who suffered at the hands of a brutish America, and I thought of Dr King, smiling down benevolently on his old college, as a new age dawned for this land.

David introduced me live on the programme, and I painted a scene of happiness and joy in the hall. At times it was so loud because of the singing and cheering, 'Yes, we can! Yes, we can!', over and over again, that I could not hear myself speak, but I carried on trying to convey down a microphone to millions of BBC viewers around the world how important this moment was, particularly for those older civil rights activists who were all around me.

Then I decided to do something I had never done before as a reporter. I felt compelled to try to convey my *own* feelings and emotions about what had just happened. It seemed to me that viewers might have wanted this, and the moment felt right. Calmly and simply, with no triumphalism, I said that for me, a black man, to be here at this place, at this time, is truly astonishing and a privilege, and it is a moment I will never forget. David thanked me then moved on. I put down the microphone and said to myself that was the most stupid thing I could ever have done. Why did I put myself into the story? It's not about me. God, I'm an idiot. Over-emotional nonsense. I berated myself. I felt stupid, idiotic and foolish.

At that moment I looked up, and a black correspondent from one of the big three American networks was broadcasting live on air and he was in tears, there was no attempt to hide *his* emotions. He was out there and proud. He could barely speak he was so overcome. I realised then that I had not been stupid in trying to convey how I felt about that night. In fact, it was one of the best things I had ever done as a BBC journalist.

One of America's founding fathers, James Madison, when writing about slavery, said it was the 'mere distinction of

colour . . . [that was] a ground for the most oppressive domin-
ion ever exercised by man over man.' The concept of race is a
construct, it is man-made, to differentiate in order to exploit.
In electing Barack Obama, Americans were finally saying
that a person's colour does not mean anything, it *should not*
matter. To quote Dr Martin Luther King, it is the 'content of
one's character' that is the most important thing.

As midnight approached, the TV screens beamed into
Frederick Douglass Hall the scenes from Chicago, at the giant
Grant Park, where close to a quarter of a million people had
gathered to hear Obama's victory speech. As he walked out
onto a giant stage along with Michelle and their two daughters, the swagger was there, the confidence and the broad
smile, and I saw before me America's First Family, and it was
black. My eyes filled with tears. What I was witnessing was a
new, updated version of the American Dream made flesh for
millions right around the world. It was made flesh for me.

* * *

On 3 April 1968, Martin Luther King gave a speech at the
Mason Temple in Memphis, Tennessee. He had been in the
city supporting black sanitation workers, who had been on
strike for higher pay and better conditions. The speech was
one of the finest of his life, and it was his last.

'I've been to the mountain top . . . I just want to do God's
will, and he's allowed me to go up to the mountain, and I've
looked over and I've seen the promised land. I may not get
there with you, but I want you to know tonight, that we as a
people will get to the promised land.'

The next day he was shot dead, assassinated while standing on the balcony outside room 306 of the Lorraine Motel. In 2018, on the fiftieth anniversary of his death, the BBC sent me to Memphis to report on the commemorations and services in his honour, and as I looked up at the balcony outside room 306, I was transported back to Morehouse College and Frederick Douglass Hall on the night of 4 November 2008. I recalled all the tears and emotion, and I wondered if what Dr King had seen when he reached the mountain top, and looked over the other side, was an image of Barack Hussein Obama smiling back at him, representing America's promise and what it could achieve.

–12–

A Health Service Fit for Everyone?

I WOKE UP covered in sweat and I could hear the dull drone of flies on manoeuvres, they were buzzing around the sink in the bathroom by the light I had left on all night. It was 19 October 2017, and as I looked down a cockroach scurried across the floor. There was no air-conditioning in my hotel room in Cox's Bazar, a coastal town in south-east Bangladesh, and the fan trying to create a breeze above my head was no match for the all-consuming heat.

I took a look out of the window and was shocked but pleasantly surprised to see the most wonderful pristine beach, stretching way off into the distance, with not a soul lounging or sunbathing, building sandcastles or wading into the water. I later found out it is the longest uninterrupted natural beach in the world. Quite a sight, a balm for half-awake eyes, compared to the horrors I knew I would encounter later as I headed for the border with neighbouring Myanmar, to record the pain of the thousands of Muslim Rohingya refugees forced from their homes by Buddhist terror squads and a vengeful Myanmar military.

As I stared, mesmerised by this ribbon of golden sand, with the waters of the Bay of Bengal calm and still, it was time to snap out of that moment of bliss and get ready to leave for the border. I made for the bathroom, scratching my bristly chin as I walked, reached for a razor in my washbag and looked in the mirror. Something was wrong. I could see a lump protruding from behind my left earlobe. I pressed it with the index finger of my right hand and it was hard and solid, but I felt no pain. Must be swollen glands, I told myself, enflamed by the Bangladeshi heat of the tropics. I am sure it will be gone in a day or two.

Our work at the border was intense, in searing heat with no shade. Access to water was limited, dehydration and heat stroke constant dangers, and I felt dizzy much of the time, but we had to get the story as a tide of humanity, tens of thousands of men, women and children, streamed out of the lush, wooded border area into the flat grasslands of Bangladesh, lucky to be alive. The Rohingya escaping Myanmar, with only the clothes on their backs, were in far worse shape than I was. For much of the time my mind was focused on their pain and suffering, which was as intense as the heat.

There were so many stories of the brutality they had endured and witnessed, of villages torched and burnt to the ground. Periodically we could see columns of smoke rising into the clear blue sky, signalling another home being transformed into embers and blackened charred ash. The stories of people being murdered with machetes, and others shot by Myanmar troops, filled the boiling hot air as I asked for recollections and narratives of the grief. It was a devastating catalogue of brutality, as the parched survivors drank from a nearby stream that was brown and filthy, emblematic of what they had been reduced to, human beings on the margins, discarded and only fit to drink dirty water like animals.

Towards the end of the day my fingers reached for the area at the back of my left ear, where the lump had sat stout that morning. The outgrowth was still there. Four months later, it had not budged.

* * *

After the war, the National Health Service had taken over the running of more than 2,500 hospitals in England and Wales and there were not enough people to staff them. Local recruitment drives up and down the country were embarrassing in the lack of interest shown by the indigenous British, and so recruiters ventured to the Caribbean.

My mum's younger sister, Aunty Chris, answered the call, moving to Lancashire from Jamaica shortly after I was born in 1964. She was twenty-one years old and nursing was what she wanted to do. She trained at Kidderminster Hospital in Worcestershire, where the hours were long and the wages low. But a bigger challenge was coping with patients who saw Aunty Chris's skin colour first, and her professional skills second. Some white patients did not want to be treated by black nurses and those training my Aunty Chris never prepared her for how patients might react. Some would slap her hand away, not wanting to be touched by her during an examination.

The daily indignities came not only from the sick, but from the NHS too. In June 2023, exactly seventy-five years after the *Empire Windrush* docked at Tilbury, I chaired a discussion for BBC Radio 4 on whether those who had travelled from the Caribbean back then had done the right thing, or should they have stayed at home and given their blood, sweat and tears to the cause of building up their own countries, not Britain.

I was struck by the dignity of one of the panellists. Now in her late sixties, a former nurse by the name of Brenda Beazer was recruited in Barbados at the age of nineteen to work in the NHS. Brenda says the Government of Barbados had a contract with the British to supply staff, and her mother had to sign over the deeds of her own home as a surety, in case Brenda decided nursing was not for her once she had begun training.

She ended up in Wellingborough in Northamptonshire and said all the Caribbean nurses were told that the white English nurses did not want to work weekends or bank holidays, they only worked 9 to 5. So it was the black nurses who did all the unsociable shifts. They also had to clean the toilets, wash out the bedpans and mop the floors. Brenda said she wanted to run away, that this was not the life she had expected.

Then she said something truly shocking, which I had never heard of before. She was trapped and could not leave, because the matron had taken away her passport. 'They had my documentation,' said Brenda, 'the matron had my passport in her office. There was nothing we could do, there was no one to talk to. All we could do was go to our little rooms and cry.' Today, this would be described as modern-day slavery. It seems that back in the 1960s and 1970s, Brenda and many other young Caribbean nurses did not own their freedom, much like their slave forefathers.

Black nurses were also discriminated against when it came to the level of qualification they could attain in the NHS. Aunty Chris was in training to become a State Enrolled Nurse.

That was the course that the overwhelming majority of black trainees had to take, involving two-years of study that led to work as what was described as 'practical support staff', though a better description might have been 'general dogsbody'. State Registered Nurses trained for a year longer, which meant they could ultimately attain the level of Ward Sister, and they tended to be white.

Regardless of their ability, most black women were only put forward for the junior SEN category, right up until it was abolished in the mid-1980s, and most individuals had no idea they were being downgraded even before they started their careers. By the time they found out, it was too late. Thousands of black nurses, hopeful of a high-status career, ended up locked in lives characterised by unsociable shifts, long hours, low pay and with little chance of promotion.

Racial inequality blighted the NHS when my Aunty was training, and it blights the NHS of today, with ethnic minority staff filling the mainly lower-paying roles, and few black people sitting on NHS Trust boards. This is the health service I had to deal with during one of the most traumatic periods for the country, and one of the most traumatic periods for me.

* * *

I remember the day very clearly. It was 14 March 2020 when I announced to viewers on the *BBC News at Ten* that the number of people confirmed to have been infected by COVID-19 was over one thousand, and another ten people had died, doubling the number of dead in the UK from eleven to twenty-one. I wondered that day how many times I would have to announce more deaths.

How high could the number of corpses go? No one had a clue. Not the government, not the scientists or statisticians. We were all flailing in the dark, not knowing what the hell was happening. Only two days later, I announced on the BBC News Channel that the number of deaths in the UK was now over fifty, and 1,500 people had been infected. But with no easily accessible test, there could be many more times that number infected, and they could all be infecting others, who were infecting others, and on and on. A nightmare replicating itself like a photocopying machine from hell – Xeroxing an outbreak into an epidemic into a pandemic into a once-in-a-hundred-years global catastrophe.

And yet, were we getting a full picture of how the National Health Service was coping with the unfolding tragedy? I was not sure. By mid-March, appalling pictures were coming out of Italy of the health service there crumbling under the weight of coronavirus cases. Hospital intensive care units were teeming with the sick. And as ICUs filled to bursting, extremely ill COVID-19 patients were having to be treated on general wards, where the patients with other ailments were being turfed out. Accident and emergency wards were taken over, as well as meeting rooms, the floors of corridors, even hospital car parks. One disease was trumping all others – the coronavirus.

The town of Bergamo in the north became the epicentre of the nation's tragedy, with so many people dying that local priests begged the army to come in to transport the corpses, up to seventy a day, to other towns and cities in giant military trucks, as the local funeral homes could not cope with the volume of cremations.

I was greatly impressed with the work of Stuart Ramsay and his team from Sky News, who managed to gain access to one ward in a hospital in Bergamo. The pictures were jaw-dropping of exhausted staff and patients gasping for air, some with giant plastic bubbles covering their entire head, a device designed to equalise the air pressure in their lungs to aid breathing. They looked like characters from an animated sci-fi cartoon show. Some of the medics nicknamed the areas full of coronavirus patients, the 'apocalypse wards'.

But why were there no pictures in the UK of how NHS hospitals were coping with COVID-19? Was the health service simply dealing with the situation better than the Italians and there was nothing to see? The truth was that reporters were not being allowed onto coronavirus wards in the UK to bear witness, so we could not tell what was going on.

It was shortly after Boris Johnson announced the UK's first lockdown on 23 March, that I approached the BBC's Head of Newsgathering, Jonathan Munro, and the Head of Home News, Richard Burgess, about trying to gain access to a UK hospital's ICU, to try to see what was really happening. Our chat was via Zoom, a mode of communication I had never used before, but it was a sign of the times.

I was anxious not to step on the toes of the BBC's other correspondents in pursuing my story. I wanted to spend several days going deeper, trying to get to the heart of the NHS battle with the virus, to record the stress on medical staff, as well as the pain of patients and relatives. This would in no way interfere with the BBC's other reporters getting daily news coverage. Jonathan and Richard were happy, and the editor of the *BBC News at Six* and *Ten*, Paul Royall, was very keen.

I approached NHS England to try to get into an ICU, and I was willing to travel anywhere in the country. Phone conversations with their communications department were cordial, but did not amount to much. I was offered an afternoon in a hospital that a couple of my colleagues had already filmed in, only a few hours one afternoon, hardly enough time to get under the skin of the story. I was then offered a few hours in another hospital, a big shiny marquee establishment and I was beginning to see a pattern.

It was becoming clear that NHS England – perhaps understandably – were steering me away from an in-depth look at COVID-19 and the health service, and they wanted to keep journalists and cameras at arm's length. I was beginning to get frustrated and found out that reporters in America were having similar problems getting into ICUs and had even made formal complaints. The authorities on both sides of the Atlantic were strictly controlling the flow of information, fearful of similar scenes being broadcast to those in Italy.

One conversation I had with NHS England over the Easter weekend of 2020 made me realise that getting the access I wanted might not be possible. I thought I might as well give up, perhaps I was aiming too high. Maybe the medical staff themselves did not want cameras in their ICUs while they were stressed and coping with the extraordinarily high numbers of coronavirus patients, and it was only fair to let them get on with their difficult work. But I was not 100 per cent convinced that was the case, and I had one card left to play.

Even after life as we knew it in the UK was completely transformed with the lockdown, as streets emptied and businesses were shuttered, it was clear that many people still did not get it. They simply did not understand, or want to understand, that this virus was not like the flu – it was a killer that had the potential to swamp and sink health services, including the NHS, right around the world. Doctors felt they had to speak out to get across the severity of what was going on, and the charge was led in America.

Medics were recording video diaries on their phones of the unbearable pressures they were under, uploading their testimonies to social media. They were talking about the daily trauma of having to see people die, that this was not what they had signed up for as medical practitioners; their job was to try to make people better, not to manage death.

Many of those making videos were imploring people to wear masks, a simple enough precaution, but somehow that proved too inconvenient for some, too constraining of their civil liberties, too much of a faff and a pain in the arse. To wear or not to wear, that was the question, and it fast became a political point of principle in America and in Britain for those who wanted to defy and question mask mandates. I can only imagine the level of frustration these medics must have felt because of the puerile selfishness of some of their fellow citizens.

In Britain, there were videos from nurses that highlighted other examples of the public's self-centred nature. Dawn Bilbrough was a critical care nurse who uploaded a video on Facebook recorded in her car. She had just come off a 48-hour shift, but could not find any basic food items like fruit and veg in the nearby supermarket. The shelves had been stripped bare by people panic-buying.

'I just don't know how I'm supposed to stay healthy,' she says, as tears well up in her eyes. She then begins to cry and looks straight at the camera. 'Just stop it,' she cries, hardly able to get her words out, breaking down and sobbing. 'Just stop it, because it's people like me that are going to be looking after you when you're at your lowest. Just stop it. Please.'

Patients in ICUs were beginning to post their own videos too, warning of the dangers of not wearing masks and not social distancing. One video showed a woman in her bed in an intensive care unit, pointing to the tubes coming out of her nose and her arms, and she is struggling to speak clearly because of her breathing difficulties. She looks straight at the camera.

'If anyone still smokes,' she says, 'put the cigarettes down, because I'm telling you now, you need your fucking lungs. And please none of you take any chances. I mean it, because if it gets really bad,' at which point she stops, tilts her head back and lets out a deep, rasping cough, an illustration of the damage the virus has done to her lungs, before continuing, 'then you're going to end up here.'

These videos and many others left a profound impression on me, and I was determined to get into an ICU, to try to tell the real story of the pandemic in Britain.

The previous autumn in October 2019, I had made a series for BBC News on knife crime, and I came across Martin Griffiths, a consultant trauma surgeon at the Royal London Hospital in the East End. He was our guide into a world of gangs and poverty and extreme violence. A proud Jamaican by birth, he did not suffer fools gladly and he hated posturing.

Every day he saw the results of good intentions when it came to tackling knife crime, but a clear lack of understanding on the part of so many people who claimed to want to fix the problem, as to what really needed to be done. He told me that it is so easy for the rest of society to dismiss and demonise the kids on the streets and ignore the fact that they are products of appalling environments – often victims with no structure in their lives, poor parenting, no aspirations, unable to escape the cage that has been built around them through no fault of their own.

I found Martin fascinating and I recall one long chat I had with him (we had so many), as we were waiting to film one day. He knew my background: grammar school, university, BBC, and he asked me directly: 'Let's give you chaotic parenting, inconsistent food, inconsistent shelter, and you're surrounded by people with the same problems – that's all they know. Then let's put a big fence around you with people outside judging you, who deem you as worthless, and let's give you no access to get beyond the fence. Let's see how you behave.'

The impression he gave was that he thought I would not be much cop at surviving in that environment, that few people would be much cop, and he is probably right. Martin liked to burst bubbles of complacency. He despised the pompous who pontificated about the poor and disadvantaged with an attitude that said they just need to 'work harder' and 'pull themselves up by their bootstraps'. I had enormous respect for Martin for what he believed in and his values; as well as the fact that as a black man, he had made it to the top of the NHS, and when we finished the series on knife crime to great acclaim, I realised that I wanted to work with him again.

So, in March 2020, I sent him an anguished email, explaining that my attempts to get into an ICU to make honest films about how the NHS was coping with COVID-19 had so far failed, and did he have any contacts in the ICU at the Royal London, who might be able to help.

I waited for a reply, this was my last throw of the dice. A week passed and there was no word from Martin. I told myself that if I did not get into the Royal London's ICU I would give up and let the pandemic pass me by, leaving the coverage to the health and medical correspondents who knew so much more about the crisis anyway than I did.

Another week passed and there was no word from Martin. Then he got in touch. Good news. He said the medics in the ICU *really* wanted to talk. They had seen the series on knife crime and trusted that I would represent their work fairly. In fact, they were disappointed we had not approached them to film earlier in the pandemic. We agreed the hospital would lobby NHS England from the top, and I would keep chipping away from the bottom, a pincer movement.

Finally, NHS England got back to me, fed up with being harangued, saying rather wearily that they were willing to allow a BBC team to film for four days in the ICU. I chatted with the communications department of Barts Healthcare Trust who run the Royal London. They said, 'Don't worry, behave yourself and we'll slip you in for longer.'

There was an unreality to that time, and yet so much was painfully real. Life was suspended, still it carried on. Old certainties were no longer certain, but we were all convinced life could/should/must return to normal. For many millions of us, before Astra Zeneca, Moderna and Pfizer changed everything, the coronavirus years were a hiatus and interruption in time, merely a break in continuity. But for others it really was the end.

I admit I was a little nervous setting foot on the Covid ward at the Royal London Hospital for the first time. The nurse who had been tasked with chaperoning us looked closely at the chart on the wall before we entered. She was not going to get this wrong and possibly endanger my life. It was a small poster outlining the correct way to put on personal protective clothing, or PPE. We were at the so-called 'donning' station, the point of no return, a white door plastered in stickers coloured red that warned DANGER, KEEP OUT, IS YOUR PPE ON CORRECTLY? as well as the chart telling you how to dress.

'Right, I'm going to make sure this is done properly, I know how to do mine, but let's be sure,' said the nurse reassuringly.

We followed her instructions to the letter. We took off our civvies and put on scrubs, a basic blue top and pants with nothing underneath. We popped on white plastic clog shoes familiar to anyone who loves a TV medical drama. We washed our hands and arms thoroughly up to the elbow. Then we put on a white smock, making sure it was securely tied at the back, our arms fully covered. On top of that we had to wear a white plastic disposable apron, writing our names on the front with a black marker pen.

Next we tied on a blue head covering, and pulled on two sets of gloves, a tight-fitting pair in blue, and then a flesh-coloured pair on top. Then the mask went on, hospital grade, thick and padded, the elastic ends tight around our ears keeping them locked in place, but digging the whole covering uncomfortably into our skin. Finally, a pair of thick clear Perspex goggles completed the battle dress, an impregnable barrier, we prayed, against an enemy we could not see but was everywhere; my overall anxiety compounded by the fact that I am black.

My work pattern during the pandemic was no different to the calmer days before the storm. It had been made clear to all of us in the BBC newsroom that no matter what happened, the Corporation would produce the nightly news as expected and without fail, as a public service in this time of crisis. Viewers needed the most up-to-date information on what was going on, including any public health messages the Government and the nation's scientists needed us all to know.

What I noticed, though, making my way into the BBC's headquarters in central London on the Tube or on a bus, was that my fellow travellers also heading to work during the lockdowns were by and large black or Asian. They were the bus drivers and cleaners, hospital porters, security guards, refuse collectors and road maintenance staff. They kept working while millions were furloughed, and some of them were paying a heavy price.

At the start of the pandemic, if you were from a black, Asian or ethnic minority background like me, you were almost twice as likely to die if you became infected. But black and Asian people were still going to work despite the presence of the virus, and on hospital wards, black and Asian medical staff were more likely to be interacting face to face with infected patients, working in the lower tier jobs of the NHS.

I will never forget that first trip to the coronavirus ICU. The door to another world opened, and the first thing that struck me was how quiet the place was. Just the sound of ventilating machines beeping every now and again, and medical staff talking through their masks, audible only if you were near, so the conversations were low level, like whispers. But the images my eyes were processing shouted at me. Patients were lying helplessly all around, maybe ten, twelve or so in this ward, the same number through a door in another ward. They were lifeless. Brains functioning, hearts beating, but lumpen inanimate objects.

Their faces were devoid of colour, gaunt, like death masks. Plastic tubes fed oxygen through noses and mouths and holes punctured in throats. They were like deep sea divers tethered to oxygen bottles. What were they dreaming? We know that while on ventilators patients have profound hallucinations, drifting in floating worlds, and yet the activity around their beds is precise and real, as nurses and doctors and consultants check vital signs, log crucial numbers on charts, and measure oxygen levels every single minute.

We watched in awe as the drifting, slow-motion world of one patient collided with the urgent world of the staff treating him. The monitors of his ventilator were beeping. Red lights flashed. We were interviewing the consultant Dr Parjam Zolfaghari, known as PJ, when a nurse came up and grabbed him by the arm.

'You're needed urgently,' she said in a whisper, trying not to let the words reach our microphone. He turned to us and apologised, saying he would be a couple of minutes, but we followed him into the next ward as I signalled to my colleague Davy McIlveen to keep his camera rolling. PJ is a gentle, softly spoken man, originally from Iran, with a bedside manner reassuring in its calm. The doctors and nurses he joined were clustered around a man whose machines were now going crazy, beeping and bleeping, signalling, flashing and buzzing. The doctors were clearly worried. I could see it in their eyes through their goggles. Their conversations were hushed, but our microphones picked up everything.

'I don't think he's going to make it through the night,' said PJ to one doctor. 'We need to think about calling his family.'

The patient lived in the local borough of Tower Hamlets. He had been on a ventilator for several weeks and overnight he had developed pneumonia. I saw an X-ray of his chest and I could not see his lungs; they were covered in what looked like thick smoke. I was reminded of the billowing smoke of industrial chimneys from factories in the area where I grew up in Lancashire. Thick and dense and choking. PJ told me it was the accumulation of secretions from his lungs. The organs were not working properly, the virus was eating them away as we spoke, which meant oxygen could not get around his body and the ventilator, which had been doing his breathing, was now unable to cope with the onset of pneumonia. COVID-19 did this.

PJ whispered again to his colleagues and they pulled up the patient's gown to expose his chest. They started massaging his flesh to try to dislodge the fluid. Time was running out, not only in the frantic real world of the doctors and nurses, six, seven, eight of them, now clustered around this bed, but also in the patient's floating world, where his sleep was heading towards a permanence. His lungs were beginning to pack up, but there was one last throw of the dice. Proning, the turning of the patient on to his front to help free up his lungs to pump oxygen.

It was a Hail Mary pass, and the kind of procedure one of the other consultants, Nick Bunker, told me was rarely used before COVID-19 came along. I counted the nurses and doctors around the bed now, ten in all, and having grabbed the sheets around the patient, they manoeuvred him, rolling him over. He was now laying on his front, arms by his side with the palms upwards, ventilator tubes protruding from his mouth. All the medics could do now was watch and wait.

Later that night, he died.

My visits to the Royal London during that time made me very conscious of my own health. Was I in good enough shape to withstand an infection? Is my throat feeling a little tight today, my chest a tad heavy? Any cough I had, or throat clearance I made, would make me think, could this be it? But as with any difficult story, our BBC team, myself, Davy and producer Sam Piranty, had all assessed the level of risk and decided it was worth it to tell the full story. But in the back of my mind was the ever-present fear that, somehow, I could be struck down because of the colour of my skin.

On shift a few days later in the Covid ward was Irene Tubuuze, a nursing student from Uganda, on the ICU for the very first time. I was bowled over by her strength and selflessness. Barely in her twenties, she told me she worried all the time that she might become infected and because she was black, she might stand less chance of survival.

'You're like, oh my God, was I careful enough?' she told me. 'Am I getting it today, will I get it tomorrow? The danger is very real here. But you just have to keep strong. I always tell myself someone has got to treat people. I mean if it were my relatives, I would want someone to care for them, so that kind of keeps me going.' Truly astonishing!

From the beginning of the first lockdown, ministers began daily briefings at 5.00 p.m., which the BBC televised, to give the latest information on the pandemic. An hour before, all the media outlets were alerted to the latest figures on infections, hospitalisations and deaths. That 4.00 p.m. information drop was like a bell tolling for the dead every single day, the last post sounding on more lives lost, week after week, for more than two years.

Research was scant at the beginning of the pandemic, but gradually over time it became clearer why people who were black or Asian were more vulnerable. Of course, the virus did not discriminate between black and white victims. Social factors like income, wealth and education affect the quality of health of all of us, and as such, poorer black and ethnic minority communities were more vulnerable.

The Office for National Statistics concluded that the higher risk of death among people of black and ethnic minority backgrounds was more to do with having a higher risk of infection, than having a worse outcome once infected. The pandemic had shone a light on an unequal Britain, and an unequal health service. One study suggested that of the 1.2 million staff employed by the NHS, 20.7 per cent belong to black, Asian and minority ethnic (BAME) backgrounds.

However, analysis of deaths of NHS staff during the pandemic showed that '64 per cent of those who died belonged to a BAME background. This disproportionately high mortality rate points up the discriminatory deployment of staff from non-white ethnic backgrounds in areas with potentially high virus exposure.' In other words, black and Asian people were more likely to come into contact with people infected with coronavirus, because they were in the lowest tiered jobs, like the role my Aunty Chris was forced into as a trainee nurse, back in the 1960s.

In the first wave of the pandemic, NHS England had originally granted us four days filming at the Royal London Hospital. We ended up being there for two weeks. In the second wave about a year later, we were filming for ten days, and after the vaccine roll out, we filmed on a now sparse Covid ward for a week in January 2022. We made nine films in all, which tried to chronicle the experience of staff and patients in one hospital and one community, in the time of COVID-19. The trilogy of films represents some of the proudest moments of my reporting career.

* * *

It was not until four months after I had noticed the lump behind my left ear, in the sweaty heat of my Bangladesh hotel room, that I visited my GP. Yes, I know, I am bloody stupid. My older brother Peter, a gentle giant of a man, had left it too late to treat the aches he was feeling in his back. By the time he had a proper medical examination, the cancer in his prostate had spread throughout his body. He was given two years to live, and he died on 14 July 2014. I miss him terribly.

When my GP was finally given the chance to examine the lump in my neck, he quickly arranged for all manner of tests to be done. Initially he feared I had some kind of leukaemia, but an ultrasound scan of the lump suggested it was a fibrous tumour. The big question, was it malignant? I did not tell Catherine what was going on. I claimed the lump, which was barely visible anyway, was merely a swollen gland after time in the tropics.

I did not tell anyone else in my family or any of my friends either. If it was benign, why put them all through the agony of the wait for the results? I did not want to do that to them, so I agonised alone, until the test results came back a week later, saying it was a benign tumour in my saliva gland and being under the age of sixty, I might as well have it removed. If I had been older, the advice was to leave it and monitor it. Catherine was upset I had not told her. I ended up spending four days in hospital, with the huge tumour that was removed being roughly the size of a squash ball. I now have a long scar down the side of my neck as a reminder of a very unhappy time.

By a strange quirk of fate, long before the diagnosis of my tumour, I had been invited to speak at a celebration in Manchester of Windrush Generation NHS workers. I ended up travelling to the north-west the week after I left hospital, and I still had a covering on my scar after the operation. I talked about Aunty Chris and the other black people who made the idea of the NHS come to life, who gave it vigour and importance. This was in late 2019, only a few months before the torment of COVID-19.

There were people dying in India, America, Brazil, Iran and so many other places, who did not have health insurance and where there was no National Health Service. The NHS is there for all of us, no matter who we are, free at the point of use, available from cradle to grave. The service is part of the origin myth of post-war modern Britain, but the pandemic gave us a glimpse into a dark future. What if there was no NHS? What if all those black nurses from the Caribbean had not appeared? With current chronic staff shortages and low morale, what can society do to repair the beating heart of our nation, an organisation that despite so many difficulties, most Britons are still extremely proud of? The Government points to record funding for the service, but admits waiting lists are too long and the pressure on services too great, as life expectancy grows and medical needs become more complex.

The NHS saved my life, but who will save the NHS?

-13-

Two Morgues, One Pandemic

AS I HAVE headed inexorably towards my sixtieth birthday, thoughts begin to shift to that moment when it all will end. Morbid, I know, and these days I hope the Sunday magazines are right to say sixty is the new forty. But such thoughts are an inevitable consequence of the years passing, the hair on my head thinning to whispers, and the stubble on my chin becoming more salt than pepper. The passing of my older brother Peter was the first death of someone really close to me, someone that I loved and cared about deeply. I know I have been lucky in that respect, not having to face such an aching absence till later in life. My wife Catherine lost her father to emphysema when she was fourteen.

The coronavirus pandemic naturally forced many people to confront the idea of their own mortality. It is the fear of death that led most of us to stick to the rules, to social distance, stay home if infected, self-quarantine, wear a mask and get the jabs. We understood that this thing could kill us.

My pet theory, based on absolutely nothing, is that the anti-vaxxers, anti-mask wearers and Covid deniers seemed incapable of this intellectual leap. They did not want to confront the possibility of dying. The newspapers and online forums were full of stories of people convinced the coronavirus was no worse than the flu, and if infected they would be able to shake it off, so no vaccine for them.

One story I read was about a 'fit and healthy' 42-year-old former bodybuilder, who loved climbing mountains and lifting weights, but died of COVID-19 after refusing to get vaccinated. His twin sister and mother were now warning others not to think they were invulnerable to the dangers of the virus. John Eyers was from Southport in Merseyside and was described by his sister as 'the fittest, healthiest person I know'. He did triathlons, and she said he had been climbing Welsh mountains and camping in the wild only four weeks before his death. But he ended up in an intensive care unit after catching coronavirus, and told doctors before he was put on a ventilator that he wished he had been vaccinated.

Intensive care medics I spoke to at the Royal London Hospital, and others interviewed around the world, said they rarely came across patients needing critical care who had received two doses of any of the major vaccines, and that it was difficult to see the regret on the faces of unvaccinated patients when they became unwell and needed to go on a ventilator. That realisation, dawning like the bright light of the sun suddenly illuminating everything, suggested they had made the biggest mistake of their lives in not getting the jab. Realisation and remorse, twin intensive-care bedfellows.

Perhaps for others the opposite can be true, that some vaccine sceptics are in fact *very* aware of their own mortality. Their fear is of the side effects that could kill them.

I did get an email recently, from a man clearly angry about our Royal London Hospital films. He wrote:

Dear Clive,

I remember that propaganda piece that you did at an ICU, showing all the unvaccinated patients in a ward. Will you now do a similar piece from the same hospital showing all the vaccinated people in there, and if they are in there for vaccinated adverse reactions, for balance?

Thanks,

Jeff.

This was my response:

Hello Jeff,

Latest Govt figures show around 145 million Covid vaccines have been administered in the UK. How many of these people are in hospital with adverse reactions, Jeff? My apologies if you or anyone you know has had an adverse reaction. That's an individual tragedy. But many, many millions of people haven't had a bad reaction and it's why life has returned to normal for much of the planet after the pandemic.

Have a great day.

I never heard from him again.

Mortuary attendants, undertakers and grave diggers are obsessed with death. It is their job to help shuffle us all off this mortal coil. Yet during the national and international emergency of COVID-19, I did not see a single interview with anyone working in these professions. I could not understand why. Surely they would be some of the *first* people to approach to ask questions like, 'What's it like dealing with all this? How are you coping? Have you had to handle anything on this scale before?'

A second wave of the pandemic hit the UK in January 2021, and the soft-spoken Ulsterman Davy McIlveen, camera journalist and wonderful, empathetic human being, agreed to team up with us again, after producing award-winning work on the first trip to the Royal London Hospital the previous year. Sam Piranty was once again the producer, one of the finest and most conscientious I have ever worked with. His emotional IQ was off the charts in dealing with the staff, patients and their families, often when they were being compelled by me to talk to us at their rawest and lowest, and most emotionally drained.

The first thing I said to Sam when we began preparing to return to the hospital was that I wanted to film in the basement morgue. He told me he would see what he could do. A few days later, he came back to me and said matter-of-factly, 'No probs, we're in.'

'Really,' I said, 'it's that easy?' I assumed because I had never seen the pandemic from the perspective of the people having to deal with the appalling levels of dead, that hospital trusts were reticent to allow access. It turns out I had never seen this perspective because no one had ever asked for it, something I still find bizarre to this day.

We returned to the Royal London in the frigid January of 2021, the coldest start to a year for a decade, and the boss, Marie Healy, a brilliant and impressive woman with a wicked sense of humour and lovely Irish lilt to her voice, greeted me with an elbow bump on the main Covid ward on the fourteenth floor.

'It's good to see you again,' said the consultant, now Divisional Director of Surgery and Critical Care.

'And it's good to be back,' I responded while looking around the ward through my Perspex goggles and fully kitted out in PPE. I must admit, as my eyes fell upon my surroundings, I was slightly alarmed.

When I was last in that long white room in May 2020, there was plenty of space between the beds for banks of monitors measuring the health of the ventilated COVID-19 patients. Their breathing tubes dangled by the side of their beds, moving in time to the breaths forced by the machines. Now there was little space. More beds had been squashed in and there were so many more nurses and doctors on the ward.

I could sense a tension in the air too, a weariness. I saw it in the eyes of the staff, behind their safety visors and goggles, and I could hear it in their voices when I spoke to them. Endless twelve-hour shifts while sheathed in layers of PPE, their facemasks put on after a fifteen-minute 'fit test' session, carried out by an independent company. The test essentially meant masks now pinched into the skin even tighter than before and looked painful to wear.

Of the more than 500 beds at the Royal London, more than 400 were occupied by COVID-19 patients, with about 140 in intensive care. There were so many staff shortages this time round that each nurse was looking after and monitoring three, sometimes four, patients. The ratio would be one-to-one in normal times. Boris Johnson, when he fell ill, had two. One nurse told me that this felt like wartime and that some of her colleagues, who were willing to stick around to help, were thinking of leaving the NHS once the pandemic was over. They were burnt out, tired, fed up and angry at the minority among the public who belittled the severity of coronavirus, who believed they could luxuriate in complacency.

It is sobering to think that at the time, the number of people who had died of the pandemic in the UK was more than 20,000 higher than the number of civilians who died in the Second World War: 94,000 and counting. The numbers were mind-boggling, and I was shocked every time I heard the latest death statistics or had to read them out on the nightly TV news. Yet I got the impression that for a lot of people, the daily stats went in one ear and out the other. The pandemic was a once-in-a-century event and I acknowledge its magnitude is hard to comprehend. But for many in the NHS, where was the outrage, the anger, and the scrupulous adherence to social distancing and mask-wearing that the calamity required?

I realised my sensitivity to the death statistics came from a working lifetime of covering wars, from Bosnia, Croatia and Kosovo to Afghanistan, Syria, Libya and Iraq. I have talked to so many war widows and orphaned children in my life, and while covering the first wave of the virus from the Royal London, I talked to bereaved relatives. But as a society, I believed we had shied away from talking about the deaths of all those lost in the pandemic, because we did not want to hear about them; somehow we pushed all that to the back of our minds. Yet mass death is the very definition of a pandemic, and that is why I wanted to visit the hospital morgue.

The year before, I went to a funeral parlour in the Navajo Nation of northern Arizona while covering the US presidential election, trying to gauge how the richest country on Earth was handling the Covid crisis. Appallingly, as I discovered.

Native Americans had suffered terribly because of the pandemic, and I spoke to the director of one funeral home as he prepared a body for burial.

The dead man's feet were sticking out from the shroud. He had well-manicured toenails. His clothes were packed in a plastic bag, with his name scribbled on it in black marker pen, resting on his chest. The mortician's name was Michael Begay. His place of work smelt of formaldehyde, a little cloying. It was immaculate, sterile and clean. Michael told me about his own trauma, of having to bury so many people from the local community.

'There was one day when I went into our storage unit and I saw all those bodies lying there, and I knew two of them. It was a hard time for me, and they were dead because of Covid. It was heartbreaking and a good friend of mine, his son died, and I'd known him since he was a little boy.' At this point Michael started shaking his head slowly. 'I got the phone call, and it was my friend, and I was saying, "Man, I can't imagine what you're going through." Then we both just cried together on the phone.'

In the UK three months later, Sam, Davy and I made our way down into the basement of the Royal London Hospital to visit the mortuary. The people who work there are not called morticians anymore, they are now 'anatomical pathology technologists'. No, I did not know that either. I met a wonderful woman named Hannah, who helped lead the small team of five who had dealt with hundreds and hundreds of bodies because of COVID-19.

We filmed her pushing metal gurneys laden with cadavers in white body bags, some with a little yellow biohazard sticker that read 'DANGEROUS – INFECTION'.

'These are the Covid deaths,' she told me. The space in the tall shiny fridges was quite tight. Hannah's assistant had to unzip one of the bags and move a dead man's right hand, which had been resting on his left arm, down to his right side so that the body bag would fit into the fridge a little more easily. There were five shelves for five bodies, with the corpses pushed in on a metal bed, feet first. The fridges were all numbered, and the names of the dead logged on a huge whiteboard. There was no smell in that mortuary, none whatsoever. It was like being in an office, or any room other than a place full of fridges with dead people inside. I found that quite strange.

Before we began the interview proper with Hannah, I chatted with her to calm her nerves, to help her to relax and make her feel less self-conscious.

'Just look at me,' I said. 'Ignore Davy behind the camera and Sam the producer off in the wings. It's just me and you having a coffee and we're just chatting. Relax.'

I say this to all interviewees, but it sounded even weirder in the middle of a mortuary in the middle of a pandemic.

As Davy set up his shot and Hannah and I waited, she said she felt bad for the relatives of those who had died, because she and her staff had not been able to offer as much support as they usually would, due to lockdown restrictions. I knew this was something that pained her, and I told her it was not her fault.

Davy started rolling, Sam was listening in making sure we were getting the interview we needed, and I began to ask Hannah some questions. She told me that she managed to get through the first wave the previous spring, but spent much of the summer worrying about the second wave that some had predicted would come. So while most of the rest of us were enjoying renewed freedoms after the easing of lockdown restrictions with many 'eating out to help out', and as the sun warmed summer skies day after day, Hannah said all she could think about was the second wave. The dread. A sense of foreboding consumed her that lots and lots of bodies would flow into her mortuary.

'You've been doing this job for more than twenty years, was there anything that could have prepared you for what you've seen during this current second wave?' I asked her.

'How do you ever prepare for people just dying and dying and dying, you know?' she replied. 'Though it's our job and we deal with dead people all the time, every day, this level I think has taken its toll.'

'Does it feel like a conveyor belt?' I ask.

'It does, it does in a way, yes. I hate to say that, as I hate to think of it like that. But yes, it is almost, yes.'

I remembered our first conversation. I knew she felt guilty about the families of the bereaved and I tried to give her comfort.

'That's what the pandemic has done. I mean it's no one's fault,' I told her.

'Yes,' she said. Then she averted her gaze and looked into the middle distance. I can only imagine the thoughts and images that crowded into her head at that split second. Bodies and more bodies, a conveyor belt of misery she could not stop, a tap that could not be turned off. Distraught families crying, some angry perhaps, some pleading, begging to have a final goodbye.

But Hannah could not help them. The tears began to well up in her eyes and her forehead furrowed and her face went a pale scarlet, and she began to cry. She raised up her arm to hide the tears as she walked out of camera shot to the side to weep. I cried too. Davy and Sam's eyes filled with tears. It was so heartbreaking, raw and real. Months and months of suppressed emotion burst out.

Her apprentice, Kelly-Ann, came forward and hugged Hannah. She was also crying.

'I've never seen her cry,' she told us.

As Hannah wiped away her tears, she said that no one outside the mortuary had ever asked her how the pandemic made her feel. She told me she did not discuss her work at home, or with friends or anyone outside the tiny circle of five people who take care of the dead. 'No one wants to talk about death,' she said. 'It does tend to kill conversation.' She laughed as she composed herself and re-fixed her face mask, wiping away the tears from her cheeks. She was right. No one really wants to talk about all the dead in the pandemic.

A tiny minority of people criticised us for filming in the mortuary, and elsewhere for filming gravediggers and cemeteries. But I am proud of what we did, giving a voice to workers like Hannah, who had endured the utter hopelessness of the pandemic in a cocooned world of their own, with little moral support from the rest of society, which did not want to know.

Hannah's colleagues sent us a message of thanks after our film was broadcast on the *BBC News at Ten*. Members of the public sent them flowers. They said they had never been featured in any of the media, working as they do in the

When Catherine and I arrived in Singapore in 2001, we were desperate to live in a 'shophouse' in the Little India area of the island. We eventually found one on Petain Road, above. We lived a privileged expat life, in stark contrast to squalor and pain of many of those who featured in my assignments as Asia Correspondent.

Reporting on the violence between the Dayak people and the Madurese in Borneo was a harrowing experience.

As an eleven-year-old, watching footage of the Soweto Uprising on TV made me aware for the first time of the terrible inequities of life for black people in South Africa under apartheid.

Over a quarter-century later, I visited South Africa to report on the funeral of Nelson Mandela. I hoped his story of courage and sacrifice would somehow live on in this new South Africa.

On my first foreign assignment for BBC Television, covering the civil war in Liberia. I'd traveled abroad before on reporting trips, but only for radio. I was so excited and nervous too. I didn't want to mess it up.

Iraq, 2003. When we arrived in Basra, the country's second largest city, we found civilians looting local hotels, even nicking off with ceiling fans. It was an intense assignment, embedded with the Royal Marines of 40 Commando. Protocol dictated I be given the rank of captain.

Filing a report from the BBC Bureau in Afghanistan. A group of fighters had only weeks earlier taken over the country. They were hardline Islamists called the Taliban.

On 4th November 2008, I was in Atlanta, Georgia, the birthplace of the civil rights movement, reporting on Barack Obama's victory in the presidential election. I tried to convey to millions of BBC viewers around the world how important this moment was, not just to America, but also to me.

Obama's victory in the 2008 presidential race led me to reflect on the long history of racism in America, and all those who came before him. From lynching survivor James Cameron (above), Emmett Till, Frederick Douglass, Harriet Tubman, Rosa Parks, to Dr Martin Luther King, brave men and women fought for a better world.

In almost thirty years of reporting from the US, I've covered so many mass shootings I've lost count. The tragedies include the deadliest committed by a single gunman in American history, the 2017 Las Vegas massacre at a music festival (above). Sixty died and hundreds were wounded.

I'm holding a semi-automatic rifle in a gun store... In some states the age when you can buy a drink is twenty-one, to get one of these, it's eighteen.

President Obama cries in the aftermath of the Sandy Hook Elementary School shooting. His tears acknowledged that while he was the most powerful man on the planet, when it came to gun control in his own country, he had little power at all.

Watching footage of the murders of Eric Garner and George Floyd at the hands of police officers made me feel physically sick. Their murders compelled me to make two documentaries; the first on race in America and the second on the death of George Floyd and the Black Lives Matter movement.

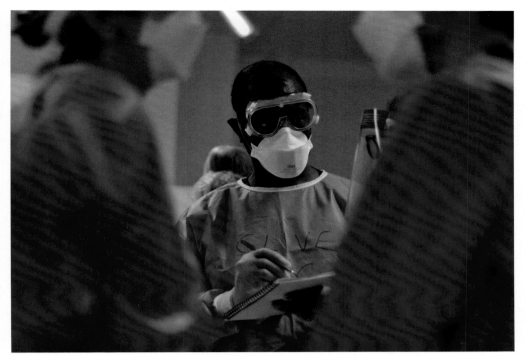

Reporting from a Covid ward in 2020 was a surreal experience. Many of my friends and colleagues asked me if I was scared, but I was determind to document how our National Health Service was coping with the crisis.

My hometown of Bolton, pictured above, was one of the worst-affected areas of the country with COVID-19. Nationally, people from black, Asian or ethnic minority backgrounds were almost twice as likely to die if they became infected.

In February 2022, I flew to Kyiv to report on the threat of a possible Russian invasion of Ukraine. The next morning they attacked by land, sea and air, and in a short few days were twenty miles from the centre of the capital, with its stunning gold domed churches and cathedrals. Wearing a flak jacket became second nature.

In President Zelenskyy's bunker in the first few weeks of the war. It took several days before members of his inner circle and the leader himself managed to get their families out of the country. It was a perilous time.

basement of the hospital. No one ever wanted to talk to them, to ask how they were coping. But for me, they are the very people we as journalists should be talking to, and they must never be forgotten.

Hannah's story touched many, and among the goodwill messages was one from America, from Navajo Country. It was from Michael Begay, the mortician we filmed months before in Arizona. He said he had watched our film from the Royal London Hospital online and he saw Hannah's interview. He said he 'felt incredibly emotional' hearing her story. He added, 'It's nice to know I'm not alone.'

−14−

The Barrel Children

AT THE HEIGHT of the Covid pandemic, I was really worried for my older sister, Judith. She has lupus, a chronic and incurable illness of the immune system, which causes inflammation and pain in any part of your body. Rather than fighting viruses or bacteria and infection by producing antibodies, her body starts to attack and destroy healthy cells, tissues and organs.

I was five years old when I first met her, along with my two half-brothers Lionel and Peter. The three of them had remained in Jamaica after my parents arrived in the UK. To have established a completely new life in a new land with three children in tow would have been very difficult, even for my resourceful mum and dad. The plan was always that they would send for the kids in due course. Leaving them behind was heartbreaking for my mum, but in her mind it was a necessary evil. She says she knew her sadness would be temporary, that she would be able to heal the fracture in the family and eventually have all her children by her side. But what were the effects of the separation on the minds of my brothers and sister?

When the appropriate time came, my siblings made the journey. Judith came first on her own in January 1969, aged seven, right in the middle of winter, which must have been an awful shock coming from the Caribbean, and Lionel and Peter arrived a little later. It was hard enough for adults to leave everything they knew and a world they understood, to create a new beginning in Britain. So, imagine what it must have been like for children who had been growing up with their grandparents, to have to adjust once again to a new life with parents they hardly knew.

Lionel and Peter were a good six or seven years older than me, and Judith a couple of years. That wider age gap with my older brothers meant there was perhaps not a closeness to our relationship growing up, but I did very much see them as 'big brothers' and protectors. They were my blood and I saw them now as part of our family in our home in Bolton. But to be fair there was a distance between us, not helped by the testy relationship the teenaged Lionel and Peter developed with my father.

While a few thousand Windrush children accompanied their parents when they made the journey to Britain in the three decades after the war, there were many more, tens of thousands like my half-brothers and sister, who were left behind by the *Empire Windrush* and successive ships and planes carrying Caribbean migrants to the new world. Tiny tots and preschoolers, tweens and teenagers, left behind on Jamaican, Barbadian or Trinidadian quaysides, waving goodbye, no doubt in tears, being comforted by relatives and wondering when they would see their parents again.

No doubt some of these children felt abandoned and lost, others were perhaps angry and resentful. These children were destined to live the next few years as if they were orphans, charges of their grandparents and other members of the extended family. Many were left wondering if their parents loved them.

They were referred to as 'barrel children', the kids whose link to their parents thousands of miles away came through letters, parcels and care packages, or 'barrels' of goods, sent back from Britain. At the end of every month, my parents would send money back to Jamaica, and every Easter and Christmas there would be a parcel, usually with new clothes, shoes and some toys. It was a comfort for my parents to know that they were still providing for their children, even though they were so far away. It was a sign of *their* continued love.

In Jamaica, as early teens around the age of twelve and thirteen, Lionel and Peter would have been well on the way to manhood. They would have established an independence and self-confidence and begun defining the parameters of their own lives, rather than having parents around telling them what to do. Grandparents might have been a little more forgiving of errant behaviour than their parents would, and that naturally meant conflict ensued when Lionel and Peter did come to Britain, newly bound by the strictures of living in our home.

My father, suffering his own problems of alienation and unhappiness living in Britain, was often in no mood to tolerate any kind of misbehaviour. As Lionel and Peter found adjusting to life in Britain trickier and trickier, perhaps on occasion bunking off school, coming home late and so on, the fights became worse. My dad failed to understand the discombobulation and trauma Lionel and Peter were experiencing at having to adjust to their new lives, suddenly having to yield to the will of someone they did not really know.

I saw all this unfold in our home, the shouting and arguments, the slammed doors and anger. How at times Lionel, Peter and Judith too, were perhaps subconsciously 'othered' by my father. How the three of them might have felt the other children including me, who were born in Britain, were more highly prized by our parents. I know they grew up in Bolton often feeling like outsiders in their own home, and this was a common experience for many of the newly reunited 'barrel children'. Their accents were Jamaican and flavoured with patois, while the other kids, me included, sported a Lancastrian brogue.

They admit they found the adjustment hard. The behavioural grammar of children, talking about the latest toys and games, sporting heroes and pop music, all that was alien to my half-brothers and sister, who were desperately trying to fit in and make new friends, trying to survive. Lionel kept a broad Jamaican accent for a long time, a defiant stand in a land that he believes never truly accepted him or Peter. How right he was, as they were both going to find out to devastating effect many years later. Their rejection at home and at school was to be mirrored by a rejection by Britain itself.

What I gradually came to understand over time, as it became clear Lionel and Peter did not really look like me, was that my father was not their biological father, and this might well have underpinned his behaviour towards them when we were all growing up.

* * *

Just like my half-brothers and sister, I have often wondered where I belong. The reverence and longing my parents had for the Caribbean, whilst living in Britain, sometimes made me think that was perhaps where I should be, even though I had never been to Jamaica. Years of travelling as a BBC foreign correspondent have made me feel that maybe I am simply a citizen of the world, which according to one disapproving former British Prime Minister, apparently might make me a citizen of nowhere. What utter nonsense! But as indicated earlier in this book, most of the time I feel very English and very British and proud to be so, but I am of course of Jamaican stock and deeply wedded to my roots in the Caribbean.

I am a Black British Caribbean, and that is how I responded on my census form in 2021, an identity I share with most black Britons who grew up in the UK in the 1970s and 80s. The 2021 census found that 18 per cent of the population identify as being black, Asian, mixed or other ethnic group. Being a member of this minority will always bring challenges, and there will forever be some among the 82 per cent of people in England and Wales who identify as white, who will never accept me as being British. Knowing that is how some people feel is always at the back of your mind, buried deep but ever present. That no matter how much you might want to belong, there are others who say you never will.

The glorious summer of 2012, during the London Olympics, was a time when I have never felt so 'at one' with Britain, where those feelings of being in the minority in this country were the furthest from my mind, or deepest in my subconscious. I was tasked with reporting on the non-sporting side of the games for the *BBC News at One, Six* and *Ten*. My job was to chronicle the excitement of the world's biggest global gathering and sporting event. For those two glorious weeks in July and August, it felt like I genuinely lived in a colour-blind society. We were *all* British. Black, white, Asian, Christian, Muslim, Hindu, immigrant or native.

It is difficult to describe the atmosphere at the time, but looking back, it was truly blissful. Who can forget the sense of pride at watching Danny Boyle's opening ceremony. It celebrated everything I love about this country, and I was not the only one moved to tears. Mr Bean, the Beatles, the NHS, the Windrush Generation, Shakespeare, the Red Arrows, James Bond.

The sun shone on cue, everyone was in a good mood and smiling. Even the traffic in central London was down, because many people left the city anticipating big crowds for the Games. And of course, our athletes, black and white, were a credit to our nation. We were a diverse people, talking about what united us, not what could divide us. Our common cause was supporting Team GB. It seemed we *all* had a rightful place in these islands.

Yet behind the scenes, a quiet catastrophe was taking shape, borne out of the words of the then Home Secretary, Theresa May. They are words that were repeated in different settings, including an interview with the *Daily Telegraph*, only two months before the ecstasy of the Olympics. She said, 'The aim is to create, here in Britain, a really hostile environment for illegal immigrants.' The problem is that *legal* immigrants were also caught up in the aggressive new policy, and for several years, no one seemed to care.

* * *

There is an obvious literary comparison to make between the innocent victims of the Windrush scandal, and Franz Kafka's bank officer, Joseph K., in *The Trial*. Kafka's protagonist is arrested, but it is never explained why. If a crime has been committed, it is not one of which Joseph K. is aware. His predicament is baffling and inexplicable. It's a tale of existential angst, and the dehumanised implacability of an all-powerful and faceless bureaucracy. Joseph K. must defend himself against a charge about which he can get no information. The computer always says no.

I interviewed a man called Mike Lord in the summer of 2020, a modern-day Joseph K., at his home in the suburb of Hartcliffe, on the southern edge of Bristol. It is an area consisting mainly of council houses developed after the war and is one of the poorer parts of the city. When I was a BBC regional TV news reporter in the early 1990s, I often filed reports from Hartcliffe on the social deprivation and lack of jobs in the area, after the decline of local industries, most notably the closure of the Imperial Tobacco factory in 1990. Now, thirty years later, I was back and in Mike's garden, talking to him for a film about the colonial legacy of the British Empire and his travails living a twenty-first-century version of *The Trial*.

Mike spoke with a broad West Country lilt, rolling his 'Rs' like a true native. Bespectacled, there was not a line on his face, despite being halfway through his sixth decade. He had the look of a Jay Blades about him, wearing a dark, *Peaky Blinders*-style cap. He was fit and healthy, after years of working on construction sites as a lorry driver and digger operator, but he was much less well-composed on the inside. He was fed up and weary of a long battle with the Home Office to prove he had a right to live in Britain, despite having been in the country for more than half a century.

He was born in Barbados and arrived in the UK in 1960, aged six years old. He was a barrel child, left behind in the Caribbean by his parents while they established themselves in the UK – his mum as a nurse in the NHS and his dad as a fireman.

'I was crying my eyes out,' he told me. 'I just didn't want to come to the UK, giving up everything I knew back home. It was cold here, I was shivering when I first arrived.'

Mike had travelled on his godparents' passport and had full rights of entry and settlement under the 1948 Nationality Act, just like my parents. He had no other paperwork proving he had a right to live in Britain, and he did not need any. He arrived in the UK perfectly legally.

However, a desire on the part of successive governments to halt the numbers of people coming in, amid growing anti-immigrant sentiment among some voters, prompted a tightening of the rules in the early 1970s. Anyone who could prove they arrived in the UK before 1973 was fine, but if you did not have any paperwork, you were liable to forced deportation. Mike had no documents.

'I felt like a leper,' he said, 'I may just as well have had a tag on my back saying I'm not British.'

Employers would not go near him, worried they would be in trouble for hiring an illegal immigrant. Mike struggled to make a living, flitting from short-term work here, to piecemeal work there. Keeping his head down, he managed to eke out an existence.

Then in 2012, the year Britain patted itself on the back with the London Olympics, the 'hostile environments' policy was announced. The pressure on the Conservative half of the coalition government to cut net migration from around a quarter of a million to 'tens of thousands' had been intense, and the UK Independence Party was gaining in the polls. The Home Office decided to try to make life so unbearable for illegal immigrants, they would want to pack their bags and leave. The problem was that ministers and officials cast such a wide net to catch illegals, they ended up scooping up thousands of people who had every right to be in Britain, but who simply did not have the paperwork to prove it.

Undocumented migrants were cut off from using fundamental services, losing access to benefits payments, the NHS and the police. It was made illegal for them to work or to rent property. Doctors, landlords, police officers and teachers were tasked with checking peoples' immigration status and carrying out ID checks. If they did not comply with the new rules, they were liable to fines of up to £10,000.

Often anyone who looked or sounded 'foreign' was asked to show their papers in order to rent a home or get medical treatment. Many people lost their access to bank accounts and driving licences. Some were placed in immigration detention, prevented from travelling abroad and threatened with forcible removal, while others were deported to countries they had not seen since they were 'barrel children'.

The Home Office was now the faceless bureaucracy of Kafka's *The Trial*, and there were around 15,000 Joseph K.s of the Windrush Generation from Jamaica alone. People like Mike Lord were now caught in a surreal 3-D version of an Escher painting, with dead-ends, wrong turns, blind alleys and staircases leading nowhere, as they tried to find the paperwork to prove they had a right to live in Britain.

Like Joseph K., they were not aware of any crime they had committed – don't forget they had been allowed to enter the UK without hindrance back in the 1960s. They were then told their crime was not having the paperwork, but they were not required to have any paperwork to enter the country, or to live in the country, in the first place. No matter. Now they were being hounded.

Then, around 2016, I received a panicked phone call out of the blue from my brother Lionel. He wanted to know if I happened to have any pictures of him as a schoolboy. I did not and when I asked him why he needed them, he said they were for the Home Office official who said they were necessary to prove he had been living in the UK since 1973. My older brother was another Joseph K.

We chatted some more, then said our goodbyes. He then rang round the rest of the family, looking for evidence that he attended the English Martyrs School in Bolton. This would be the proof that he did arrive from Jamaica before the immigration rules were changed in the early 1970s. He had no other paperwork. Peter was in the same mess, with no documentation, as both had travelled to Britain on Jamaican passports, as did Judith.

Ah, ha! I hear you cry, surely there would be a record of the date of their arrivals on official landing cards? Yes, indeed, except that a decision was taken by the Labour Government in 2009 to destroy the thousands of landing card slips, stored in the basement of a government tower block in Croydon, and it was the coalition government led by the Conservatives that implemented the destruction in 2010. Franz Kafka would have found that twist delicious.

The Government's hostile environments policy was in full swing. Peter was anxious to get a British passport so he could take his daughter Maisie to see his homeland before he died of prostate cancer. If he travelled on just his Jamaican passport, despite having lived in the UK for over forty years, he would not have been able to return to Britain. By now, he had been told he had two years to live. Meanwhile Lionel had been denied benefits and access to the NHS despite illness, and he was finding it hard to get a job. Judith had sorted out her paperwork several years earlier, shortly before getting married in 1989, so she had already secured a British passport.

What was galling for Lionel and Peter was that they firmly believed they were British, because they had not been led to think otherwise until it was too late, and the burden of proof was now on them to show their residency predated 1973. They had to find at least one official document from every year they had lived here, a terrible and in so many cases impossible burden.

Then, thanks to the quiet, brilliant journalism of Amelia Gentleman at the *Guardian*, the scandal of what had been happening to the Windrush Generation for several years was exposed, and the Government was forced to loosen its hostile environments policy. A compensation package for all those affected was agreed, but payments have been painfully slow.

Lionel's case for restitution, after years of not being able to find work and the denial of benefits and healthcare, was bolstered when he managed to find a photograph in the archives of the *Bolton Evening News* of him in the choir at his school on a special presentation night, dated before 1971. I asked Lionel to sum up what the last few years have been like for him. He paused for a few moments, then said they had been 'fucking awful'. I was similarly angry and also ashamed of my own country.

Judith has recently moved back to Jamaica, building her dream home in the St Thomas parish in the north-west of the island, a lush, secluded corner of the world. She says for the first time in a long time, she now feels truly at home.

As for Peter, he died before he was able to get a British passport to show the land of his birth to his daughter Maisie.

–15–

Confederacy of Dunces

HISTORY RECORDS THAT Barack Obama has cried in public on seven occasions. He was never a gusher, no boxes of tissues and bawling, in fact usually he is a reserved man in public, very clinical, calm and collected in policy speeches, rarely relying on emotion. For some, he was a little too professorial, lacking the 'I feel your pain' empathy of a Bill Clinton. So when Obama cried, it really meant something. Like when he was moved by a surprise appearance from Aretha Franklin, on stage at a tribute ceremony he was attending in New York in 2015. She sang 'You Make Me Feel Like a Natural Woman' to her own accompaniment on piano.

Sitting next to Michelle, as the Queen of Soul serenaded her husband in front of thousands of people in the hall, Obama's right hand went up to his left cheek, and with his index finger he flipped away a single tear. To date, the footage of that night has been viewed online 18 million times. He also cried when he made his farewell speech as president, in his hometown of Chicago in January 2017, and on three occasions he cried in public over the loss of people very dear to him: while paying tribute to his grandmother on her death in 2008; at the funeral of Dorothy Height, the prominent civil rights activist who marched with Dr King, in 2010; and on the death of his political mentor and friend, the Hawaiian US senator, Daniel Inouye, in 2012.

But Barack Obama has shed more public tears for one group of people than any other. He was not close to them; in fact, he had never even met them. But their deaths were so pointless, so needless, and ultimately in his mind and those of many millions of people in America and around the world, eminently preventable, that their loss was as profound as anything he had known. On two occasions, separated by four years, he wept in public over the deaths of twenty children, aged between six and seven years old, as well as six teachers, shot dead in a mass shooting at the Sandy Hook Elementary School, at Newtown in Connecticut in 2012.

At the White House during a news conference on the day of the tragedy, he addressed the families of those who died, crying for the first time. 'I can only hope it helps for you to know that you're not alone in your grief,' he said. 'We have wept with you; we've pulled our children tight.' And with that his right hand moved up to his left eye and wiped away a tear.

Others did weep for the families of those who died. I cried too, and it was the moment I fell out of love with America, unable to comprehend what its values really are. I assume the president was thinking, what if? What if it had been his daughters Sasha and Malia who were in the gunman's sights. I thought of my own nephews and nieces, what if it was them who had been mercilessly cut down in their classroom, where they should have been safe.

Yet it seems not enough Americans have been able to ask that simple question down the years, to put themselves in the shoes of the families of gun violence victims and ask, 'What if?' For if they had done, America would have sensible, tough gun controls. It appears not enough Americans really care.

I have only ever had reason to pick up an assault rifle once in my life. It was in 2004, and I was at a gun show in Virginia, reporting on the imminent demise of federal legislation that had been in place for a decade, banning nineteen different types of military assault weapons, including AK-47s, Kalashnikovs and Uzi rifles, as well as high-capacity ammunition magazines holding more than ten rounds.

'Go on, try it,' said the guy running one stall. Curious despite my abhorrence of guns, I picked it up, an M4 assault rifle. It looked a bit like the one Sylvester Stallone uses to devastating effect in *Rambo*. I thought, what the fuck is this? Why would *any* civilian feel the need to buy one of these weapons, which were clearly designed for the battlefield? The thing in my hands, the stall, the gun show, the people milling around prodding and picking up the weapons, as if checking out the firmness of avocadoes at a Sunday morning farmers market – it all seemed so immoral and wrong.

These are weapons of war; they are killing machines. And yet America's legislators were about to allow them to be released back onto the open market, for any Tom, Dick, and/ or Dirty Harry to buy. I said to the guy who let me handle the M4 assault rifle, 'Why would anyone want a semi-automatic weapon?'

His response was simple and spoke to America's obsession with guns for sport, hunting and self-defence. 'Why not?'

The federal ban had been introduced by Bill Clinton in 1994, after a spate of mass shootings in the previous few years, including at a school in California when a teacher and thirty-four children were shot, five of whom died, by a man firing a semi-automatic Kalashnikov AK-56. The public was angry and scared and asked the question I asked myself years later, why would any civilian feel the need to buy one of these weapons? To get the ban through Congress, the deal Clinton made was that it would last just ten years, and then lawmakers would decide if it should be extended. But the Republican-led Congress was not minded to keep the law, so it was about to lapse.

Guns are a poison Americans like to drink, but why? The hunting and fishing argument was always nonsense. How many ducks do you need to kill at any one time with a 9mm Uzi, accurate at 200 metres? Another argument is that guns and shooting are part of the great American outdoors, they are emblematic of frontier culture, woven into the fabric of society. The same could be said of Canada, Australia or New Zealand, but they are not awash with weapons the way that America is. Why not have comprehensive background checks and keep the civilian gun market to traditional hunting rifles, if you really feel the need to go kill a moose? That is what they do in much of the rest of the world.

In 2020 in Canada, 37 per cent of all homicides were gun-related. In Australia it was 13 per cent, and in the UK only 4 per cent. In America it was 79 per cent. The estimated number of firearms per 100 residents in the US is 120.5, and the only country that comes anywhere close is Yemen, with 52.8 per cent, but they have been fighting a brutal civil war for close to a decade. There are more guns in America than people. The country is armed to the teeth.

I came fully to understand what the real reason might be in 2016, when I travelled to Orlando in Florida, to report on the mass shooting of forty-nine people and wounding of over fifty others at a gay nightclub. I was filming at a local gun shop, and history was repeating itself. Just as I had done in 2004, I asked the owner why anyone would feel the need to buy a semi-automatic weapon, designed for the battlefield and soldiers, not for suburbs and everyday citizens.

His response was startling. 'We need the most powerful weapons we can get our hands on, because if the federal government comes after us, we need to be able to fight back.'

'The federal government?'

'Yes, you try to limit our freedom, you try to deny liberty, you will be punished. The government has big guns, we need big guns too.'

What pure fantastical nonsense, I thought at the time. Now I am not so sure, given the January 6th storming of the US Capitol Building in 2021. This belief in a God-given right to defend oneself against the tyranny of Government is played upon with great skill by the gun lobby group, the National Rifle Association. It claims that any attempt to take away high calibre weapons is the thin end of a wedge, and a slide towards *all* guns being taken away, leaving citizens defenceless against a tyrannical leader.

The NRA acts on behalf of gun manufacturers with the aim of shifting as many weapons as possible, regardless of the detrimental effects to society. It spends many millions of dollars buying the support of lawmakers in Congress, in order to stifle any meaningful attempt to introduce gun controls, no matter how appalling the latest mass-shooting atrocity. In America, more men, women and children killed in school shootings does not instinctively lead to a belief that fewer guns might be the answer, but perversely, that *more* guns are the solution.

The NRA always ends up calling for schools to be better prepared, with suggestions that even teachers should be armed, or for there to be more armed security guards. What underpins this madness is a familiar and catchy NRA refrain: 'The only thing that can stop a bad guy with a gun, is a good guy with a gun.'

Whenever I hear that phrase, I am reminded of the Jonathan Swift essay, 'Thoughts on Various Subjects, Moral and Diverting', where he writes, 'When a true genius appears in the world, you may know him by this sign, that the dunces are all in confederacy against him.' It has always struck me that the geniuses are those ordinary Americans who believe in sensible gun controls and assault weapons bans, and the dunces are the ones who refuse, despite all the evidence.

Numerous studies have shown that the 1994 Federal Assault Weapons Ban caused the number of deaths from mass shootings to fall. Even including the 1999 Columbine High School massacre, the deadliest mass shooting during the period of the ban, there were slower average annual rates of both mass shootings and deaths than before assault rifles were taken off the streets. The evidence is also clear that there are higher rates of mass shootings (defined by the FBI as the deaths of four or more people) in the US states with more relaxed gun laws and higher rates of gun ownership. What kind of person would ignore such evidence and fight for more guns, not less? A dunce! Pouring more fuel on the fire is surely not the way to put it out.

Because of the power of the NRA and its deep pockets, the dunces keep winning and people keep dying, and I was finding it more and more difficult to care. I remember one time in 2019 when there had been more mass shootings than days in the year and getting fed up with reporting on the slaughter. I began to think that if Americans themselves did not feel strongly enough about their fellow citizens dying to do something about it, why should I, and one day in the newsroom, I said that we should not keep covering mass gun attacks in the US, because frankly they were two-a-penny and no longer 'newsworthy'.

My comments made the editor think, but were never followed through, and so my frustration at the constant victories of the Confederacy, despite the ever-rising death numbers, was deeply depressing. I started to lose sight of why I fell in love with America many years before, and why I ended up spending more of my working life there as a foreign correspondent than any other country.

It was America's endless capacity for optimism that I fell in love with, the belief that tomorrow would always be a better day. But how on earth could that belief remain relevant, if the fear is that tomorrow you might get cut down by someone wielding an AK-47? Now, tomorrow would always be worse.

I also sensed a fatigue on the part of viewers about coverage of yet more mass shootings across the Atlantic, and I did not want to add to the ennui. So, in October 2018, for the one-year anniversary of the deadliest mass shooting in modern US history, when sixty people died and nearly 500 were injured, I suggested a reporting trip to America, not to

231

interview the grieving relatives and remember those who died, but to talk to the survivors.

The people who escaped death, but who were tragically maimed, blinded, crippled and psychologically damaged. Those whose lives were irrevocably transformed by that cruel night of high velocity violence. America's walking wounded are its dirty little secret; tens of thousands of people every year left worse off by the country's obsession with guns, who are never talked about by the media and the rest of society, like the lepers I reported on in Japan at the start of my career.

I returned to the scene of the hideous crime in Las Vegas from where I had reported the year before. I stood beneath the gleaming glass tower of the Mandalay Bay Hotel and looked up, counting as my eyes ascended the building, one, two, three, four, eventually reaching the 32nd floor, from where the killer in the adjoining rooms, 134 and 135, camped out for six days, usually sleeping much of the day and gambling in the in-house casino at night.

Then on 30 September, he put a 'Do not disturb' sign on the doors of both his rooms, and on the evening of 1 October, used an arsenal of more than twenty high calibre weapons to fire over 1,000 bullets down onto the site below, where a music festival was taking place. There were thousands of people in his eyeline, enjoying a live concert. The singer Jason Aldean was on stage with his hybrid brand of rock/country music. The killer liberally sprayed bullets down onto the people below, like he was shooting fish in a barrel. He would have been too far away to see their faces and the fear in their eyes.

They were just indistinct figures in the gloaming moving beneath his hotel room window, illuminated by the lights of the concert stage. Those people meant nothing to him, their lives, hopes and fears, their families and friends, their jobs, needs and wants, their humanity, none of that meant anything. *His* need was simply to kill, and America had no problem giving him the means to do that.

When I arrived in Las Vegas the year before to report on the tragedy, many of the billboards on the Las Vegas strip, that gawdy stretch of boulevard forested with shiny high-rise resort hotels and casinos, carried words of condolence after the massacre. 'Our thoughts and prayers are with you,' or words to that effect. Two days later when I left, those words of acknowledgement of what had happened had disappeared, and it was back to the ads flogging the resorts, spas, casinos and restaurants with their buffets for $9.99 plus tax. It took only forty-eight hours for Las Vegas to move on; after all, tomorrow will always be a better day.

My mission a year later was to talk to those who could not move on, so I visited one of the local hospitals that received scores of the wounded on the night of the massacre. Rosemarie Melanson was one of them, and she was chirpy the day I went to see her, as her two daughters were visiting, joining her husband who was already sitting by her bed.

In her mid-fifties, Rosemarie had spent much of the year since the shooting in and out of hospital. One of the gunman's bullets went through her chest and into her stomach, then it hit her liver and spleen. Twelve months on, she was still having surgery, and doctors intended to remove a small piece of her intestine a few days after my visit.

'There were times when I thought I didn't have the strength to survive, because I was so weak,' she told me. 'But my husband stayed with me in the hospital the whole time, sleeping in my bed, and he's the one that gave me the strength to get through.' Then tears filled Rosemarie's eyes, and she began to break down. 'There were so many days and nights I didn't know if I'd make it, because I didn't feel good.'

Her doctor, Matthew Johnson, told me that few can comprehend how many people there are in America who are walking wounded as a result of gun-related injuries, tens of thousands every single year, sometimes over 100,000.

'They're psychologically traumatised, and often the injuries affect their whole way of life. They can't work and if they don't have disability insurance, they can end up on the streets having sold everything to pay medical bills.'

I visited Chelsea Romo at a beauty salon where she was getting her hair done. In her late twenties, her long blonde tresses were being straightened and blow-dried. Her hair was parted more towards the left of her scalp, allowing a long fringe to lie across her right eye, hiding the fact that it was not there. Every now and again, the stylist would fiddle with the fringe, moving it out of place and revealing the pink tissue of her eye socket, minus the eyeball. One of the gunman's bullets had shattered her right eye, and almost left her blind in the left. Three operations in ten days saw screws go into her cheek, while her right cornea was sutured shut. She told me there was so much shrapnel in her eye that it broke the machine the doctors were using to suction it out.

In fact, shrapnel was still inside her, creating hard grey spots on her face and scalp. From time to time some of the pieces would work their way to the surface, allowing surgeons to pluck them out. She says whenever she goes out, her five-year-old son, Gavin, warns her not to go anywhere she might get shot. Chelsea's medical insurance had only a few months of coverage left. Then what?

* * *

The second time President Obama cried for the victims of the mass shooting at Sandy Hook Elementary School was when he laid out the executive actions he was taking in response to the killings, four years after the attack. He had made meaningful gun control a top priority of his second term in office, and now in his last year as the most powerful man on Earth, he was announcing to the world what he was doing to stop Americans killing each other. But he knew he did not have much success to report. The fact is that gun sales went up in the year after Sandy Hook and later many states expanded gun rights, the fear being that the death of little children might finally force a reckoning on American gun laws and push Congress to act.

But the NRA did not need to worry. The Confederacy of Dunces that constituted the gun lobby in Congress shot down every proposal the White House put forward after Sandy Hook. That left the president with very little to announce to the waiting press when he entered the East Room of the White House in January 2016, this despite polls regularly showing that most Americans wanted stricter and tougher gun controls. So he chose to make the speech emotional, which for him is a rarity.

Relatives of some of the victims stood behind him with the faces of their dead children on button badges on their lapels.

Obama knew it would be *his* last word as head of state on the issue of gun control, but he did not want it to be *America's* last word. As he announced a set of paltry measures, such as executive orders closing the loopholes that had allowed fire-arm purchases at gun shows to go unchecked, his voice became more strident, angrier.

'Our inalienable rights to life and liberty and the pursuit of happiness, those rights were stripped . . . from high schoolers at Columbine, and from first graders at Newtown.' He then paused, resting his arm on the podium, with his eyes welling up. 'Every time I think about those kids it gets me mad. And by the way, it happens on the streets of Chicago every day,' as tears blemished his face and trickled down his nose. 'All of us need to demand a Congress brave enough to stand up to the gun lobby's lies. All of us need to stand up to protect its citizens.'

What Obama's tears acknowledged was that while he was the leader of the free world, the most powerful man on the planet, when it came to gun control, he had no power at all. The tears were spontaneous and a reflection of his deep sadness, but in not fighting them back, he decided it was the only way to get across to the American people that it was *they* who had the power to change things, not the president.

If they want gun control, they must vote for it, by kicking out a supine Congress in the pocket of the NRA. But the fundamental problem in America is that when election time comes around, most voters do not have gun control at the top of their list of priorities, whereas the gun advocates will *always* get out and vote for the most important issue to them, which is keeping their armouries and arsenals intact. Barack

Obama says not being able to pass meaningful gun control measures was the biggest disappointment of his presidency.

Since then, thousands of mass shootings have come and gone in America, and with every single one, I have internally railed against the Confederacy of Dunces, while announcing the killings on television. Then in 2022, at the Robb Elementary School in the city of Uvalde in Texas, an eighteen-year-old gunman shot dead nineteen children and two teachers after firing multiple rounds from an AR-15 style rifle, like the ones I saw at the gun show in Virginia in 2004. It is the weapon of choice for mass killers. I was beside myself with rage.

The police waited more than 1 hour 14 minutes before breaching the classroom to tackle the gunman. Anxious parents, knowing their children were inside the school, tried to break the police cordon to rescue their kids and ended up in scuffles with the police, whom it seemed to them were not doing their jobs. There were clearly no 'good guys with guns' willing to engage the 'bad guy with a gun'. Security camera footage released in the following weeks clearly recorded the screams of the children locked in the classroom with the killer. The gunshots are on the tape too, as the children are slaughtered. But news organisations removed those sounds, in deference to victims' families.

If one of my nephews or nieces had been in that classroom, I don't know whether I would have given permission for the screams to be heard. But I do think that if all the parents *had* agreed to release the audio, maybe, just maybe that might have snapped America out of its torpor when it comes to introducing meaningful gun controls.

Congress later decided to hold hearings into the mass shooting and the police's appalling response, and appearing before the committee was Roy Guerrero, a paediatric doctor from Uvalde, whose patients were some of the children who died. He said assault weapons did not belong in the hands of everyday civilians, especially when in America you must be twenty-one years old to buy a beer, but only eighteen to buy an AR-15.

'They've been designed as military grade killing machines,' he said. Dr Guerrero then picked up a tape recorder he had on the desk in front of him. 'The following is audio that I was given by a parent, of kids in the classroom across the hall from where the shooter was. These children survived, but this is the shrill screaming of children trying to get out, while their classmates are being murdered.'

And with that, he pressed play. The noise was blood-curdling as the chamber of the committee room filled with the sounds of children screaming and sobbing. 'Please somebody help me,' cries one girl over and over again.

A woman sitting behind Dr Guerrero closed her eyes and bowed her head sobbing, another man bowed his head too.

'If America has decided the killing of children is bearable,' tweeted the political commentator Dan Hodges, 'then the US gun control debate is over.'

Dr Guerrero's tape is the soundtrack to a side of America that I despise. A lawful, yet lawless America. A contemptible America, a selfish and mean America. A Confederacy of Dunces.

–16–

George Floyd and Gen Z

THERE HAVE BEEN a few times in my line of work when I feared I was going to die. While covering wars and natural disasters, you do take calculated risks after fully assessing the dangers, but you can never be certain everything will be okay. One incident sticks in my mind that I could not possibly have legislated for, and it had nothing to with battlefield armies or the wrath of Mother Nature.

In 1996, I headed to Afghanistan to report on the first take-over of the country by a group of fighters known as the Taliban. Travelling from Pakistan, I crossed the majestic White Mountains along what was part of the old Silk Road, through the fabled Khyber Pass, a 300km journey winding through a vista of jagged majesty, with the mountains of the Hindu Kush standing guardian over a storied history.

We weaved our way through rugged peaks recalling the adventures of Persian kings and Genghis Khan, Rudyard Kipling, the Great Game and Flashman. This was the kind of adventure I had dreamed of as a kid growing up in Bolton. The West knew the Taliban were fundamentalists, committed to their own, narrow interpretation of Islam, but Washington, London and Islamabad believed the stability they might bring to that blighted country would benefit everyone. Indeed, the militants had at first been welcomed by the Afghan population as liberators, who would safeguard peace and security after years of civil war.

However, extremist, patriarchal rule characterised their governance, with female education banned and women not allowed to work or leave their homes unless accompanied by a close male relative. On that first trip, I attended one press conference with a senior Taliban official answering questions from the world's press, and there was a lone Western female journalist there in the courtyard of the government building where the conference took place.

She was modestly dressed, no skin at all on show and her hair was covered. But every time she raised her hand to ask a question, the Taliban commander ignored her. It happened time and time again. Eventually it became so embarrassing, he had to yield in front of the cameras of the world, and he grudgingly listened and responded after she was finally allowed to speak.

The Taliban drained Afghanistan of simple pleasures. They banned televisions and music. Driving through checkpoints you would see yards and yards of unspooled tape from music cassettes angrily confiscated from motorists. Ribbons of it fluttered in the breeze draping sentry posts. I often wondered what songs the ribbons held, what they would say. The only songs in Afghanistan now were laments for freedom playing in people's minds.

At cinemas Taliban fighters would unspool reels of film, then toss the whole thing onto a bonfire. At police stations, seized TV sets were smashed. Music and dancing at weddings were banned too, along with paintings depicting living things.

Life had to be joyless in the service of the Taliban's God. Now the Taliban are back in power, for more of the same.

I have reported from the country many times since, and it was on one assignment there that I thought my number was up, and all because of a couple of fried eggs. I was eating breakfast in a café in Kabul, after the Muslim holy month of Ramadan had just come to an end. They had sold out of food very quickly and it was late morning. A Taliban fighter walked in and asked for some breakfast – two fried eggs. The café owner apologised saying he had run out of food, but the man with an AK-47 slung over his shoulder said there must be something left, he had fasted and was desperate to eat.

The café owner reiterated there was nothing in his kitchen, and when he finished speaking, the Taliban fighter reached for his assault weapon and shouted that he would kill every-one in the café if the owner did not produce two eggs. The place fell silent, while life carried on as usual outside. I thought, is this how it ends? I die over a breakfast? I started to move slowly behind a pillar, hoping not to attract the gunman's attention. The café owner stood stock-still, he didn't know what to say, and so the Taliban fighter shouted again, 'I'll kill everyone in this café!' and he pointed the barrel of his AK at the man who had told him the cupboard was bare.

I thought about trying to make a run for it, the door was open, but I would have to negotiate a couple of tables and chairs in my way, and if I stumbled and made a noise, it could be curtains. I had no idea what to do and I felt helpless. The thing is, it would have been no problem for the Taliban fighter to kill us all with impunity. It was not an empty threat and we knew it. The Taliban were now the law, there would be no consequence, and he could do exactly as he pleased.

The man raised the barrel of his gun to the café owner's face, and it was at this point he signalled to the cook in the kitchen to find two eggs, which thankfully he did, food I assume the café owner was holding back for his own family. As the Taliban fighter put away his AK and sat down to eat, I got up with my interpreter and walked away. I was so lucky I did not see anyone die that day.

I tell this story because it was a paltry couple of fried eggs that could have got me killed. Truly absurd. So were the circumstances surrounding the death of the black man Eric Garner, who died while being held down in a choke hold by several New York City police officers, after an arrest for allegedly selling suspected unlicensed cigarettes. A tragedy over a few fags. George Floyd lost his life over suspected counterfeit $20 bills. There was no accusation by the police of murder or rape, he wielded no weapons, and yet he was handcuffed and also pinned down by four Minneapolis police officers with one kneeling on his neck for more than seven minutes. All because of an alleged counterfeit $20 bill. Their deaths reinforced the belief of many in America that black lives did not matter, and seeing both videos now still makes me sick to my stomach.

What I see is another layer of meaning smudged over the tragic consequence of a huge set of complicated circumstances in New York and Minneapolis. In the brutality of the overzealous police officers, I see the distillation of my life's work as a journalist, reporting on repression right around the world. The same power to abuse that I watched in the actions of those men in police uniform, with their black boots and badges, guns, batons, stab vests and brute force, was no different to the power to abuse exhibited by the Taliban, or the Burmese military towards the Rohingya. The police officers seemed to feel they had been licensed by the state to be indifferent to the pain they were causing.

For more than seven minutes, a Minneapolis policeman had his knee on George Floyd's neck, in full view of camera phones and the watching world. But his face betrayed no shame, no sense of moral outrage, no desire to ease the pressure, no pain that what he was doing was difficult. In fact, it seemed to be the easiest thing in the world to squeeze this man beneath him, and take the life from him. It was simply a public display of the raw power that he believed was invested in his uniform and his badge. The world watches their crimes, but little is done.

Ah, but why should my heart bleed for George Floyd or Eric Garner, as some commentators suggested. They had been criminals, who had already broken *their* contract with the state that as good citizens they should abide by the laws of the land. Well, your heart should bleed because you are a human being. As my mother used to say, and as I have believed my whole life, 'Do unto others, as you would have them do unto you.'

The humanity of millions poured out in protests around the world to show their revulsion at what they saw. Large-scale demonstrations for Eric Garner across America, and massive protests for George Floyd around the world. Demonstrations for justice such as have not been seen for a generation and even further back, to the civil rights era of the

243

1960s. What was revealed in every step taken by the protestors as they marched, was not only how much black people were disgusted by what had happened, but also the disgust of white people.

I finally got to make a film for the BBC's *Panorama* programme about race in America after George Floyd's death, and I went to film one of the protests involving thousands of people. It began in Hyde Park and finished in Trafalgar Square, in the summer of 2020. I was struck by the idealism of the protestors and their sense of mission. They were not jaded like me, having seen so many black deaths at the hands of the police in America, with the killings doing little to change society or lead to police reform.

The demonstrators were mainly white people, many in their late teens and twenties, Gen Zeders who have grown up in a world of gender fluidity and diversity of all kinds. Racial tolerance is second nature to them. They really believe they can change the world. My generation did too when we were younger. I hope Generation Z succeeds where we clearly failed. A generation with so many built-in disadvantages that we did not have ... student debt, an acute awareness of climate change, unaffordability in property and rent, jobs are a problem too. And on top all that they must deal with the racial mess we left behind.

Just as in America, the Covid pandemic and lockdowns meant millions of people around the world could not walk away from the video of George Floyd being suffocated. There was no school, college or work to divert our attention. We were all a captive audience for the barbarity, our eyes glued to our TVs and social media feeds, smartphones and laptops, as morbid fascination turned to horror. The white world of affluence and privilege and success could not avert its gaze. Laid bare was a taste of what life was like in the black world and it was not pretty.

In making the *Panorama* film, which analysed the moments leading up George Floyd's death and asked whether this could be a turning point for race relations in America, I interviewed a political commentator called Charlie Sykes, a dyed-in-the-wool conservative and Republican. I had spoken with him before, for the film I made in 2016, when I talked only to white people about America's racial divide.

Then he was clear that race was not the issue activists made it out to be in America. He believed that too many black people wanted to play the race card of discrimination and prejudice to get a leg up in society. But watching George Floyd die on television had completely changed his view.

'I've been stopped by the police for a variety of things, you know like not having my taillight on or speeding,' he said. 'I never once thought that a police officer would throw me to the ground and handcuff me.'

I asked Charlie whether he and other white conservatives needed to see a video like that to make them understand what African Americans have been talking about for such a long time.

'Unfortunately, yes,' he replied. 'Yes, I did. White Americans might have thought, okay this happens but it's random, it's a few bad apples here and there. But I think what we've been seeing is that it's not just a few bad apples. It is systemic, it's incredibly widespread, and in fact we've been in denial of this situation.'

It was great for me to hear Charlie say this, but it was a

tragedy that it took the death of yet another black man, this time caught in graphic detail on camera, to school white America.

The murder was not a teaching moment for everyone. Donald Trump decided he would focus his attention on the violence of a tiny minority during some of the protests, the opportunists who were in no way marching for social justice, who seized the chance to loot stores. This was the White House stance, despite the vast majority of the demonstrations involving millions of people being peaceful and law-abiding. Some right-wing commentators and columnists on both sides of the Atlantic similarly chose to focus on the sporadic episodes of rioting, giving scant mention to the appalling murder of a human being, or the deficiencies of out-of-control police forces.

One columnist, for whom I have a bottomless well of contempt, wrote an article where he referred to George Floyd's death as 'unfortunate', then proceeded to spend the rest of the 2,000-word diatribe laying into, as he put it, the 'mob' of protestors. As with Newton's Third Law of Motion, 'To every action, there is an opposite and equal reaction', and reactionary forces in Britain and America circled the wagons after George Floyd's death.

They refused point blank to acknowledge that society had deep issues to address when it comes to race relations, and if they did acknowledge that fact, they did so grudgingly under sufferance, and then proceeded not to talk about it, analyse it, or discuss possible solutions. It is an age-old trick that perfectly explains why so little progress has been made in tackling racial issues. The reactionaries do not want to change or transform society. If they are doing okay, everyone else can go hang. So, you don't talk about change, you talk about something else.

The corporate world understood far better than some short-sighted columnists and reactionary politicians what George Floyd's death meant, and I will never forget walking down the King's Road in Knightsbridge, only a few days after he died. All the ad space on the side of the bus shelters seemed to have been bought up by Ralph Lauren, and all the products featured black models.

Defying Trump and some on the right, many blue-chip companies came out in support of the protests. Advertising companies suddenly started featuring mixed-race couples and black people more prominently.

More companies took on experts in Diversity and Inclusion, and firms analysed their hiring practices to make sure they were as inclusive as could be. The England football team and the Premier League chose to begin matches with the players all 'taking the knee', a symbolic gesture of humility and prayer pilloried by some in Government who clearly hadn't the faintest idea what it meant, or where the gesture came from. For the record, Dr Martin Luther King led civil rights protestors in prayer on the street outside a courthouse in Alabama, after some of his fellow marchers had been arrested. King kneeled to pray.

The boos that used to accompany the gesture at the start of the campaign soon turned to cheers and applause, once those on the terraces went away and took the time to find out what the gesture was all about. In the US, the multibillion-dollar American football league, the NFL, which at one time had threatened players who 'took the knee' before matches rather than standing for the national anthem, issued an apology to those players.

At the BBC, along with my fellow presenters the late George Alagiah, Reeta Chakrabarti and Mishal Husain, we lobbied both the Director-General, Tony Hall, and his successor, Tim Davie, on the BBC's commitment to improve diversity in the newsroom, an ongoing project. How can we get more black and brown people into senior positions? Are we looking in the right places for staff, are we reaching out beyond the obvious universities and colleges?

For the first time in my life, the issue of race relations and inequality was being discussed calmly and rationally right across society by everyone. My parents had come to a Britain where it was still legal to refuse a black person a job, or a room in a boarding house, simply because of the colour of their skin. Laws ended that naked outward prejudice, but now the more subtle forms of the disease, unconscious bias and soft bigotry, were finally being dealt with, despite some howling at the moon by the 'anti-change' merchants, for whom all is well, and attempts to change society for the better being denigrated as 'woke'.

It seems to me that white society actually 'woke up', and that turning back the tide of change will become progressively more difficult as Generation Z gets older and becomes even more influential.

I have interviewed the veteran civil rights leader Reverend Jesse Jackson on several occasions and his message of inclusiveness to bring about change has been constant. He has talked of a 'coalition of conscience', and his political organisation, the Rainbow PUSH Coalition, which grew out of his run for the White House in 1984, has sought to bring black and white together in the cause of racial justice. He is now encouraged to see so many young white people marching with young black people, and believes there is a lot of anguish and conscience among whites about race, and that is progress.

I last spoke with him outside the Lorraine Motel in Memphis, not far from the balcony where he stood with Dr Martin Luther King on the day MLK was shot dead in 1968. We met on the fiftieth anniversary of his death. He told me that intellectually most white people understand that race is a construct, a pseudoscience: the races should be equal, black people are not inferior and white people are not superior, simply by virtue of the level of melanin in their skin. But what the world does have is economic inequality between the races, education is not equal, access to healthcare is not equal, and access to development is skewed. The distribution of power is fundamentally unfair.

I could not agree more. These are challenges I have seen not only in Britain and America, but around the world in my work as a journalist. Which is why the death of George Floyd resonated with many millions of people globally, and addressing those challenges positively should be the lasting legacy of his passing.

'The Queen is gravely ill, can you come into the office?'

MARY WHITEHOUSE WAS not impressed with me. The social conservative activist railed against the so-called 'permissive society' of the 1960s, 70s and 80s, which she believed was embodied by the BBC, full of leftie types and hippies (no change there then!). She led a long-standing campaign against the Corporation, establishing the pressure group Clean-Up TV in 1964. A year later, she founded the National Viewers' and Listeners' Association, which for many years would slap down the BBC for what in her view was excessive bad language and portrayals of sex and violence in its programmes.

So I guess her lip must have curled and her brow furrowed when she saw me appear on BBC *Breakfast News* on the morning of 20 July 1995, broadcasting live from outside the private King Edward VII Hospital in Marylebone, in central London. I was the on-duty news correspondent, tasked with covering whatever breaking stories may have occurred overnight.

The day before, Queen Elizabeth the Queen Mother, then in her mid-nineties, had been admitted to have a cataract removed from her left eye. Despite the pretty straightforward operation, there was a little concern given her advanced years, and her doctors decided to keep her in overnight.

So, I went down to the hospital and met up with the live camera crew at around 7.30 a.m. My live 'hit' or appearance on *Breakfast News* was due sometime after 8.00 a.m. I had a quick chat with a couple of people inside the hospital and clocked a mountain of flowers and cards left by the general public, wishing the Queen Mother well and a speedy recovery. I jotted down some notes in my pad, and I was ready to go live.

The presenter back in the studio asked me a question along the lines of , 'Our news correspondent, Clive Myrie, is outside the King Edward VII Hospital in central London with the very latest. Clive, what can you tell us?'

Now I cannot remember the exact words I used, except for one. I replied something along the lines of , 'The doctors treating the Queen Mother say the operation went well. She was kept in overnight just as a precaution given that she's ninety-four, and she is expected to be discharged sometime later today. After the successful operation to remove the cataract, as she prepares to leave, the Queen Mother will be able to see clearly a . . .' Then came flying out of my mouth a word that offended the sensibilities of one particularly attentive woman watching and listening at home. '. . . able to see clearly a *hell* of a lot of cards and flowers wishing her a speedy recovery.'

'Clive Myrie, our correspondent, reporting there. Thank you.'

I wonder if watching television was ever a pleasurable pastime for Mary Whitehouse, or was it a constant vigilance that sucked any enjoyment out of the experience? By all accounts she did not actually watch a lot of the stuff on TV (especially the BBC, which she despised) that she believed might be just filth or morally deplorable. 'I have too much respect for my mind,' she was often quoted as saying.

I suspect she would have been watching BBC *Breakfast News* the morning I appeared, but without her notepad by her side ready to log any indiscretion. She may have assumed that the British TV watching public would have been safe at that time of the morning – best reserve the ink for later at night when there was bound to be telly trouble on the depraved BBC.

Maybe she did not actually watch me that morning and it was another member of the National Viewers' and Listeners' Association who 'dobbed me in', sending Mary a full read-out of my misdeed. Whatever the case, a few weeks after my 'infamous' broadcast, the NVLA sent a letter of complaint to my bosses in the BBC newsroom. The charge? That I should not have used the word 'hell' in such a context, because it is a profanity. The Queen Mother, as well as Mary Whitehouse, would have understood it as a swear word, because of its religious background. The inappropriate use of religious terms was much more taboo in the early twentieth century, when they were both born, than in the more secular society of today.

Now, curse words are more to do with sex and scatology (which I assure you, Mary Whitehouse did not like either) rather than pertaining to religious imagery. Her deeply held Christian beliefs informed her life's work of campaigning, which I respected, and though we never talked about it, my mum would not have been happy with me using the word 'hell' either, given her age and similar level of religiosity. I was a little miffed someone took the time and trouble to complain about something that was an attempt to reflect how much the Queen Mother was loved, but I am sorry if I upset anyone.

I cannot recall how the BBC responded to the complaint. By the mid-1990s the Corporation might have felt *it* was on the right side of public taste, not the 85-year-old Mary Whitehouse. I am sure the response would have been polite and courteous, and probably agreed with Mary in her assessment of my use of the word 'hell'. But what this tiny little episode revealed was a bigger truth, about a changed and changing Britain, which not only the members of the NVLA and Mary Whitehouse had to contend with, but perhaps the monarchy too.

* * *

There is silent newsreel footage from 1923 of the day Lady Elizabeth Bowes Lyons married the Duke of York at Westminster Abbey. He later, of course, became King George VI and she became Queen Elizabeth, over whom I would upset Mrs Whitehouse. At the same time as my great-uncle, William Runners, had settled back into country life in Jamaica after the trenches of France in the First World War, and that experience had set him on the road to believing the British Empire needed to free its dominions, the end of Empire would have been unthinkable in the minds of the thousands of people lining the route from the Abbey to Buckingham Palace, waving their white handkerchiefs as the wedding party passed by.

One of the captions in the newsreel reads: 'The whole Empire wishes them long life and happiness.' The United Kingdom and her dominions were forever indivisible in the minds of the British, and for many in the Empire, too. My mum and dad grew up with and understood the monarch as being Head of State of Jamaica. The Royal Family had a reassuring permanence in a changing and increasingly dangerous world. For many of my parents' generation flung across the empire, there was an easy acceptance of the stability the House of Windsor seemed to bring. My mum says that at the time of Queen Elizabeth's coronation in 1953, her feelings about the monarchy were neutral.

That year, as Britain prepared to crown a new Queen, my mum was a kindergarten teacher in Jamaica, at the Revival School in Sheffield, on the western edge of the island, not far from where my family hailed from in the parish of Westmoreland. All the schools in Jamaica were going to celebrate the Coronation and bunting and banners were strewn along the balconies of official buildings, draped from monuments, courthouses and across schoolyards.

My mum remembers the special stamps that came out for the big day, a black and white picture of a very young, demure-looking Elizabeth wearing a tiara, in an oval setting with crosshatch green surrounding the image. JAMAICA ran along the bottom and all the dominions had similar special stamps. Malaya's crosshatching was pink, Bermuda's a navy blue, the Bahamas sky blue, the British Solomon Islands a light black. All the lands over which the Queen would now be sovereign, unified under her rule, the coming together of a shared colonial heritage one lick at a time.

Twenty-four hours before the oath and ermine, the cloth of gold, anointing of Holy oil and the fixing of her crown, the young Elizabeth made a radio broadcast to her global realm, where she pledged her devotion to its people. She said, 'Throughout all my life and with all my heart I shall strive to be worthy of your trust.' For many of my mum's generation that call to service resonated, regardless of the legacy of empire. On Coronation Day there was no talk of slavery and displacement, of subjugation and white supremacy. In my mum's school there was a celebration for the new Queen, a tea party with sandwiches. Each child was given a special little cup, bluey green in colour, with the Queen's head on one side.

There was a desire on the part of many Jamaicans to see in the flesh the woman who decorated the stamps and the side of their coronation cups. There was a fascination for my mother too: who was this young thing thrust into the limelight to rule over us? That is why six months after the Coronation, when the Queen embarked on the longest royal tour ever and reached Jamaica, my mum joined an estimated quarter of a million people, one sixth of the population, to welcome the new sovereign to the island, after the royal plane touched down at Montego Bay.

My mum had got a lift with some of her friends up from Sheffield on what was a fine day, though some rain was forecast, and she took a place among the crowds ready to see the newly crowned monarch. So many Jamaicans thought of Britain as the Mother Country, benevolent and wise, so the stories filtering back at the time from the early Windrush pioneers, of frosty receptions and racism, did not really make much sense. All that was pushed to the back of peoples' minds, and across the two days of the Queen's visit, she was made to feel most welcome everywhere she went.

This was the first time that Jamaicans ever had a chance to glimpse their sovereign, and many were proud she took the time to visit, with Bermuda the only other stop on the royal tour of Britain's Caribbean possessions. By her making the effort, Jamaicans felt special, part of something larger than themselves. It was recognition that Jamaica was not just this insignificant little island miles away from Buckingham Palace and the House of Commons and Lord's Cricket Ground, it mattered, because the Queen came to say hello, or 'how di do' in Jamaican patois.

My mother says at Montego Bay she saw a slight young woman and wondered how she might handle the weight of Queenship with its heavy burdens on such slender shoulders. Apparently, the man standing in front of my mum in the crowds remarked how pretty the young Queen looked.

Perhaps Elizabeth's relatively young age, only twenty-five, helped endear her to my mother's generation. She had no baggage and plenty of time to prove her worth. It is complicated, yes there is a dreadful legacy of colonialism that blights Jamaica and the Caribbean to this day, but the Queen somehow transcended all that for my mum and dad and millions of others like them, who came of age at the start of the new Elizabethan Age.

* * *

Prince Philip was the first Royal I clapped eyes on at close quarters. It was in the mid-1970s, and I would have been around fifteen or sixteen. I had managed to get a Duke of Edinburgh's Award, the scheme for adolescents and young adults to complete a set of exercises building character and self-worth. Usually involving a sport, some kind of outdoors activity like camping in the wild for a few days, performing a community service, and so on. Nowadays the list of tasks young people can take part in has grown enormously, and the scheme is now global in over 144 countries. For me it was fun as well as tough, and I learned the importance of working hard to achieve one's goals, and that effort is rewarded if you keep pushing.

It was the Duke himself who gave me my award and little badge, along with several others at my school. He landed a helicopter on our playing fields in Bolton, and I can still picture him bounding over as we all stood in line feeling a little nervous. But he had an easy charm and was very friendly. Tall and athletic looking, he was lean and trim, the very model of the kind of character his scheme was designed to create: confident 'go get 'em' youths. I was impressed, and in recent years I have been giving out the badges myself at receptions for Duke of Edinburgh Award Scheme winners, at St James's Palace and Buckingham Palace, and I have talked about my own experience of taking part.

It was quite a while before I got anywhere near the Queen. Fast-forward to the year 2000 and a Commonwealth Heads of Government meeting in Durban in South Africa. As Head of the Commonwealth, the Queen was there to welcome all the leaders and corral cooperation, and she did this simply by virtue of her presence. I was maybe a couple of metres away from her at a daytime reception, and like my mum, I was struck by her diminutive stature. The difference this time, of course, was that almost half a century had passed, and those slender shoulders had indeed borne so much in the service of her nation.

The respect she had garnered worldwide throughout all that time was immense. She won respect from the most unlikely quarters, her quiet diplomacy on show for example with that stunning handshake with the former IRA commander, Martin McGuinness, on a visit to Northern Ireland in June 2012. The greeting lasted around four seconds, but the symbolism lives on to this day, as a sign of the progress made in bringing Republican and Loyalist communities together. McGuinness said later, 'I liked her courage in agreeing to meet with me, I liked the engagements that I've had with her . . . I like her.'

Nelson Mandela was similarly impressed with the way the Queen operated. One of the things I loved about Sussex University during my time studying there was its activism, especially when it came to denouncing the amorality of apartheid. I attended sit-ins and went on marches, and I got my first bank account with the Midland Bank, refusing to sign up with Barclays, because of their significant interests in South Africa. In fact, the country's dependence on foreign investment meant it was particularly susceptible to banks taking a stand. Britain was the most important source of foreign capital to the country and was home to the parent companies of South Africa's two largest banks.

In 1964, students marched from Brighton to London, to hand in a petition with hundreds of signatures. Leading the march was a 22-year-old economics undergraduate at Sussex by the name of Thabo Mbeki. He would go on to become South Africa's second black president, after Nelson Mandela.

The petition called on the Conservative prime minister at the time, Sir Alec Douglas-Home, to pressure the South Africans after the treason trial of several ANC activists, including Mandela and Mbeki's father, Govan. They had all been found guilty and were expected to be sentenced to death.

Sussex was a new university at the time (it had only been granted its Royal Charter in 1961), but was gaining a reputation as a home of radical thinking, and ended up helping to lead the way in the struggle against apartheid. Several exiled South Africans managed to study at the university, and as a result, many Sussex alumni went on to serve in Mandela's first government.

But that road to black majority rule was a rocky one. In 1986, when the likes of Ronald Reagan and Dick Cheney were denouncing the ANC as terrorists and rejecting tough sanctions and travel restrictions on the regime in South Africa, Mandela was left to rot in jail. Twenty-three years had passed of what would ultimately be a twenty-seven-year prison sentence. Some in the Western world had finally acknowledged the true horrors of the country's brutal racial oppression, as well as the ANC's work to end the suffering. In fact, 1986 was the year the leaders of the Commonwealth nations came together to agree on a programme of economic sanctions against the South African government.

Forty-eight of the forty-nine nations signed off on a plan. The one holdout, to its shame, was Britain. Despite Mandela himself making it clear that sanctions were vital and it was important to make South Africa an international pariah, Margaret Thatcher, alongside Reagan and Cheney, thought they knew better than him.

There is absolutely no evidence that the three of them supported white minority rule in South Africa, indeed by all accounts, behind the scenes Thatcher would give the regime in Pretoria grief over apartheid, including telling them to release Mandela. But why would they do that if there was no pain, or change a system that was serving them very nicely? And why did she not condemn apartheid publicly?

As a student, I was embarrassed and disgusted by the Government's attitude. Thatcher disapproved of economic sanctions of any kind. She felt denouncing apartheid and advocating economic pain would damage Britain's own interests, and sanctions were 'a crime against free trade'.

This was despite the United Nations imposing an arms embargo on South Africa in 1977, in response to the massacre of schoolchildren in the black township of Soweto. Chase Manhattan Bank called in its loans in 1985, with other banks in Europe and America following suit over the next several years. The US Congress, then state and local governments, halted investments, trade and lending, and perhaps most egregiously for the white South African leadership, international sporting bodies boycotted and shamed the country that valued that particular connection to the outside world. I found Thatcher's stance utterly appalling and morally reprehensible. History will not be kind.

One person who disagreed vehemently with Britain's stance was none other than the Queen. In official documents declassified in 2017 by the Republic of Ireland, she was so enraged by Thatcher's refusal to back sanctions that she considered scrapping their weekly audience. She felt the Prime Minister had damaged 'her Commonwealth' by refusing to support a tough line against the racist apartheid regime. After becoming South Africa's first democratically elected president, Nelson Mandela cultivated a close relationship with the Queen, and the two spoke often on the phone, using their first names as a mutual sign of respect and affection. I for one believe that her stance on apartheid marked her out as being generous of spirit, compassionate and wise.

I saw these traits on display again in her rallying cry to the nation during the darkest days of the first wave of the Covid pandemic. I was about to go inside the Royal London Hospital to see for myself what was happening to the NHS, and in a national address at a time of great unease, the Queen's words provided a kind of glue binding us together, splintered as we all were into individual households during lockdown.

'Together we are tackling this disease,' she said. 'If we remain united and resolute, then we will overcome it . . . We will be with our friends again. We will be with our families again. We will meet again.'

I will never forget those words, and for me they helped to justify the very essence of why in an age of cynicism, atheism and republicanism, there was a point to the Royal Family.

* * *

On 8 September 2022, I was preparing to fly to Italy the next day on a filming trip, when I received a call from the Acting Director of News at the BBC, Jonathan Munro. He would usually drop me an email if he wanted to chat about something, so instinctively as soon as he said, 'Hi, it's Jonathan,' I thought something was up. Did I go too far on Twitter? Was there a new Mary Whitehouse taking me to task for something I said on air? Whatever, it was probably not going to be something pleasant he wanted to discuss. What Jonathan ended up talking about never entered my head as a possibility, even though it had been in the back of my mind, a nagging expectation, a sad inevitability, for several years.

I came off the road as a full-time foreign correspondent to become a presenter in 2009. Ever since and perhaps for a few years before, the BBC had been preparing for the death of Queen Elizabeth, as were the Metropolitan Police, the City of London, the Church of England, and the authorities at Westminster Abbey. It would be a moment no one could get wrong, and periodically the BBC would have rehearsals and be ready for the moment.

Over the years there had been tweaks and adaptations. How formal should the coverage be in the modern age? Do we behave as if we are in the 1950s, solemnly reporting events, or must there be a nod to modern vernacular and style? The rehearsals, a few times a year, were to check the technical aspects of what would be one of the biggest undertakings BBC News would ever be involved in, but also to nail down the tone of the coverage.

The world would be tuning in, all eyes would be on the BBC, and getting the tone exactly right would be key. Getting it wrong would see the vultures circle, particularly critics in the mainstream press, as well as politicians on the left and right who frankly do not believe in objective journalism or truth, but want propaganda for their side. They would be queuing up to slam the BBC if it messed up.

We all knew that in the newsroom, the scrutiny and pressure would be intense like the heat of a furnace, and during some rehearsals staff were extremely nervous, even though it was not the real thing. The run-throughs usually involved the whole senior management team being in the newsroom, inspecting every detail. It was nerve-racking for some, because it was clear if you messed up on rehearsal day, you would probably not be trusted with the main gig.

Jonathan in his phone call did not stand on ceremony, there was no small talk. He was clear and to the point. 'The Queen is gravely ill, can you come into the office?' It took me a split second to fully process what he was saying. *The Queen, gravely ill, can you come into the office,* all in the same sentence. Roughly an hour later, I was at the BBC's New Broadcasting House studios in central London, and I did not leave until around ten hours later, presenting late in the afternoon and for much of the evening.

It was the most surreal time; the newsroom was calm and in complete control. Everyone knew their roles and what they had to do. Slowly, more information would come in from Scotland about the state of the Queen's health, and when it became clear members of her family were flying up from London and Windsor to Balmoral, we knew it was only a matter of time before the official announcement, which came at 6.30 p.m., around seven hours after Jonathan first got in touch and asked me to come in.

I was not sure what my involvement would be in the coverage after that. Big state events are usually taken over by the huge beast in the BBC called the Special Events department, which has little to do with news.

On the passing of the monarch, the heir automatically accedes to the throne. But for hundreds of years there is a ceremony, formally proclaiming to the world the new sovereign and their regnal name. There had been suggestions for a few years that Prince Charles might take the name of George on becoming King. After all, Charles I had his head chopped off, and Charles II was known as the 'Merry Monarch', because of the rather hedonistic style of his court – to put it mildly. But it soon became clear after the Queen's death that the Prince of Wales would become King Charles III.

The formal Proclamation of Accession of the new King and their regnal name would come after a meeting of the ceremonial body, the Accession Council, at St James's Palace, due two days after the Queen had died, but it was unclear whether the meeting would be televised. The day before, I received a rather casual phone call from the BBC, telling me I was going to be broadcasting live from St James's Palace when the Accession Council met, for a BBC One special programme. 'Not a problem,' I said, as I put down the phone, but for the first time in the whole of the BBC's coverage of the death of the Queen, I felt nervous.

Despite hours of live broadcasting on the day she died and the day after, I had battled the nerves by telling myself that this was just another story. I was not going to let the weight of history of the events I was describing prey on my mind. This was how I had handled the death rehearsals over the years, trying to relax into the moment, blanking out the fact that one day millions of people around the world would be watching. I told myself I was covering any ordinary event and I simply had to do my job to the best of my ability.

But the Proclamation Accession somehow felt different, and I really did feel the weight of history on my shoulders. This ancient ceremony had never been televised before, and this time it was marking the end of the Elizabethan and the beginning of the Carolean Age. But that was the point, it was the *beginning* of something new, so this was an opportunity to look forward, not back, and no matter what one's view of the Royal Family might be, surely most people would want to wish Charles well.

That was my attitude on the day as I broadcast live among the crowds at St James's Palace, while the Accession Council, made up of former prime ministers, members of the Cabinet, senior Church of England clergy, the great and the good, gathered to ratify the accession.

Outside, clear skies greeted thousands of people who had gathered to witness the spectacle, armed with selfie sticks and smartphones. There was this weird crossover of the old and the new, the ancient and the modern. The State Trumpeters of the Household Cavalry in their fine red and gold livery waited to proclaim the new King and the atmosphere was one of nervous expectation, a much less sombre feel than the previous few days surrounding the Queen's death.

At one point, I got out my own smartphone to take a snap of the trumpeters as their fanfare pierced the late morning air, and the Garter King of Arms at St James's Palace read out the Proclamation of Accession: 'The Prince Charles Philip Arthur George, is now by the death of our late Sovereign of Happy Memory, become our only lawful and rightful Liege Lord, Charles the Third.' The Garter King then took off his hat and bellowed, 'Three cheers for His

Majesty the King, Hip, hip!' and the crowd as one shouted three times, 'Hooray!'

* * *

One early evening after I had presented the *BBC News at Six* and I was preparing to present the *News at Ten*, a colleague in her twenties approached me asking if she could have a word in private. I said of course and we went to a quiet corner of the newsroom. The Queen's state funeral was only a few days away, but she said she had been perplexed by the BBC's over-all reporting. I asked why, and she said she did not feel the newsroom had spent enough time exploring the legacy of imperialism and colonialism, and the crimes committed in the name of the Royal Family in years gone by.

I understood her point of view, but asked her to remember that the while the Queen's death was a public event, she was also a mother, grandmother and great-grandmother, and the public grief of millions of people was also the private grief of her own family. Now was not the time. The BBC had *of course* discussed the legacy of colonialism in its coverage, and I myself had a long, fascinating discussion with the eminent historian, Sir Simon Schama, on the very subject, live on the BBC, and related to him the feelings of affection my Windrush Generation parents had towards the Queen, despite their colonial history in Jamaica.

'Best wait till the period of mourning is over, imagine if it was your mum who was being attacked, and she hasn't even been buried,' I told my colleague, and she fully understood, now was not the time.

A few months before the Queen died, Prince William and his wife Catherine went on an official tour of the Caribbean, visiting Jamaica, and they recreated a scene from the 1953 Commonwealth tour of his grandparents, which my mum saw first-hand. Standing and waving, they rode along in an open-top Land Rover for a military parade, exactly as the Queen and the Duke of Edinburgh had done all those years ago. Kate in a pretty dress, William in white military uniform.

It was a disaster and poorly received by many Jamaicans. The world had moved on since 1953. Jamaica now wanted to remove the Queen as Head of State and so evoking imperialist images was unfortunate, to say the least. I felt sorry for William and Kate and by all accounts his gut instinct was that recreating the tableau would be foolhardy. His ear was closer to the ground of what a new generation might be thinking about the royals, but others at the Palace, no doubt older and thinking they were wiser, perhaps overruled him. A whole new generation of people had grown up indifferent to royalty, and like my colleague at the BBC, they feel the monarchy has done more harm than good.

But my dad told me he cried when he heard the Queen had died.

'It's very sad,' he said. 'I never heard her once have a bad word to say about anyone. She was a good woman.' My mum was sorrowful too. 'The brightest diamond in the Crown jewels is dimmed,' she told me. My parents' generation admired and respected the Queen, partly because she symbolised certainty and stability in a crazy world. For them, things seem a little bit more uncertain now.

−18−

Ukraine and Russia:
Another Log on the Fire

THE WINDOWS RATTLED in their frames; powerful thrusts of disturbed air threatened to smash the glass. 'Oh, fuck,' I said, with the phone line to the BBC newsroom in London still open and senior producer Lesley Roy on the other end.

'What's going on?' she said, and I could tell she was worried. The rattling suddenly ended.

'Okay, it's stopped now. Wow, that was heavy, man,' I said, relieved.

'Is it still okay to talk, should you be heading down to the bunker?' she inquired.

'Must have been a missile strike on one of the suburbs, but it felt really close.' Then the windows rattled again, this time more violently. 'Oh, fuck,' I said again, as the tremor lasted this time for three or maybe four seconds, which may not sound like much, but it felt like a very long time and was nerve-racking.

We were two weeks into Russia's invasion of Ukraine, and from the tenth floor balcony of our hotel, where the BBC had set up a makeshift office and television studio, we often heard and saw explosions and fires off in the distance, maybe ten or fifteen kilometres away. But this was the closest the war had come to us, right in the heart of the capital, Kyiv.

269

I was in two minds whether to head down to the bunker, the basement car park of our hotel, but we were only a couple of hours away from broadcasting live for the *BBC News at Ten*, and shlepping down to the basement would eat up valuable prep time. I had already spent two or three nights sleeping in the bunker on a mattress tossed on the floor, after one cacophony of air-raid sirens, coupled with credible intelligence passed to the hotel, suggested a missile strike was on the way. It was hot down there, people were restless and one man snored quite loudly, which was okay, but it all made getting any sleep difficult. What did I expect? We were right in the middle of the biggest war on the Continent of Europe since 1945.

Communism always looked better to me in the sunshine, and as a young reporter I had little desire to have to layer on clothing to report the latest numbers of tractors produced in Poland, or the grain harvest of Romania. Russia did hold an attraction as the capital of the land of Tolstoy, Pushkin and Dostoevsky, and I had always fancied a trip to St Petersburg, Russia's 'window on Europe'. But of all the BBC's main bureaus around the world, Moscow is the only one where I have never worked, nowhere near the top of my to-do list. Communism in the cold struck me as being particularly joyless and soul-destroying.

The life-denying politics of collectivism and authoritarianism were also not helped by my ignorance of Eastern European cuisine. The clichés of lumpy soups and tasteless stews lacking the enlivening qualities of hot peppers, chillies and spices were not appetising. Cuba, Mozambique, Angola and Vietnam – YES. Ukraine, Hungary and Latvia – NO.

There was another reason I had little desire to report extensively from Eastern Europe, and that was the suspicion that racial tolerance was not a high priority for the peoples of those lands. Despite the Soviet propaganda posters showing happy workers and peasants of all colours, united and living harmoniously in a socialist utopia, by the time the Iron Curtain came down, Central and Eastern Europe was pretty much ethnically and religiously homogeneous.

In the West by contrast, at the end of the Second World War, major labour shortages in northern Europe, including in former colonial powers like the UK and France, meant a drive for migrant foreign workers was vital for post-war reconstruction, and this is how my parents joined the Windrush Generation. Even West Germany from the 1950s had a Gastarbeiter or migrant worker programme, which explains the presence of the vibrant Turkish community in the unified Germany of today.

Over on the other side of the line cutting north to south across Europe – 'from Stettin in the Baltic to Trieste in the Adriatic' – to quote Churchill's Iron Curtain speech, there was no similar experience in scale or intensity of mass influxes of foreign workers. The bottom line is that black people never ventured to these lands in sizeable numbers, and the legacy of that is an Eastern Europe with a seemingly lower tolerance for people who are not white. Eastern European racism is shameful, evidenced by the chants on the football terraces, and the rise of far-right parties and right-wing governments with 'compassion deficits' for refugees escaping the wars of the Middle East, such as Hungary, Poland and Slovakia.

But so too are there racist chants on the football terraces, far-right parties, and the 'compassion deficits' of a growing number of governments in Western Europe. Having said all that, it would be unfair and incorrect to tar whole nations with the brush of racism and my visits over the years to Poland, the Czech Republic, Hungary, Croatia, Albania, Moldova, Serbia and Kosovo have all been happy ones.

It is in this context in early 2022, when Vladimir Putin was gradually building up his forces on the border with Ukraine, that my blind spot for Eastern Europe was evident. Frankly, it had not occurred to me to suggest to the BBC that I should go, and it was only a phone call asking me to consider it from Jonathan Whittaker, one of the deputy editors of the *News at Ten*, which made me think, well, why not? This was as good an opportunity as any to see a land I had never visited, and a sense of adventure had always been part of why I became a journalist in the first place.

I also did not think the Russians would invade. I could not see Moscow getting anything out of a full-scale war. If he attacked, I believed Putin would simply embolden frontline states like Finland to seek NATO membership. He would threaten the lucrative trade in Russian gas and oil exports to Europe, heap more crippling international sanctions on his people, unite the European Union against him, push Ukraine politically even further into the orbit of America and the West, and he would lose for ever the one thing that he craves, global respect for Russia. As I write this, all the above has come to pass, and for much of the world, the land of Tchaikovsky and Chekhov is a pariah state.

Two weeks before the windows rattled and our hotel shook, I arrived in Kyiv on a glorious late winter's day on 23 February 2022, fully expecting to be returning to London in two, maybe three days' time, after Putin had made his point with his military build-up and pulled his troops back from the border. I had arrived in Ukraine on a scheduled Ryanair flight from Stansted, with the ticket costing peanuts.

Expecting a short trip, I took only a little carry-on suitcase, hoping to keep costs down for the BBC, forsaking any luggage going in the hold (you know what low-cost airlines can be like when charging for extra weight). So I left at home my flak jacket, believing I would not be needing it anyway. As I walked out onto the tarmac to board the flight, there was a young couple ahead of me in the queue. In their early twenties, they were laughing and goofing around, clearly happy to be heading off for a quick break. They were posing for selfies in front of the Ryanair jet.

As I watched them, I thought it was a bit odd that they were heading into what could perhaps become a conflict zone. Yes, I felt a shooting war was unlikely, but it still struck me as strange that the happy couple would take the risk. I am sure they fully expected to arrive in Kyiv, have a few laughs, enjoy great food and visit some amazing bars, marvel at the beauty of Ukraine's magnificent Orthodox churches, do a little shopping and return home. Not one of us, the scores of passengers boarding that plane, thought that this would be one of the last civilian flights into Kyiv for the foreseeable future. I have no idea if the happy couple managed to escape once the war started, only twenty hours later.

Millions of people had used Ryanair and other low-cost airlines to experience Eastern Europe, and millions were going the other way. In the four years leading up to Russia's invasion, Michael O'Leary, Ryanair's chief executive, was part of a wave of airline bosses who had helped to transform the economies of many Central and Eastern European countries in the early 2000s. They also helped to create new migrant and tourist flows to Western Europe, introducing travellers from the former Eastern Bloc to places like Paris, London, Madrid and Rome.

A younger generation became more attracted to the West, turning their back on their traditional ally Russia and the East, and imbibing notions of true democracy and the rule of law. Dangerous stuff for an autocrat like Vladimir Putin, leading the kleptocracy that is modern Russia. A truly free Ukraine on his western border could threaten his own rule at home. He has always wanted to turn the clock back, right back to the seventeenth century, holding what has been described as an 'irredentist' view of what constitutes Russian lands. He advocates the restoration to Moscow of any territory that once belonged to it and that includes, of course, Ukraine.

For Putin, Kiev as the Russians call it, rather than Kyiv as the Ukrainians refer to the capital, is an errant child that has wondered off for a moment and must rejoin the family. In Putin's mind, Russia and Ukraine are indivisible, they are one land, as he explained in a 5,000-word treatise published in 2021, called *On the Historical Unity of Russians and Ukrainians*. As one former senior US government official once put it, Vladimir Putin is determined to shape the future to look like his version of the past. The problem is, Ukraine was fast acquiring a mind of its own and looking to shape its own future.

I arrived in Kyiv with producer Annie Duncanson and we headed for the hotel in the centre of the city where the BBC was based. We were both starving, having passed on the airline food, and so made a dash for a nearby restaurant. As we sat down to lunch in the very trendy little eatery, the world passed by outside seemingly without a care. The sun was high in the sky and the streets and shops were full of people living their lives, fashioning their own destinies. But as we ate, with the infrastructure of war massed on the border by Putin and his generals, the Russian leader had already calculated when he would strike, believing that the West, which had done little to curb his aggression in the past, would once again acquiesce.

It was around 4.30 a.m. the next morning that I was startled awake by an announcement over the hotel PA system, with the general manager sounding breathless and declaring in effect that the Russians were coming.

The next few days were frightening. Could I be a target standing on the hotel roof broadcasting live to millions of viewers back home? When would the Russians enter the city and perhaps storm the hotel to silence the international media reporting their every move? Surely it was only a matter of time, possibly a few hours, no more than a few days. A big decision was looming. If the BBC could organise a convoy of vehicles to escape the city, should I jump aboard?

The person in charge of our team in Kyiv, Kate Peters, was a calm, unflappable fluent Russian speaker, whom I had known for close to two decades and trusted wholeheartedly. We all had individual meetings with her to explain whether we wanted to stay or go. I had already made up my mind, but I wanted to chat with Kate before declaring my hand.

The Russians invaded on Thursday 24 February, and with the airspace closed, a convoy of vehicles leaving the city to head for neighbouring Poland was being assembled for Saturday 26th. I found Kate on the tenth floor of our hotel on the Friday morning. Others had already spoken with her and made it clear they wanted to leave. One woman was in tears saying she had never signed up for this, she did not want to be in the middle of a shooting match. Kate and I chatted quietly, away from everyone else.

'If Russian troops enter the city and they get into the hotel, what do you think they'll do?' I asked, hoping she would fall back on her years of experience living in Moscow, knowing the Russian mindset.

'They'll probably just kick us out,' she replied, 'they'll be brusque and firm, and order us to leave.' That made sense to me, but then I asked Kate another question, which was unfair, because I did not want her to think her response would determine my decision whether to stay or go.

'Is there much of a chance they'd perhaps want to kill us?'

'I don't know,' came the reply. 'I just don't know.'

I had already made up my mind to stay. To be part of the biggest story on the planet, to see up close how the whole thing would pan out. It was exciting too and my timing had been perfect, arriving in Ukraine on the very eve of the invasion. My thoughts turned to Catherine back home, and she knew I would have wanted to stay. That to pull out would go against all my journalistic instincts, and along with my other colleagues who had chosen to remain in Kyiv during the country's darkest hour, I would believe it was vital to get to the truth of what was going on.

In an age of social media and lies, spin and propaganda, with no comebacks and no price to pay for deceit, that was the point of what we do as reporters, to try to guide the public towards the truth.

But what was that truth? For me in the first few days of the war, and increasingly as the conflict dragged on, it was a simple story. The irredentist Putin was trying to reconstitute the Russian Empire and so attacked his smaller neighbour Ukraine to bring it to heel, contravening a whole host of international agreements and making a mockery of the rule of law. That is it. There is nothing more to it.

There are claims and counter-claims about whether, in the wake of the collapse of the Soviet Union, there had been an oral promise made by NATO to Mikhail Gorbachev, the former Soviet president, that there would be no eastward expansion of the security alliance. However, in interviews, Gorbachev was inconsistent in confirming such an agreement. Even if there was a deal, what concern was that of the millions of people in Eastern Europe, who had just won their freedom from Moscow?

That was the whole point of the referendums and plebiscites on whether the constituent states of the Soviet Union and neighbouring Warsaw Pact countries should leave Russia's grip, after the fall of the Iron Curtain. These people wanted to determine their own futures and alliances, and control their own destinies. If Poland, Romania, Estonia, Latvia, or Lithuania wanted to join NATO at a later date, why should that not be allowed?

The terrible fact is that even as the Soviet Union was dying, it was still seeking to control the lives of the people in the newly independent states, who had already made it clear they wanted nothing more to do with Russia. It is this arrogance that Putin embodies. That like Peter the Great, he should be the master; he should be in control.

Some argue the West needs to understand Russia better and its paranoias. The country has suffered three major invasions in its history – the Mongols in the thirteenth century, Napoleon in 1812 and Hitler in 1941 – and the experience of those encounters has fashioned a particular mindset and survival instinct. Its people feel cornered, surrounded by potential enemies on its flanks in Europe and Asia.

The problem is that down the centuries, that insecurity has led Moscow to launch several wars of choice, unprovoked offensive actions of which Ukraine is just the latest. There is a culture of war in Russia, that offense is the best defence. But it is this very culture that Eastern Europe is afraid of, and why so many countries have sought NATO's protection. It is not outsiders, but Putin and the Russians themselves who are their own worst enemies.

And what possible right can there be in Ukraine for Russia to kill, rape, maim and torture, to abduct children, to burn homes and bomb hospitals, maternity units and schools? To disfigure and destroy? Why should the innocent people of Ukraine be sacrificed on the altar of Russian paranoia? A monomania and persecution complex fed twenty-four hours of every day by Putin's state-controlled media apparatus, an all-encompassing cloak of propaganda and lies, shrouding Russia in darkness since the early 2000s, leaving a people starved of objective information and truth.

The day the windows of our hotel rattled and shook, Ukrainian troops were engaged in fierce battles with Russian invasion forces on the outskirts of Kyiv, trying to prevent them entering the city. The Russians had already managed to seize a few areas on the fringes, and had entered some of the outer suburbs. Their occupation was characterised by a reign of terror that I have no doubt will form the basis of war crimes prosecutions when this horrible conflict is over.

But the war was getting too big for me, there were geopolitical ramifications, the possibility of Washington and Moscow being sucked into a direct confrontation. Putin began talking ominously about Russia's stockpile of nuclear weapons, even at one point ordering his military to put his nuclear deterrence forces on high alert. I wanted to take what was going on back down to a more manageable level, on a more human scale, to better get across to the public the tragedy of events for ordinary Ukrainians. So I hit upon the idea of looking at the war through the eyes of one family living on one road that had been occupied by the Russians.

I was struck by the pretty names for some of the streets in the city of Bucha to the north of Kyiv. Peach Blossom and Apple Tree were a couple, which looked as suburban as you can get: lace curtains and well-maintained front yards, with garages off to the side. Chestnut trees stood proud along the road, shielding dwellings of colourfully painted clapboard. Bucha formed part of a popular commuter belt area around Kyiv, and the air was one of quiet affluence and domesticity. I was reminded of a thousand English suburbs, as birdsong filled my ears.

But I chose to focus on Railway Station Street, because in the road on the day we arrived was a long column of Russian military vehicles, which had been incinerated by attacking

Ukrainian troops. The burnt-out hulks of tanks, armoured personnel carriers and other mechanised vehicles lay broken and mangled beneath the chestnut trees, for as far down the road as the eye could see. A destroyed tank sat outside No. 13, instead of the usual suburban family 4x4. There was another tank outside No. 15. An APC sat in the road outside No. 17, and on and on.

Ukrainian troops were assessing the damage, having made the area safe and determined that none of the smashed-up Russian vehicles had been booby-trapped. The charred corpses of Russian soldiers lay undisturbed in the web of wreckage, beneath all the bent metal. As Davy filmed the scene, I thought about what the noise must have been like for all the residents cowering in the basements of their pretty clapboard houses on either side of the street, as the vehicles blew up, exploding in volley after volley of artillery fire.

The gate to No. 31 Railway Station Street was slightly ajar, so I pushed and entered, calling out to anyone who may be there. I noticed a man was on the roof. 'Hi,' I shouted up to him and he responded with a wave and clambered down his ladder.

His name was Viktor Herinenko, and he was repairing the roof after shrapnel from the firefight in the street smashed through the tiling. A few weeks before we arrived, he was making the same repairs, but the person calling up to him was a Russian soldier and Bucha was under enemy occupation. Tall with sandy hair, he was very welcoming and keen to tell his story. Behind us chickens in a pen were clucking.

Viktor installed video security equipment for a living. 'I put surveillance cameras on many of the houses in the street,' he told me.

I asked him if he had video footage of the Russians.

'No,' he said, 'the soldiers ripped out all the cameras, and ordered everyone to hand over any footage they may have filmed. Mobile phones were seized. They wanted no one to capture them on tape.'

It is thought one of the main Russian Army units that occupied Bucha was the 64th Motor Rifle Brigade, and it could well have been three of its soldiers one day in March 2022, who ordered Viktor, his fifteen-year-old son, and a neighbour who was helping him, off the roof.

'They fired shots into the ground to hurry us up,' he told me. 'They said they were going to kill us. Then they ordered us to lie face down on the ground. Put your pig faces in the dirt, they said. Then they fired some shots close to my head. I could feel the sand that the bullets kicked up touch my hair. Then I heard the soldiers say we can get rid of the two older ones and spare the younger one. But the third soldier said no, they were just fixing the roof, let them go.'

As my interpreter translated Viktor's words for me into English, I shook my head in disbelief. It was a mock execution Viktor was describing, in this ordinary little street of pretty houses and chestnut trees.

Viktor's wife Tanya then appeared, having fed the chickens, and she recounted what she saw that day: her son and husband and family friend all standing with their hands up, as the soldiers pointed guns at their heads. It was clear Tanya was still traumatised by the experience, as she told me how the Russians ordered her to stay put and not to follow the men into the street.

'You go outside, I take you down,' said one of them.

So she stood in the yard, terrified of what might happen next, helpless and unable to save her husband and son. Then two shots rang out.

'It was so hard,' she told me. 'I thought they were dead.' Tanya looked off into the middle distance, lost in her thoughts and those painful memories. 'I don't know how I'm going to walk around these streets anymore, after everything that's happened. I'll remember the blasts and explosions, us trying to hide, and the shrapnel and bullets flying.'

She paused and looked as if she was about to cry. I wanted to put my arm around her, to offer some comfort, but I did not know what to say or do to help.

'I can't explain everything I feel,' she said, after composing herself. 'I can't explain everything we went through here.'

I cannot explain it either, the snipers picking off civilians at random, leaving bodies littering the streets. The backyards and basements turned into torture chambers. The women kept as sex slaves, raped when needed on demand, then shot in the head, with torn condom wrappers left beside their bodies. The old people's home where residents died of starvation, unable to get food or water. Just like Tanya, I cannot explain why any of this happened. The brutality of it all.

Throughout my working life I have tried to understand the hatred of others, the will that drives some to hurt and kill and despise whole groups of people. I really wanted to understand the Russian mindset in Ukraine and hoped to report from Russia itself on the thinking behind the war. Now I am officially banned because of my reporting. My name is on a list of undesirables issued by the Russian authorities. Some have said to me it is a badge of honour. I don't see it that way. I am just very sad that the Russians are not interested in the truth.

In April 2023, I was asked by the British Library to interview the eminent historian, Sir Antony Beevor, in front of a packed lecture theatre, about his latest book chronicling the struggle for control of Russia after the fall of the Tsarist empire. The White movement, versus the Red Army of Trotsky and Lenin. This was also a brutal war that saw unbelievable levels of savagery, reminding me of events in Ukraine, with its horrors and cruelties, even sadism.

Sir Antony pointed out that the same levels of brutality were not evident in the Spanish Civil War as happened in Russia between 1917 and 1921, and he also highlighted the cruelty of the Red Army towards German civilians as it advanced on Berlin in 1945, including the brutal, mass gang rapes of some two million German women. Is there something in the Russian character, I asked, that lends itself to waging war on the basest of terms with conspicuous cruelty?

He said there is always a temptation to talk about a national character, but such a thing does not exist. There can be a national self-image, however, which can affect behaviours and even the culture of armies. He highlighted the conspicuous cruelties of the Mongol invasions of the thirteenth century, of which he said the Russian troops fighting today are perhaps the inheritors. This acceptance that war is brutal, and it must be fought brutally. Then Sir Antony said something that I found fascinating and was clearly in evidence in Ukraine.

'Russian leaders and commanders are as pitiless some-times on their own soldiers, as they are on the enemy.'

'I've heard it described as throwing another log on the fire,' I replied, 'the way their generals will simply toss more and more troops onto the battlefield, regardless of the level of casualties, because they have an almost inexhaustible supply of men.'

Sir Antony pointed out that it was a winning mindset at Stalingrad in 1943, and that a Western commander would probably have failed against the Germans, because he would not have been willing to sacrifice well over a million men.

* * *

In the first forty-eight hours of Russia's invasion of Ukraine, there was a blanket curfew in Kyiv, no one was allowed out. There was a real fear that foreign saboteurs were moving among the population, and anyone caught outdoors would have been arrested. Eventually people were allowed out for a few hours during daylight to find food, though most shops were closed. The night before, all we had to eat at the hotel shelter was pasta smothered in tomato ketchup.

One day Davy and I went out to film, the streets were mostly deserted, but I noticed an old woman was out feeding some pigeons. I did not really see her face, but at her feet were several cooing birds. Every now and again, a shower of birdseed would tumble from her hand. She was wearing a heavy-looking grey coat, keeping out the late morning winter chill. I motioned to Davy to take her picture, but she seemed to sense he was approaching, and emptied the brown paper bag of birdseed and walked briskly away. It was clearly something she felt she had to do despite the threat of being bombed. A gesture of kindness to the birds, which brought solace and comfort amidst the cruelty of war.

Later that day, I visited the magnificent Saint Sophia Cathedral, a stunning riot of frescoes and gold, and I watched an interfaith prayer service for peace: Orthodox, Catholic, Jewish, Muslim, all united.

A little later, Ukraine's interior minister, Denys Monastyrskyy, turned up in a bulletproof vest, seeking divine guidance. He was ashen-faced and looking very tired, no surprise given he was in charge of the Ukrainian police and other emergency services in the middle of a full-scale war. Four heavily armed Ukrainian army soldiers were protecting him, and I asked if faith was what underpinned the Ukrainian belief that they could defeat the second-largest army on the planet. Speaking softly, he was unequivocal and clear-eyed.

'God is on our side,' he told me with deep conviction. 'We will win.' And to drive home the point, he repeated those words in Ukrainian: '*My vyhrayemo.*'

Also attending the prayer service was military chaplain Oleksandr Mishura. He had a yellow armband on his right bicep, the insignia of the volunteer brigades – or citizen soldiers. He said morale was high among the troops to which he ministered, and that the soldiers had no choice but to fight to defend and protect the country. He took my arm and looked me straight in the eye, sharing a sentiment that I suspect many in Ukraine believe. 'We all know what the Bible says, when the enemy is wicked, God will always intervene.'

I think all the time about the people I have met in Ukraine, hoping they have managed to survive this horrible war. Like the mother and her eighteen-year-old daughter who shared our underground shelter. One morning, the teenager's crying woke me up. She had received word that her father, who had been living near the Chernobyl nuclear plant, had apparently been harmed by a group of Russian soldiers. They had ransacked his house looking for cigarettes and alcohol. His family feared the worst. Throughout the day she tried to call her father, but he was not picking up the phone. All of us in the shelter prayed he was still alive. When word finally came from his neighbour that he was safe and unharmed, it felt like a tiny victory for all of us.

I think about the other basement dwellers that I spent time with, like the woman with a very large, white fluffy cat, and the children who would run around the mattresses playing games, oblivious to the madness of adults above ground.

As I write, I am aware of only one person whom I met on my numerous trips to Ukraine who has since died in the war. Denys Monastyrskyy was killed when the helicopter he was travelling in crashed near a children's nursery on the outskirts of Kyiv. The aircraft was flying towards front-line positions in eastern Ukraine when it came down. I remember hearing the news and although I had only met him for a brief amount of time, I was pained he was dead. To date, he is the highest-profile Ukrainian casualty since Russia's invasion.

I have no idea if the lady I saw feeding the pigeons is still alive.

–19–

Mastermind and a Changed Britain

THE COMEDIAN JIM Davidson was the last person I expected to get a well done and good luck message from. He was a man who made a living on stage and on television in the 1970s caricaturing black men, with a comic character named Chalky White. Davidson would put on an exaggerated West Indian accent, and in chronicling the character's adventures, pandered to a stereotype of black laziness and mild drug-taking.

So I was surprised when I was told he had posted a message of congratulations on his YouTube channel in the summer of 2021, after the announcement that I would be taking over from John Humphrys as the interrogator on the quiz show *Mastermind*. 'Clive, a black man, is gonna be presenting *Mastermind*,' he said, 'and do you know what, I couldn't think of a better person to do it. I'm thrilled for you, and please don't take any notice of anyone who says it's a box ticking exercise.'

His comments made me think about popular culture in the 1970s and how insensitive those times were, and how much things have changed. *The Black and White Minstrel Show*, for example, where white men would sing and dance in black face, was a primetime hit on BBC One, regularly scoring over

14 million viewers a night from 1957 to 1978. It was finally cancelled after a number of complaints, most notably from black people. It is shocking to think now that such a programme was ever broadcast, or to think that Chalky White was ever allowed on TV.

That could never happen again, along with the sexist mother-in-law jokes that were stock in trade of comedians in the 1970s, and comedy demeaning to Irish people, who were exclusively portrayed as either a bit thick and simple, or IRA bombers. All were grotesque caricatures that made the dominant class, white men, laugh. Sure, others found the jokes funny too, but the narrative was mainly controlled by white male comedians, or white male TV executives.

It was interesting Jim Davidson said I was not to 'take any notice of anyone who says it's a box ticking exercise'. Out of the many hundreds of messages I received after my taking over *Mastermind* was announced, I could count on the fingers of one hand those who suggested I only got the job because I am black, and though I have no proof, I suspect that they were all white men of a certain age. Jim is a white male, deep into his sixties and part of that world, a culture that might see the worst in my appointment, not the best.

The same people would never say John Humphrys only got the job because he was white. It would not cross their minds, but if they did think about it, the assumption would be that he got the job on merit. A woman, however, or a black man getting the job? Well, in the minds of some white men, it *could* be a box ticking exercise, perhaps, an attempt to pander or meet an undeclared quota. It could, in the current parlance, be *woke politics.*

Inevitably, given there had been only three presenters of *Mastermind* on BBC television in its near fifty-year history, Magnus Magnusson, John Humphrys and me, there was intense media attention over the appointment. I did count-less interviews for newspapers, magazines, and on TV and radio. Yet only one solitary interviewer asked the question, 'What would you say to those people who might think you only got the job because you're black?' And guess what? That person was a white male over the age of seventy.

British culture has been transformed in the last half century, to the point where a black man can be appointed to front a major television institution like *Mastermind*, with little fuss. I joined the BBC on a training scheme after Sussex University in 1987. One day a filming crew from the *Panorama* programme turned up. They were looking at ethnic diversity in a number of British institutions, including the BBC. Out of the twelve people in my year on the course, three were black and one was South Asian. We were taken aside to be inter-viewed, and the reporter asked us if we were sure we had not been selected simply because we were black.

The interviewer was, you guessed it, a white male, and there was no similar question to the women trainees, or the Welsh trainee. A black journalist, a woman journalist, a disa-bled journalist or an LGBTQ journalist would not have felt the need to ask such a question, because they are not part of the dominant group whose position in society is threatened. It is the underrepresented who are the beneficiaries of a Britain that is finally including their experience as part of the national story, and who are now being told they have value in society.

I have always thought of culture as the dynamic interplay between the old, the current and the new. All three bleed into each other and are ever shifting. 'Culture' is not a settled, static thing. Old ideas and conventions inform the present day, while new ideas emerge to challenge current thinking.

As a kid growing up in Bolton in the 1970s, our family used to watch many of the popular TV comedies of the age. *Love Thy Neighbour, Rising Damp, George and Mildred, Mind Your Language, On the Buses, The Les Dawson Show, Are You Being Served?* Most would never be commissioned now, as new ideas have transformed the parameters of what is acceptable on television.

The writers often tried to capture the interplay between old, present, and new ideologies with varying degrees of success. *Love Thy Neighbour*, for example, chronicled the adventures of a white working-class couple living in a London suburb, whose new next-door neighbours are black. Britain at that time no longer had an empire, but notions of racial superiority were still prevalent. White men dominated society, as represented by the white male householder in the show, who could say anything he liked towards black people, including using words like sambo, nig nog and gollywog.

But newer ideas were emerging to challenge old assumptions of racial superiority. Diversity and inclusion were concepts that were beginning to develop, as embodied by the two wives, one black, one white on the show, who would not dream of using insulting or demeaning language towards one another. Conflict is the essence of drama and comedy and there was plenty of conflict here.

The sitcom *Mind Your Language*, set in an adult education college in London where different people from around the world are trying to learn English, is another example. The show was cancelled after three seasons because it was deemed to be offensive. Revolving around racial stereotypes like the humourless German, passionate Italian, hypersexual French woman and so on, past prejudices and notions of British superiority over other nations is evident, along with a 1970s willingness to accept the stereotypes and laugh along.

I have to say my family enjoyed *Love Thy Neighbour*. We were as British as anyone else and enjoyed the bigoted white neighbour in each episode getting his comeuppance. But many people were offended and hurt by all these programmes. A new kind of comedy was needed that did not find laughs in belittling people, that did not find humour in laughing at others.

What is interesting is that *Love Thy Neighbour* first went on air in 1972 and ended in 1976, lasting eight series. *Mind Your Language* first went on air a year after *Love Thy Neighbour* ended in 1977, and lasted just three seasons. A new breed of television executive was taking over the controls as the 1980s approached, and they saw a new ideology of greater tolerance and acceptance of ethnic minorities as a positive way forward, in time paving the way for my appearance as the host of *Mastermind*, via the likes of Sir Lenny Henry and Sir Trevor McDonald. Television has changed beyond recognition, to the point where someone like me is now accepted.

Just as the minutes of that Tory Cabinet meeting in 1955 suggested, it was inevitable that mass immigration from the colonies would transform the character of Britain, reshape its culture and redefine its values. Old attitudes to race could not be sustained, not only because ethnic minorities were offended, but because a growing number of white people, for whom multiculturalism was the norm, also became offended.

Any decent society worthy of that description had to represent all those within it fairly, no matter their race. And from racial tolerance grew acceptance and acknowledgement of the worth of others who were marginalised, such as women, the disabled, the LGBTQ community, and now the debate has moved to the treatment of people who are trans.

The BBC has had to navigate these tricky waters with skill and alacrity and from time to time has bashed against a rock or two. It is a national broadcaster owned and funded by licence fee payers and has a duty to represent everyone. The public must feel it has a stake in the Corporation if the licence fee is to be justified, and that means programming and presenters that represent diverse Britain. Catering to older, more traditional audiences, who are used to things being done in a certain way, is extremely hard while trying to appeal to future licence payers who are more digitally savvy and expect edgier programming. Get the balance wrong and you lose both audience and licence payers.

What should a TV executive do, if he or she has a hit show, popular with many, but offensive to some? The battle over *The Black and White Minstrel Show* is a case in point. David Hendy, author of *The BBC: A People's History*, writes that in May 1967, the Campaign Against Racial Discrimination submitted a petition calling for the show to be cancelled.

The minutes of a BBC Board of Management meeting reveal that the Corporation's head of publicity, rather unscientifically, used the *Daily Mail*'s letters page to gauge the public's 'general view', and concluded that 'the programme was not racially offensive'. What is worse, the Director-General, Hugh Carleton Greene, decided that 'no further action was necessary', based on this evidence, and the show continued for another decade.

David Hendy writes that the very last edition was broadcast in 1978, and by then, the Controller of BBC One, Bill Cotton, realised he could not defend the show any longer. Inevitably there was grumbling from fans, but they were told firmly that the 'racist implication' of its minstrelsy was now obvious to all.

'It's all very well people who are not black saying they didn't think about it that way,' he told them. 'It's the people who *are* black whose views surely needed to be taken into account.' The BBC's shift mirrors that of society as a whole, as Britain transformed multiculturally. The fact that asking white people whether *The Black and White Minstrel Show* was racist is pretty stupid. It is the people who are affected by racism whose view is the most relevant, and remember, this was a debate coming a full three decades after the arrival of the first of the Windrush Generation.

The BBC has been my employer for more than thirty years, and I have felt comfortable working in its newsrooms all over the world. Much of the time I am the only person of colour, though the situation has improved since I first joined the corporation. There are more people from ethnic minority backgrounds, particularly on screen, but the Corporation itself would admit that stocking the front window is not enough. There are still too few senior producers or members of management who are black or Asian.

While I am used to being one of the few faces of colour, for outsiders it can be a shock. At the 2012 London Olympics, I was reporting for BBC News. There was a tremendous amount of interest in anything to do with Usain Bolt, who was destined to set a new Olympic record and become the first person to win the 100m and 200m in successive Olympiads. Jamaica's Shelly-Ann Fraser-Pryce won the women's 100m too.

The BBC asked me to make a feature on the phenomenon of the little Caribbean island's dominance of world-class sprinting, so I thought it would be good to interview a reporter from Jamaica, who had been over in London covering the Games. I eventually interviewed Lance Whittaker, one of the leading Caribbean sports commentators. But another Jamaican journalist was very impressed with the fact that the mighty BBC had asked me (a black man) to cover the Games for the main news programmes.

'Any chance I could come over to see the famous BBC's offices?' he said. Of course, so I took him over to the BBC's workspace. It was huge, considerably larger than anything the Jamaicans had seen, covering almost an entire floor of the main Media Centre, with scores and scores of people at work. I showed him around, but he was awfully quiet.

When we left a few minutes later, he grabbed my arm and said, 'How do you work there?'

'What do you mean?' I replied.

'All those people are white. You were the only black man I saw. It must be hard,' he said apologetically, with concern. I said I had not noticed; I am used to it.

In the BBC newsroom, there is now an LGBT and Identity

correspondent, as well as a Disability Affairs correspondent. One of the Corporation's biggest entertainment hits is *RuPaul's Drag Race*, where drag queens compete in challenges to be crowned the 'next drag superstar'. Oh, how times have changed! The BBC has tried to keep pace with our ever-shifting culture, reflecting back to viewers the sensibilities of the nation in which they live.

For some, however, change can be too quick on TV, no matter how relevant to wider society. The colour-blind casting of an adaptation of Charles Dickens' *Great Expectations*, for instance, where a black actor played Mr Jaggers in the costume drama and a black actress played Estella, garnered criticism for being in the minds of some too 'woke'.

One person is quoted on an entertainment website as complaining, 'I figured they'd insert some woke nonsense, but the casting of Estella is just ridiculous.' Another viewer, clearly riled up, complained that 'Woke *Great Expectations* is a crime against humanity.' 'My expectations of the BBC's *Great Expectations* were proved right,' harrumphed a third. 'Woke casting with black actors is just as expected.'

Another disgruntled viewer blasted, 'One hundred and sixty-two years after writing the novel, Charles Dickens' *Great Expectations* is adapted into a woke version of the classic novel, replete with Britain bashing content and some characters that have undergone personality changes and even changed their skin colour. Is nothing sacred?'

One person claimed to know their history, saying the 'casting of Estella as a black leading woman is not believable for the time and the culture the story is set in. It's stupid woke pandering.' This is complete tosh, of course, there were some very posh black Victorians, a hidden history that has been unearthed in recent years.

One also has to wonder if the complainants objected to Shakespeare's *Romeo and Juliet* being switched to New York as *West Side Story*, with a bunch of Puerto Ricans representing the Capulet family? Does it *really* matter that Estella is black, as long as the actress playing her is good in the role? Might some of those now complaining, on another occasion, have grabbed a pen and paper and with furrowed brow written to the letters section of the *Daily Mail*, protesting that *The Black and White Minstrel Show* was not racist?

When it was announced in 2021 that I had been chosen to replace John Humphrys as the new host of *Mastermind*, I walked into the newsroom at New Broadcasting House in London and the *News at Six* and *Ten* team gave me a round of applause. It had still not sunk in what a big deal this appointment really was. George Alagiah, a man so many of us look up to in the newsroom because of his brilliant journalism, warmth, kindness and generosity, took me to one side. He said this is a wonderful moment, that a person of colour is being given one of the BBC's crown jewels.

'Do you understand how important this is?' he said.

I was slightly overwhelmed by his words. 'No pressure then,' I replied, as I realised how far the children of Empire had come.

The following year, the Prince of Wales and the Duchess of Cornwall attended a reception at New Broadcasting House, celebrating the ninetieth anniversary of the World Service, and I was introduced to them both.

'You're the man off the roof,' said the Prince, smiling as I shook his hand, referring to my stints presenting out in Kyiv. I thought to myself, it is nice to know that he gets his news from the BBC.

Then in June 2023, a few weeks after the Coronation at Westminster Abbey, I received a special invitation in the post. It was from the Master of the King's Household, and I was being 'commanded' by Their Majesties to attend a reception at Buckingham Palace to celebrate the seventy-fifth anniversary of the *Empire Windrush* reaching British shores. The other invitees were also members of Britain's Afro-Caribbean community, from all walks of life – the arts, film, television, sport, business, science, music and politics. Oh, how times had changed.

As I prepared to see the King, and checked in my coat next to the famous Picture Gallery on the first floor, where the reception would take place, I thought back to my mum in 1953, going to see the new Queen Elizabeth in Montego Bay. Two generations of Royals and two generations of Myries, and in between a radically changed Britain. I was now standing in the King's Picture Gallery, in Buckingham Palace, and I was there to drink champagne and nibble finger food, not to hang pictures. Among those waiting to speak to the King was Sir Trevor McDonald, and as we chatted it seemed fitting that we were there together.

As I write, a Hindu man of Indian descent is the British prime minister. What would Queen Elizabeth's first prime minister, Winston Churchill, have made of that, as an arch defender of Empire?'

The Home Secretary is a Buddhist woman, also of Indian descent. The Foreign Secretary is a mixed-race man whose mother is from Sierra Leone; the man who is fifth in line to the throne has married a black American woman; a female bishop who is black, Rose Hudson-Wilkin, helped officiate in King Charles's coronation service; the Mayor of London is the Muslim son of a bus driver; Oxford University now has a Professor of LGBTQ+ studies; and in another first, there is a Professor of Social Mobility at the University of Exeter. On top of all that, a black man whose parents emigrated to Britain in the 1960s from Jamaica is the presenter of the television quiz show *Mastermind*.

This period of enormous change has defined my almost sixty years on this Earth. The once marginalised are now being allowed a voice in the story of these islands. Though some baulk at this transference of power from white, old, male elites, what is gratifying is that most people have embraced the change.

Britain has perhaps gone further and faster in this transformation than any other mature democracy. The Americans may argue that the election of Barack Obama as the 44th President was but one example of how the marginalised have assumed some of the most important roles in their society. But having lived in the United States for several years, my feeling is that deep in its marrow, America is still a white, Protestant country, where the success of someone like Barack Obama is an exception to the rule. In other words, America's transformation is skin-deep, in my view, whereas in Britain I believe it is much more fundamental.

And yet the change is not by any means complete. On 22 April 2023, I attended the thirtieth anniversary memorial service for Stephen Lawrence, at St Martin-in-the-Fields in

London. I filed into the church chatting away with a trail-blazer, Britain's first black woman MP, Diane Abbott, and the black TV presenter, Brenda Emmanus.

What we all agreed was that so little seems to have changed in relation to how the police treat the public in the decades since Stephen was stabbed to death in a racist attack by a group of white youths, outside a bus stop in south-east London. The McPherson report into the handling of the subsequent murder inquiry found that the Metropolitan Police investigation was incompetent, and the force was institutionally racist.

As more people filed into the church to honour Stephen, it was not only McPherson's inquiry that was on everyone's mind. A month earlier, Baroness Louise Casey had carried out another inquiry into the toxic culture of the Met. Her review came in the wake of the conviction of one officer for the kidnapping, rape and murder of Sarah Everard, and another who clearly believed his position as a Metropolitan Police officer made him 'untouchable', as he raped, assaulted and inflicted 'irretrievable destruction' on at least twelve women before intimidating them into silence. Both men are now in jail.

So, what was Lady Casey's finding? That the Metropolitan Police was not only institutionally racist, but also sexist, homophobic, and as established by an earlier inquiry in 2021, institutionally corrupt. All the people that our society now recognises have a claim on what it means to be British are still being treated by the nation's biggest police force as if they have no claim.

At the memorial service, Stuart Lawrence was the first to

speak in honour of his brother. In a quirk of fate, he was played by my nephew, the actor Jorden Myrie, in a television adaptation of the family's fight for justice after Stephen's death. Stuart said that thirty years on after the murder of his older brother, the big question is still, why did it happen? A question sadly asked many times, he said, but one that still has no answer.

It is the question I have asked myself throughout my journalistic career and throughout this book. Why different societies or groups are unwilling to live and let live; why they would rather destroy. I have tried to understand this through episodes in my own life, analysing my thoughts and feelings. If I have learned anything, it is that we all have the capacity for compassion and empathy, but it takes courage, wisdom and humility to mine the goodness in us all.

Acknowledgements

MY SINCERE THANKS go to all at Hodder & Stoughton for being a part of this project, particularly Rupert Lancaster for steering things along. Many thanks also to my literary agent, Toby Mundy, and my business manager, Lorraine Ellison, for your help and guidance. To Martin, Annie and Neil, my closest friends, for being a big part of my life. To Lio, Peter, Judith, Garfield, Sonia and Lorna, for being wonderful brothers and sisters, and to my wider family for their ever-present love and support. To my mum and dad, Lynne and Norris, for teaching me right from wrong and the importance of always trying to live a life of humility and dignity. To my loving wife Catherine for always supporting me, no matter how hare-brained my schemes, and to Fiona Brownlee for introducing us at the cheese and wine party in 1992. Sincere thanks to Kate Bush for allowing me to use the lyrics from Army Dreamers. A final 'how-di-do' to all in the Windrush Generation, pioneers who helped to rebuild Britain, making it a better place.

Picture Acknowledgements

Inset 1

Page 1: Author collection

Page 2: Author collection

Page 3: (*top*) Author collection (*bottom*) © Bax Walker Archive / Alamy Stock Photo

Page 4: (*top*) © Everett Collection Inc / Alamy Stock Photo (*bottom*) © Pump Park Vintage Photography / Alamy Stock Photo

Page 5: (*top*) Author collection (*middle*) © Cornell Capa/The LIFE Picture Collection/Shutterstock (*bottom*) © Gibson Moss / Alamy Stock Photo

Page 6: (*top*) © ITV/Shutterstock (*middle*) © Keystone/Hulton Archive/Getty Images (*bottom*) Author collection

Page 7: (*top*) © Patrick Eagar/Popperfoto via Getty Images/ Getty Images (*bottom*) © ITV/Shutterstock

Page 8: (*top*) © James Gray/Daily Mail/Shutterstock (*middle*) © Daily Express/Archive Photos/Getty Images (*bottom*) © Steve Taylor ARPS / Alamy Stock Photo

Inset 2

Page 1: (*top*) © travelib prime / Alamy Stock Photo (*bottom*) Associated Press / Alamy Stock Photo